W9-CGX-670

Living
the
Psalms

ENCOURAGEMENT *for the* DAILY GRIND

CHARLES R.
SWINDOLL

WORTHY
PUBLISHING

Copyright © 2012 by Charles R. Swindoll, Inc.

Published by Worthy Publishing, a division of Worthy Media, Inc., 134 Franklin Road, Suite 200, Brentwood, Tennessee 37027.

HELPING PEOPLE EXPERIENCE THE HEART OF GOD

eBook available at www.worthypublishing.com

Audio distributed through Oasis Audio; visit www.oasisaudio.com

Library of Congress Control Number: 2011944877

All rights reserved. No part of this publication may be reproduced, stored in a retrieval system, or transmitted in any form or by any means—electronic, mechanical, photocopy, recording, or any other—except for brief quotations in printed reviews, without the prior written permission of the publisher.

The content of this book was derived from the previously published *Living Beyond the Daily Grind*, Books I and II.

All Scripture quotations, unless otherwise indicated, are taken from the New American Standard Bible®. Copyright © 1960, 1962, 1963, 1968, 1971, 1972, 1973, 1975, 1977, 1995. The Lockman Foundation. Used by permission.

Scripture quotations marked ESV are taken from the Holy Bible, English Standard Version. Copyright © 2001 by Crossway Bibles, a division of Good News Publishers.

Scripture quotations marked KJV are taken from the King James Version.

Scripture quotations marked MSG are taken from *The Message*. Copyright © 1993, 1994, 1995, 1996, 2000, 2001, 2002. Used by permission of NavPress Publishing Group.

Scripture quotations marked TLB are taken from the Living Bible.

For foreign and subsidiary rights, contact Riggins International Rights Services, Inc.; www.rigginsrights.com

Published in association with Yates & Yates, www.yates2.com

ISBN: 978-1-936034-70-3 (hardcover w/ jacket)

Cover Design: Chris Gilbert, Gearbox
Cover Image: Thinkstock (sheep)
Interior Design and Typesetting: Kimberly Sagmiller, Fudge Creative

Printed in the United States of America
13 14 15 16 17 LBM 8 7 6 5 4 3

CONTENTS

ACKNOWLEDGMENTS

Before getting underway, I must pause and express my gratitude to Byron Williamson of Worthy Publishing. Byron has been far more than a business associate in the publishing business. He is a true friend whose sincere affirmation fuels my fire. Along with him I thank Mark Gaither, my son-in-law, who is also my excellent editor. His careful attention to detail has been of inestimable value and my gratitude knows no bounds. And I also want to mention Sealy Yates, my longtime friend and literary agent, who has no equal in diligence or in commitment.

Words fail me as I attempt to describe the depth of my gratitude to my wife for her understanding, unselfishness, and encouragement. Without her willingness to adapt to my writing schedule; to listen patiently to my incessant reading of what I have written; to prod me on during the dry spells; and to tolerate the late-night, middle-of-the-night, and early-morning flashes of insight that kept the light burning over the desk in my home study—there is no way I could have reached this milestone.

INTRODUCTION

Without a song the day would never end;
Without a song the road would never bend;
When things go wrong a man ain't got a friend,
Without a song.

I got my trouble and woe,
But sure as I know the Jordan will roll,
I'll get along as long as a song is strong
In my soul . . .[1]

Even though this song was composed before I was born (which makes it a real oldie), I often find myself returning to the tune. It slips out in places like my shower at the beginning of a busy day, between appointments and assignments in the middle of a hectic day, and on the road home at the end of a tiring day. Somehow it adds a touch of oil to the grind, smoothing things up a bit. Willie Nelson blew the dust off the old lyrics when he recorded it. I still sing them to myself . . .

Without a song the day would never end;
Without a song the road would never bend;
When things go wrong a man ain't got a friend,
Without a song.

True, isn't it? The right combination of words, melody, and rhythm seldom fails to work like magic. And given the pressures and demands folks like us are forced to cope with on a daily basis, we could use a little magic. Most of the people I know are never totally free of a relentless daily grind.

---

1 "Without a Song" words and music by Edward Eliscu, William Rose, and Vincent Youmans. Copyright © 1929 (renewed 1957) Miller Music Corporation and Vincent Youmans Co., Inc. Published by Miller Music Corporation by arrangement with Vincent Youmans Co., Inc. All Rights of Miller Music Corporation assigned to SBK Catalogue Partnership. All rights administered by SBK Miller Catalogue and Vincent Youmans Co., Inc. International copyright secured. Made in USA. All rights reserved. Used by permission.

- The homemaker with ever-present children at her feet faces fourteen or more hours a day in the grind of meeting deadlines, making decisions, competing with strong wills, and completing an endless list of chores.
- The professional experiences a grind of a different type: people, people, people . . . especially dissatisfied people who would rather scream and sue than smile and solve, which only intensifies the drain brought on by increasing expectations and decreasing energy.
- The truck driver has an altogether different but equally exhausting routine: the grind of traffic snarls, weather hazards, thoughtless drivers, and monotonous miles.
- Then there is the grind of repetition the athlete must live with: unending hours of practice, weight training, road work, watching films, perfecting technique, fierce competition, injuries, loneliness, boredom, exhaustion . . . only to wake up to another day of the same song, fifth verse.
- And who can deny the exacting requirements of academic pursuits? Students and faculty alike must live with the ceaseless, cyclical grind of daily preparation and assignments, attending class, doing projects, choosing electives, cramming for exams, grading papers, and (hopefully) earning a degree or tenure.

Fact is, the grind is not going away! The salesperson has to live with a quota. The performer must constantly rehearse. The therapist can't escape one depressed soul after another. The pilot has to stay strapped in for hours. The preacher is never free of sermon preparation. The broadcaster cannot get away from the clock any more than the bureaucrat can escape the hassle of red tape. Days don't end . . . roads don't bend . . . Help!

Instead of belaboring the point, since we cannot escape the grind, we must find a way to live beyond it. The question is, how?

The answer is, a song. Remember? "Without a song the day would never end." But not just any song! Certainly not some mindless, earsplitting tune yelled at us by a bunch of weird-looking jerks with blue and orange hair, dressed in black leather and spikes, and microphones stuffed halfway down their throats. No, not that. I have in mind some songs that are really old. We're talking ancient. In fact, they are the ones inspired and composed by our Creator-God—the original Rock music with a capital R. They're called psalms.

These are timeless songs that have yielded delicious fruit in every generation. They're not silly ditties, but strong, melodious messages written with life's daily grind in mind and specially designed to help us live beyond it. That's right, *beyond* it. To borrow again from the songwriter, "We'll get along as long as a *psalm* is strong in our souls." I really do believe that. Why else would God have inspired those age-old compositions? Surely, He realized the lasting value of each musical masterpiece and therefore preserved them to help us persevere. They drip with the oil of glory that enables us to live beyond the grind.

I could go on for pages. In fact, that is exactly what I intend to do! Since God's Book is full of such songs, I am convinced it is worth our while to spend our time pondering and applying these wise words and timeless principles woven through the Psalms.

To help make them stick, let's not try to digest too great a meal in one sitting. Seems to me these songs are like rich food to be savored slowly. Too much, too fast would be counterproductive. Let me urge you to take your time, to read each section carefully, to give your mind time to digest each daily provision slowly, and to enter into my reflections methodically and meaningfully. Let's sing David's song through each day of the week. I believe these time-tested lyrics will add just enough oil to our days to enable us to live out the truths of these psalms. Otherwise, our long days would never end and the wearisome road before us would never bend. How grateful I am for these inspired songs!

And now . . . let's press on. The weeks stretch out in front of us, and God's insightful songs await our appropriation. My desire is that these months of study and reflection on His Word will enable us to do more than plod along a tiresome path. If my weekly game plan works, we'll soon be living the Psalms on a daily basis.

THE GRIND OF COMPROMISE

How blessed is the man who does not walk in the
  counsel of the wicked,
Nor stand in the path of sinners,
Nor sit in the seat of scoffers!
But his delight is in the law of the LORD,
And in His law he meditates day and night.
He will be like a tree firmly planted by streams of water,
Which yields its fruit in its season
And its leaf does not wither;
And in whatever he does, he prospers.
The wicked are not so,
But they are like chaff which the wind drives away.
Therefore the wicked will not stand in the judgment,
Nor sinners in the assembly of the righteous.
For the LORD knows the way of the righteous,
But the way of the wicked will perish.

(Psalm 1)

Day 1: *Psalm 1*
Compromise and Erosion

The Hebrews' ancient hymnal begins with a song that addresses one of life's most common grinds: compromise. Please understand, I'm not referring to those give-and-take times so necessary for living in harmony with one another. Without that healthy kind of compromise, nations could never find a meeting ground for peaceful coexistence and family members would forever be at each other's throats.

I'm thinking, rather, of compromising with wrong, allowing the slow-moving tentacles of evil to wrap themselves around us, squeezing the joys and rewards of obedience from our lives. It happens so silently, so subtly, we hardly realize it's taking place. Like an enormous oak that has decayed for years from within and then suddenly falls, those who permit the eroding grind of compromise can expect an ultimate collapse.

I recall reading years ago of the construction of a city hall and fire station in a small northern Pennsylvania community. All the citizens were so proud of their new red brick structure—a long-awaited dream come true. Not too many weeks after moving in, however, strange things began to happen. Several doors failed to shut completely and a few windows wouldn't slide open very easily. As time passed, ominous cracks began to appear in the walls. Within a few months, the front door couldn't be locked since the foundation had shifted, and the roof began to leak. By and by, the little building that was once the source of great civic pride had to be condemned. The culprit proved to be a controversial coal extraction process called "longwall mining," deep in the earth beneath the foundation. Soil, rock, and coal had been removed by the tons so that the building sat on a foundation that had no support of its own. Because of this man-made erosion, the building began to sink.

So it is with compromise in a life. Slowly, almost imperceptibly, one rationalization leads to another, which triggers a series of equally damaging alterations in a life that was once stable, strong, and reliable. That seems to be the concern of the psalmist as he composes his first song, which encourages us to resist even the slightest temptation to compromise our convictions.

The Passage and Its Pattern

The First Psalm is brief and simple, direct and profound. Even a casual reading of these six verses leads us to see that it is filled with contrasts between two different walks of life—the godly and the ungodly. A simple yet acceptable outline of Psalm 1 would be:

I. The Godly Life (vv. 1–3)

II. The Ungodly Life (vv. 4–6)

Written between the lines of this ancient song is evidence of the age-old battle in which all of us are engaged: compromise—the erosion of our good intentions.

Making It Strong in Your Soul

Take just a few moments now to review your priorities. Family. Career, vocation, or calling. Job (not necessarily the same as career, vocation, or calling.) Health. Finances. Possessions. Friends. Spiritual development. Feel free to expand the list. As your eyes landed on each word, did your conscience react to anything? Did you mentally flinch or cringe? Compromise occurs when our behavior fails to reflect our priorities. In what ways have you compromised, and how can you get back on track?

Day 2: Psalm 1
The Godly Life

In the first three verses of Psalm 1, the psalmist describes the one who chooses to live a righteous life, the one who consciously resists the subtle inroads of compromise. He envisions a person who remains wary of anything that might erode commitment to a godly life. His song begins with three negative analogies to illustrate the importance of resisting compromise with evil, lest the evil become a habit of life. Then, in verse 2, he shows the positive side of godliness and the means by which it may be attained. Verse 3 describes the benefits of a righteous walk. Now let's do some in-depth analysis.

How blessed is the man who does not walk in the counsel
   of the wicked,
Nor stand in the path of sinners,
Nor sit in the seat of scoffers! (v. 1)

The first word, "blessed," is somewhat bland in our English language. The Hebrew term is much more descriptive, especially with its plural ending. Perhaps a workable rendering would be, "Oh, the happiness, many times over. . . ."

What is it that causes such an abundance of happiness? It is the uncompromising purity of a righteous walk with God. We see this by analyzing the three categories of remaining terms in this verse.

walk .... counsel .... wicked
stand .... path .... sinners
sit .... seat .... scoffers

The psalmist has spiritual erosion in mind. The word pictures illustrate how easily our intentions toward righteousness slow to a standstill or a complete stop as they are worn away by the company we choose to keep.

Walk

"Walk" is a term that suggests passing by or "a casual movement along the way." With its entire phrase, it implies the idea of one who does not imitate or "go through the casual motions" of wickedness. The word translated "counsel" comes from the Hebrew term meaning "hard, firm." Here, it means a definite, firm, planned direction. Consider this paraphrase of verse 1:

Oh, the happiness, many times over, of the one who does not even casually go through the motions or imitate the plan of life of those who live in ungodliness.

It is not uncommon to flirt with the wicked life, periodically imitating the motions of those without Christ. We may, in jest, refer to the fun and excitement of ungodliness or chuckle at our children's questionable actions. David warns us against that. He tells us that we will be abundantly happier if we steer clear of anything that could give the erosion of spiritual compromise a head start.

Stand

The Hebrew word for "stand" has the idea of coming and taking one's stand. The word "path" comes from the word meaning "a marked-out path, a certain and precise way of life." Can you see the progressive deterioration toward more involvement in sinful living? The casual passerby slows down and, before you know it, he takes his stand.

On the other hand, by taking a firm stand for righteousness, we will be "like a tree firmly planted by streams of water"—one that cannot be eroded by the winds of wickedness and unrighteousness.

Sit

The next word the psalmist emphasizes is "sit." This suggests a permanent settling down, an abiding, a permanent dwelling. It is made even clearer by the use of "seat," meaning "habitation" or "permanent residence." Don't miss this: the way of life is in the sphere of "the scoffer," the one who continually makes light of that which is sacred—the blasphemous crowd.

Can you see the picture in the writer's mind? We shall be happy many times over if we maintain a pure walk, free from even the slightest flirtation with evil. If we begin to "walk" in "the counsel of the wicked," it is easy to slip slowly into the habitation of the scoffer.

Making It Strong in Your Soul

Mentally review the past twelve months paying special attention to your "walk." How has your manner of life changed from years past? Is your walk more pleasing to God, or less? Consider your willingness to take an unpopular "stand." Can you be firm? And what about your attitude? Have you taken a comfortable seat among those who do not value the Word of God?

wisdom calls aloud – But who listens

Day 3: Psalm 1
An Uncompromising Walk

As I read Psalm 1, three illustrations from the Bible flash into my mind. Two men flirted with evil, then fell; but there was one other who refused to begin a "walk in the counsel of the wicked." The first two illustrations involve Lot and Samson; the third is Joseph. People the world over are familiar with Samson, whose life is best described in Proverbs 5:20–23:

> For why should you, my son, be exhilarated with an adulteress,
> And embrace the bosom of a foreigner?
> For the ways of a man are before the eyes of the LORD,
> And He watches all his paths.
> His own iniquities will capture the wicked,
> And he will be held with the cords of his sin.
> He will die for lack of instruction,
> And in the greatness of his folly he will go astray.

Most people are not as well-acquainted with Lot, Abraham's nephew. With Psalm 1:1 in mind, note Genesis 13:

> So Lot chose for himself all the valley of the Jordan, and Lot journeyed eastward. Thus they separated from each other. (v. 11)

Lot *"walked in the way of the ungodly."*

Abram settled in the land of Canaan, while Lot settled in

the cities of the valley, and moved his tents as far as Sodom. Now the men of Sodom were wicked exceedingly and sinners against the LORD. (vv. 12–13)

He "came and took his stand among sinners."

And in Genesis 19:

Now the two angels came to Sodom in the evening as Lot was sitting in the gate of Sodom. (v. 1)

He now lived among them with his dwelling in "the seat of the scoffers."

How different was Joseph! He refused to allow the daily grind of compromise to take its toll even though Potiphar's wife continued to make her sensual moves. Please stop and read Genesis 39:1–12. The man literally ran from her alluring advances. I find it most significant that every time sexual sins are mentioned in the New Testament we are told to "flee." Psalm 1:1 assures us we will be happy many times over if we check the first signals of compromise with evil. Happiness is maintaining unblemished, moral purity.

The ancient song goes on: "But his delight is in the law of the LORD, and in His law he meditates day and night" (v. 2).

This verse begins with "but," a word of contrast. While the first verse was negative, this is positive. In contrast to compromise and erosion, the godly believer occupies himself with God's Word.

Why does David mention the Law here? Because in order to change our path of living, we need an absolute standard, clear direction. God's Word gives us that sense of direction. We understand the Law to be a reference to God's written Word, the Bible (Ps. 119:9). The psalmist claims that the godly person "delights" in the Lord's Word. He doesn't look upon the Word as irksome or a burden or an interruption in his day. Rather, day and night he meditates on it.

Verse 1 of Psalm 1 gives us a promise of happiness; verse 2 provides the means for experiencing it. Now verse 3 declares the end result:

> He will be like a tree firmly planted by streams of water,
> Which yields its fruit in its season
> And its leaf does not wither;
> And in whatever he does, he prospers.

I am impressed that we shall *be* something rather than *do* something as a result of delighting in and meditating on God's Word. Without any fanfare, yet surely as the rising of the morning sun, we shall become treelike in four specific ways. We will be:

1. Planted—fortified, stable, rooted, solid, and strong
2. Fruitful—production naturally follows being planted and growing
3. Unwithered—even during days of difficulty, the treelike soul is undaunted
4. Prosperous—fulfills the goals God has designed for his life

I have said for years: "The roots grow deep when the winds are strong" (cf. Jer. 17:5–8). Let me encourage you today to maintain a pure, uncompromising walk; delight yourself in His Word, and you'll grow into a stable, reliable "spiritual tree."

There is no shortcut to spiritual growth. Like physical growth, it occurs on a daily basis, depending upon the food and proper surroundings. With the right kind of spiritual diet and climate, you can experience "happiness many times over." And best of all, the daily grind of compromise and its erosive effects can be checked.

Making It Strong in Your Soul

As you consider your own circumstances, what does "walking in the counsel of the wicked" look like in practical terms? What choices are involved? On the other hand, what practical steps can you take to cultivate a "delight" in God's Word? List them and establish some specific deadlines.

♆

Day 4: *Psalm 1*
The Ungodly Life

A key observation in Psalm1:4–6 is contrast. Don't miss the many things that are quite the opposite from the preceding verses. "The wicked are not so, but they are like chaff which the wind drives away."

"Not so!" That is exactly how verse 4 begins in the Hebrew Bible. It is an emphatic negative assertion. Literally, it says, "Not so, the wicked!" It refers back to the three preceding verses describing the righteous, godly believer, who:

- is happy many times over (but "not so, the wicked!")
- delights and meditates in the Word (but "not so, the wicked!")
- is like a tree (but "not so, the wicked!")
- is fruitful and prosperous (but "not so, the wicked!")

Instead, the psalmist uses a single term that portrays the life of the ungodly—"chaff," the paper-like skin of the grain seeds which separates at the time of threshing. Chaff is completely worthless. In contrast to the firmly rooted, fruit-bearing tree, chaff blows away during the winnowing process. The Hebrew word for "blow" means "to drive asunder, disseminate, diffuse, strike, or beat."

After comparing the lives of the "godly" and the "wicked," David considers the fate of those who reject the Lord. "Therefore the wicked will not stand in the judgment, nor sinners in the assembly of the righteous" (v. 5). The first word connects this verse with the previous verse—"Therefore (or on account of their inner worthlessness and instability) . . . the wicked will not stand in the judgment."

The Hebrew verb translated "stand" is not the same as the previous term rendered "stand" in verse 1. This particular Hebrew term means "to stand erect, to arise." The idea in the mind of the songwriter is an inability to stand upright before God's judgment. A parallel statement follows: "nor sinners in the assembly of the righteous."

The one who has never come by faith to the Lord and trusted Him alone for eternal life and a position of righteousness in God's eyes has no part among the assembly of believers. Again, let me remind you of yet another contrast. In destiny, there is a great difference between the godly and the ungodly. But so many unbelievers live healthy, moral lives . . . even sacrificial and dedicated lives. How can anyone say they won't be among the eternal assembly of the righteous? Verse 6 answers that question: "For the LORD knows the way of the righteous, but the way of the wicked will perish."

You'll observe it is the Lord who does the judging. He alone sees the heart. He alone; not man. Only God is capable of being just and fair. But doesn't the first part of this verse bring a question to your mind? Doesn't He know the way of the ungodly as well? He certainly does! But this sixth verse is explaining why the ungodly will not be able to stand up under judgment nor stand among the righteous assembly (v. 5). Why? Because the Lord takes special interest in the righteous. Because the Lord is inclined and bound to the righteous by special love. He will not allow an intermingling between the righteous and the unrighteous. That is not His plan.

The verse concludes with the severe reminder that the way of the unrighteous will perish. What a jolting climax to the psalm! Again, another vivid contrast. Instead of prospering, the ungodly will ultimately perish just as the little red brick city hall was ultimately condemned.

Making It Strong in Your Soul

God doesn't demand perfection from believers; all of us fail from time to time. Fortunately, grace abounds. Nevertheless, at least one indication that our faith is genuine is a sincere desire to obey. If you do not "delight" in pleasing God by obeying His Word, perhaps now is a good time for some soul searching. Go there.

Day 5: *Psalm 1*

A Life beyond Compare

The central lesson in Psalm 1 is this: there is not the slightest similarity between the spiritually accelerating life of the righteous and the slowly eroding life of the wicked. Take time to ponder the bold contrasts:

Godly	Ungodly
Happiness many times over	Not so!
Uncompromised purity	Driven by the wind
Has a guide—Word of God	No guide
Like a tree	Like chaff
Stands erect before God	Unable to stand erect
Special object of God's care	No right to stand among righteous assembly
Destiny secure, safe, prosperous	Perish

Let's bring this week's study of Psalm 1 to a close with an expanded paraphrase:

Oh, the happiness, many times over, of the man who does not temporarily or even casually imitate the plan of life of those living in the activity of sinful confusion, nor comes and takes his stand in the midst of those who miss the mark spiritually, nor settles down and dwells in the habitation of the blasphemous crowd. But (in contrast to that kind of lifestyle) in God's Word he takes great pleasure, thinking upon it and pondering it every waking moment, day or night. The result: He will become treelike—firm, fruitful, unwithered, and fulfilling the goals in life that God has designed for him.

Not so, the ungodly! They are like worthless husks beaten about and battered by the winds of life (drifting and roaming without purpose). Therefore, on account of their inner worthlessness without the Lord, the ungodly are not able to stand erect on the day of judgment, nor do they possess any right to be numbered among the assembly of those declared righteous by God, because the Lord is inclined toward and bound to His righteous ones by special love and care; but the way of the one without the Lord will lead only to eternal ruin.

Making It Strong in Your Soul

Read Psalm 1 again, this time aloud. Pay close attention to the "walk . . . stand . . . sit" picture in the first verse. Honestly now, have you begun to tolerate a few compromises you once rejected? What will it take to get that cleared up? Never doubt the dangers brought on by spiritual, ethical, or moral erosion.

THE GRIND OF DISCOURAGEMENT

For the choir director; for flute accompaniment.
A Psalm of David.

Give ear to my words, O LORD,
Consider my groaning.
Heed the sound of my cry for help, my King and my God,
For to You I pray.
In the morning, O LORD, You will hear my voice;
In the morning I will order my prayer to You and
      eagerly watch.
For You are not a God who takes pleasure in wickedness;
No evil dwells with You.
The boastful shall not stand before Your eyes;
You hate all who do iniquity.
You destroy those who speak falsehood;
The LORD abhors the man of bloodshed and deceit.
But as for me, by Your abundant lovingkindness I will
      enter Your house,
At Your holy temple I will bow in reverence for You.
O LORD, lead me in Your righteousness because of my foes;
Make Your way straight before me.
There is nothing reliable in what they say;
Their inward part is destruction itself.
Their throat is an open grave;
They flatter with their tongue.
Hold them guilty, O God;
By their own devices let them fall!
In the multitude of their transgressions thrust them out,
For they are rebellious against You.

But let all who take refuge in You be glad,
Let them ever sing for joy;
And may You shelter them,
That those who love Your name may exult in You.
For it is You who blesses the righteous man, O LORD,
You surround him with favor as with a shield.

(Psalm 5)

Day 1: *Psalm 5*
A Song of Circumstance

S ongs are usually born out of surrounding circumstances that so affect the thinking of the composer, he cannot help but burst forth with a melody and an accompanying set of lyrics describing his plight. This is certainly the case with the blues and jazz of yesteryear as well as the old spirituals of days gone by and the romantic love songs of any era. The same has often been true of gospel songs and sacred hymns; their historical settings explain their message.

Psalm 5 is no exception. As we read it, we can detect that it emerged out of an atmosphere of strife and oppression. David was down in the dumps . . . discouraged. Whatever his pressures were, they prompted him to compose this ancient hymn in a minor key.

I seriously doubt that there is any subject more timely than discouragement. So many people I meet feel like the soundtrack of their lives is nothin' but the blues. A relentless, grinding discouragement follows each unachieved goal or failed romance. Some try to whistle a happy tune in the darkness of a failing marriage, a relationship that began with such promise but now seems hopeless. Declining health can discourage and demoralize its victim, especially when the pain won't go away. And who can't identify with the individual who bravely risked something new, only to suffer the sting of criticism from a gallery of self-appointed critics?

The discouragement brought on by several back-to-back criticisms can scarcely be exaggerated. It could be that David was just picking himself up off the mat when another sharp-worded comment knocked him back to his knees . . . hence the birth of Psalm 5. Many a discouraged soul has identified with this song down through the centuries. Frequently, the words just above the first verse (which comprise the superscription) establish the historical context of the song.

If you glance just above verse 1 in the King James Version of the Bible, you will see that David desired this song to be played "upon Nehiloth." A nehiloth was an ancient woodwind instrument many associate with today's flute. Because many of the "lament psalms" feature the nehiloth, I think of the oboe, a sad-sounding, double-reed instrument. The wistful tone of the oboe prompts many composers to feature the instrument in doleful or contemplative pieces.

Interestingly, David did not play the *nehiloth*, but rather a stringed instrument similar to the harp (see 1 Sam. 16:23, KJV). David wrote this sad song of discouragement to be played on the instrument best suited to express the feeling of discouragement that gave birth to this song.

Making It Strong in Your Soul

Sometimes, words aren't enough to express the sorrow we feel in the depths of difficulty. How do you express yourself when words do not suffice? Would you consider your behavior productive—something that might be helpful to others? Or is it destructive—actions that harm others?

Day 2: *Psalm 5*

The Psalmist's Plea

Some psalms are difficult to outline; others easily lend themselves to an organized layout. Psalm 5 falls in the latter category. It begins with a *plea* (vv. 1–3) directed to the Lord, whom David addresses, 'O LORD . . . my King . . . my God . . . O LORD." It concludes with a *promise* (v. 12). Sandwiched between the plea and the promise are four descriptions. An outline would look something like this:

     I. A Plea (vv. 1–3)

    II. Four Descriptions (vv. 4–11)

        A. What the Lord is like (vv. 4–6)

        B. What the psalmist is like (vv. 7–8)

        C. What the enemies are like (vv. 9–10)

        D. What the righteous are like (v. 11)

   III. A Promise (v. 12)

Take a look at David's introductory plea:

Give ear to my words, O LORD,
Consider my groaning.
Heed the sound of my cry for help, my King and my God,
For to You I pray.
In the morning, O LORD, You will hear my voice;
In the morning I will order my prayer to You and eagerly watch.
(vv. 1–3)

I observe three things in this plea.

First, it was a "morning" prayer. Twice in verse 3 David mentions that it was "in the morning" that he met with his Lord.

Second, it came from one who was becoming increasingly

discouraged. Look at the first two verses and notice how they grow in intensity: "Give ear to my words . . . consider my groaning . . . heed my cry!"

Hebrew poetry can be a complicated study, but some things about it are easy to grasp. One rather simple yet meaningful technique used in these two verses is what scholars call "synonymous parallelism." As the line progresses, each thought restates the previous one while compounding the intensity. If this were a musical score, the notation would call for a crescendo. David is pleading: "Give ear!" Next, he becomes more burdened: "Consider!" He then grows stronger in his plea with the request that the Lord "Heed the sound of my cry for help!" To enter into the depth of this hymn, you cannot afford to miss the growing discouragement in the writer's heart. Let yourself imagine his inner groaning. Picture his intensified misery as you mentally relive his situation.

Third, the psalmist anticipated God's intervention. By faith, he counted on the Lord's help. I see two statements in verse 3 that reveal this: (1) "I will order my prayer to You," and (2) "I will eagerly watch."

The Hebrew verb translated "order" means "to make an order." The statement could read, "In the morning I will place my order with You." While that might sound presumptuous at first, maybe even a little bossy, it's said in the spirit of someone holding a menu. He's merely choosing something the Lord has offered. David looked upon the morning as the time to "place his order" from the Lord's menu of blessings.

He then said, "I will eagerly watch" (literally, "look forward"). After placing his order, he eagerly anticipates an answer from his Lord. David refused to stumble about stoop-shouldered, carrying his burdens throughout the day. On the contrary, he took his needs to the Lord each morning.

When we think of "placing an order," we remember one thing that is essential: we have to be specific. Too many prayers suffer from timidity and vagueness. God invites us to pray with bold expectation when we ask for what He has promised or anticipate what we know to be His will.

After David placed a specific order each morning, he anticipated answers. He expected God to "fill his order" and then looked forward to that throughout the day. When our outlook is dim in the morning, when discouragement worms its way in, a good remedy is to focus our attention upward. And what a difference it makes in our day! Throughout Scripture, spiritual turning points occur at morning time. Darkness gives way to light as contemplation yields insight. For example:

> For His anger is but for a moment,
> His favor is for a lifetime;
> Weeping may last for the night,
> But a shout of joy comes in the morning. (Psalm 30:5)

> But I, O LORD, have cried out to You for help,
> And in the morning my prayer comes before You. (Psalm 88:13)

> The LORD's lovingkindnesses indeed never cease,
> For His compassions never fail.
> They are new every morning;
> Great is Your faithfulness. (Lamentations 3:22–23)

> In the early morning, while it was still dark, Jesus got up, left *the house*, and went away to a secluded place, and was praying there. (Mark 1:35)

David's cries became more desperate as he continued to suffer and continued to seek God's intervention. Then, he prayed with confidence in the Lord's sovereignty and goodness. In fact, he decided to begin each morning this way; he greeted each new day by "placing his order" and resolving to wait with confidence for God's response.

Making It Strong in Your Soul

What has you most discouraged right now? How has discouragement affected your prayer life? Perhaps, like David, you might pray with confident expectation and complete trust in the Lord's sovereignty and goodness. That's hard to do at first but, eventually, your attitude will become like your prayers.

Day 3: *Psalm 5*
The Attributes of God

After the plea in Psalm 5:1–3, David begins to think through the day that spreads out before him, giving extra consideration to those he would encounter. His song addresses four specific realms of interest (vv. 4–11).

1. David meditates on the Lord Himself (vv. 4–6).
2. David describes himself (vv. 7–8).
3. David describes his enemies (vv. 9–10).
4. David describes the righteous (v. 11).

Let's examine each realm of interest, beginning with the first: God Himself.

> For You are not a God who takes pleasure in wickedness;
> No evil dwells with You.
> The boastful shall not stand before Your eyes;
> You hate all who do iniquity.
> You destroy those who speak falsehood;
> The LORD abhors the man of bloodshed and deceit.

He mentions seven specific things about his Lord:

a. He takes no pleasure in wickedness.
b. No evil will "dwell" with Him (literally).
c. Arrogant boasters will not stand before Him.

d. He hates workers of iniquity.

e. He destroys those who lie.

f. He abhors murderers.

g. He abhors deceivers.

Why does David review these things? Because it is therapeutic to review the attributes of God—to remind ourselves that He is always good, and that He is always right in His ways. His love for us never fails and His timing is perfect. Many of the pent-up angry feelings and frustrations of our inner emotional tank are diffused as we review God's character and remind ourselves that He is *for* us, not against us. Focusing on His character helps dispel discouragement! Furthermore, we are reminded that our enemies are really God's enemies. He is more powerful than any evil and more persistent than any difficult circumstance. As for those who try to harm us, the Lord is far more capable of dealing with them than we are.

Making It Strong in Your Soul

In the midst of discouragement, it's difficult to count your blessings. So, instead, create a list of God's attributes from Scripture. (This psalm is a good place to start.) Then, pray through the list, praising God for each attribute. As an experiment, try praying this way for an entire week without asking for anything. Record your experience in a journal for later use.

Day 4: *Psalm 5*
Agents of God's Will

Having reviewed the attributes of God, focusing on His sovereignty and goodness, David examines himself (vv. 7–8).

But as for me, by Your abundant lovingkindness I will
  enter Your house,
At Your holy temple I will bow in reverence for You.
O LORD, lead me in Your righteousness because of my foes;
Make Your way straight before me.

Verse 7 begins with a strong contrast. The Hebrew is exceptionally strong, literally: "But me . . . as for me!" In contrast to those whom the Lord would destroy (v. 6), David enjoyed a spiritual position, which is mentioned in the latter part of verse 7 as "Your holy temple," a poetic reference to intimate fellowship with the Lord.

Verse 8 is the major prayer of this song. Everything before this verse could be considered preliminary. Here is the kernel of his request: "Lead me in Your righteousness because of my foes; make Your way straight before me."

What does this mean? David didn't want to resort to the tactics of his enemies, so he prayed that the Lord would lead him throughout the conflict, causing him to do things God's way. He wanted to follow God's righteous way, first and foremost. Not too many years later, the princely prophet, Isaiah, spoke to Israel on behalf of God:

"For My thoughts are not your thoughts,
Nor are your ways My ways," declares the LORD.
"For as the heavens are higher than the earth,
So are My ways higher than your ways
And My thoughts than your thoughts." (Isaiah 55:8–9)

When discouraged, we naturally pray for relief . . . we beg the Lord to act on our behalf. What if, instead, we asked for the opportunity to do something for Him? How might our perspective change if we began to see ourselves as agents of God's will, acting on His behalf and carrying out His desires, rather than always expecting Him to serve us?

When is the last time you asked the Lord for an opportunity to do something for Him? Perhaps now is a good time, especially if you're struggling with discouragement. When you pray for the ability to carry out His will, it's likely your sense of powerlessness will quickly fade.

Day 5: *Psalm 5*
God's Shield against Discouragement

Sometimes we suffer discouragement because of difficult circumstances caused by no one in particular: natural disasters, disease, economic downturns, injury. Frequently, however, we suffer because enemies cause us harm and refuse to stop. That was David's lament in Psalm 5. He knew discouragement can easily escalate into resentment, bitterness, hatred, and finally retaliation. He feared becoming like his oppressors. So, David reflected on the Lord's character and asked Him for the ability to do things His way. David then considers the character and actions of his enemies (Ps. 5:9–10).

> There is nothing reliable in what they say;
> Their inward part is destruction itself.
> Their throat is an open grave;
> They flatter with their tongue.
> Hold them guilty, O God;
> By their own devices let them fall!
> In the multitude of their transgressions thrust them out,
> For they are rebellious against You.

In his mind, David deliberately hands his enemies over to God, who has the sole authority to dispense justice or mercy. He also asks God to allow them to "fall by their own devices." When dealing with those who oppose righteousness, it's helpful to remember that they are fighting against the Lord, not you. Consequently, you can be sure He will not allow evil deeds to continue forever. He will limit sin and hold the sinners accountable. If left alone in their own counsel, they will fall by themselves!

Paul the apostle says it straight in Romans 12:17–19.

> Never pay back evil for evil to anyone. Respect what is right in the sight of all men. If possible, so far as it depends on you, be at peace with all men. Never take your own revenge, beloved, but leave room for the wrath *of God,* for it is written, "VENGEANCE IS MINE, I WILL REPAY," says the Lord.

The daily grind of discouragement is lessened when we trust that the Lord will fight our battles for us.

Finally, having celebrated the righteous character of God, having requested the ability to remain on God's side of the issue, and having considered the ultimate fate of evildoers, David imagined the future joy of the righteous (Ps. 5:11).

> But let all who take refuge in You be glad,
> Let them ever sing for joy;
> And may You shelter them,
> That those who love Your name may exult in You.

The key thought through this verse is joy. How are you doing regarding your countenance—is it joyful? Do you really live above the pressures? Is there an evidence of peace written across your face? If you fight your own battles without the Lord, you'll become bitter, severe, cranky, and ultimately your face will bear the marks of the battle.

Have you ever taken note of Cain's response to God's refusal of his offering? A most significant statement appears in Genesis 4:5:

"So Cain became very angry and his countenance fell." Another way of translating the Hebrew text adds a bit more color: "And Cain burned with anger exceedingly and his face fell." When anger and resentment are harbored, our faces show it. Our jaw tightens with clenched teeth. Our eyes narrow. It is impossible to hide inner discouragement! "Fallen" faces reveal discouraged hearts. David wanted God to take his inner burden and replace it with inner joy.

Finally, the composer mentions a promise we frequently forget:

For it is You who blesses the righteous man, O LORD,
You surround him with favor as with a shield. (Psalm 5:12)

David closes his song with his eyes turned toward the Lord and away from the sources of his discouragement. Having given God his "morning burden," David's discouragement fled. The shield he mentions at the end of his song here in verse 12 was the largest of warriors' shields, covering the entire body. So what is the promise? God will bless the one who looks to Him for protection. How? He will do this by giving him favor and by providing him with His large, protective (yet invisible) shield. Up with the shield . . . out with discouragement!

Making It Strong in Your Soul

As you meet with the Lord—preferably in the morning—and you pray to overcome discouragement, follow the guidelines of Psalm 5:

- Describe your attitude and how deeply you hurt.
- Review the attributes of God.
- Ask for opportunities to do things His way.
- Be specific in your prayers.
- Remind yourself of His defense.
- Recall the Lord's promises.

And when you're too down to pray for yourself, ask for someone to join you in prayer on your behalf.

THE GRIND OF FEELING OVERLOOKED

For the choir director; on the Gittith. A Psalm of David.

O LORD, our Lord,
How majestic is Your name in all the earth,
Who have displayed Your splendor above the heavens!
From the mouth of infants and nursing babes
    You have established strength
Because of Your adversaries,
To make the enemy and the revengeful cease.
When I consider Your heavens, the work of Your fingers,
The moon and the stars, which You have ordained;
What is man that You take thought of him,
And the son of man that You care for him?
Yet You have made him a little lower than God,
And You crown him with glory and majesty!
You make him to rule over the works of Your hands;
You have put all things under his feet,
All sheep and oxen,
And also the beasts of the field,
The birds of the heavens and the fish of the sea,
Whatever passes through the paths of the seas.
O LORD, our Lord,
How majestic is Your name in all the earth!

(Psalm 8)

Day 1: *Psalm 8*

The Value of God's Creatures

All of us need to be needed. We want to be wanted. God created us with a desire to know we can contribute something valuable and to have a significant impact in the lives of others. In years past, great men and women longed to leave their marks on the world, to create a legacy that would continue after they have passed away.

In our youth, we tend to derive a lot of self-worth from our ability to contribute to others or to assist others in their need. Being in the swirl of activity, resourceful and responsive, our youthful exuberance blinds us to the fact that it will someday end. Then, ever so slowly through a chain of events or sometimes abruptly without warning, we find ourselves sidelined and no longer in demand. One circumstance or another can seize our usefulness and leave us reeling in its devastating wake. Injustice can take our freedom. Slander can take away our reputation. Illness can take away our strength. Bad fortune can take away our wealth. Depression can take away our hope. And let's not forget the steady incursion of age on our vitality. Merely growing older can move us out of the fast lane. By being passed over for a promotion or being benched because a stronger player joins the team, we feel overlooked. It hurts.

No one wants to feel set aside.

The eighth song in God's ancient hymnal is a great one for those times in our lives when we feel bypassed, set aside, overlooked. It highlights the value God places upon His creatures, and none more than humanity.

Making It Strong in Your Soul

How do you measure your worth, your own value as a person? Be honest right now; this is just between you and the Lord. How much does your monetary worth factor into your self-worth? How about your position—your power or authority? Does your ability to impact the world or have influence in the lives of others give you a sense of increased worth?

♬

Day 2: *Psalm 8*
The Majesty of God

As I observe Psalm 8, three introductory observations leap off the page. First, it is a psalm of David, written under the Holy Spirit's direction. These are not merely the idle reflections of a creative artist. He was given this song as a gift from God to humanity. These are the words of God.

Second, I note the superscription "on the Gittith." The etymology of this Hebrew term is a subject of debate among scholars. Many believe *Gittith* is derived from Gath, the ancient Philistine city and hometown of David's most famous enemy, Goliath. The giant he slew hailed from Gath (1 Sam. 17:4, 23). The term could refer to the musical style associated with that culture or a musical instrument commonly used in Gath. Regardless, the expression "on the Gittith" or "according to the Gittith" appears above two other psalms of celebration (Psalms 81 and 84). The Scriptures tell us that after David's victory over Goliath the people of Israel sang and danced as they celebrated the triumph (1 Sam. 18:6–7).

I suggest—and it is only a suggestion—that this psalm was composed by David as a hymn of praise in honor of God who gave David that epochal triumph over Goliath of Gath. As you read the Eighth Psalm, you'll see that it seems to fit that historical backdrop. This is a song of celebration, so if you have a giant to slay—in this case, a personal giant of feeling insignificant—take heart! This song is for you.

My third observation is that Psalm 8 begins and ends with identical statements: "O Lord, our Lord, how majestic is Your name in all the earth." This repeated praise offers three implications worth noting:

 1. The psalmist speaks on behalf of the people of God, not just himself, hence *our* instead of *my*. This tells us he represents a group of people as he composes this song of victory.

 2. The name of YHWH is identified with *majestic*, which derives from the Hebrew word *adar*, meaning "wide, great, high, noble." David pictures our Lord as One who is gloriously magnificent, absolutely majestic!

 3. The Lord's works and attributes are not limited to Israel or to the Land of Canaan. They are universal in scope. The Lord God is no national or tribal deity secluded from all else.

The Passage and Its Pattern

Because seven and a half verses of Psalm 8 fall between repetitions of the same statement, we should understand that the twice-repeated statement is the central theme of the psalm. David worships the living Lord as the majestic and glorious Lord of all. In fact, an outline of the song could resemble a public worship service all of us have attended:

 I. Doxology (v. la)
 II. Worship (vv. 1b–8)
  A. Praise (vv. 1b–2)
  B. Message (vv. 3–8)
   1. Man's Insignificance: "What is man?"
   2. God's Grace: "You crown him."
 III. Benediction (v. 9)

We'll follow this outline as we examine David's song of celebration, beginning with the doxology:

O LORD, our Lord,
How majestic is Your name in all the earth. (v. 1)

This first word in the Hebrew text embodies the transcendent majesty and glory of God. While most Bibles render the first word as "Lord," it is actually His Hebrew name, represented by the four capital letters YHWH. Because this name was—and still is—so holy to the Hebrews, they *never* spoke the name audibly. Consequently, no one knows the correct pronunciation! Gentiles typically defer to *Yahweh*. The second "Lord" is the Hebrew word *adonai*, which is a title of respect in recognition of authority or sovereignty. The Jews typically pronounce the word *adonai* when reading Scripture out loud and encounter the Lord's Hebrew name, YHWH. The word translated "majestic" is a superlative, meaning "mightier than everything else."

By combining these three terms, David celebrates the supreme power of God over everything. He declares from the beginning that God has no rival. He is subject to no other power and He reigns supreme.

Making It Strong in Your Soul

What is the most powerful force in the universe? An exploding star? A black hole? God is more powerful, by far, than either of those. In fact, the combined energy of every star in every galaxy in the universe cannot rival the power of its Maker. As you consider God's omnipotence, what effect does it have on your feeling of being overlooked?

Day 3: *Psalm 8*

A Song of Praise

Having worshiped God in a short doxology, David reflects on the greatness of his God and, in doing so, offers praise. Observe as King David takes his place before a congregation of believers to lead them in worship.

[You] have displayed Your splendor above the heavens!
From the mouth of infants and nursing babes You have
    established strength
Because of Your adversaries,
To make the enemy and the revengeful cease. (Psalm 8:1–2)

The difference between praise and petition is the absence of self. David leaves himself out of the picture in this expression of praise. He declares that the majesty and glory of God are "displayed" in the heavens. The Lord has invested the physical universe with the awesome splendor of His majesty. Psalm 19:1 verifies this fact: "The heavens are telling of the glory of God; and their expanse is declaring the work of His hands." And, again, Romans 1:20:

For since the creation of the world His invisible attributes,
His eternal power and divine nature, have been clearly seen,
being understood through what has been made.

David then goes on to illustrate his concept of God's glory by the other extreme; he considers the powerlessness of babes and how God can use even tiny infants—even those still nursing—to silence those who stand against Him. God shows Himself majestic and glorious in His love for the powerless.

I have an obstetrician friend who testifies that even before he became a Christian he could not ignore the power of God as he delivered and then held in his hands one tiny, screaming infant after another. He testifies that this ultimately led him to search for answers in the Bible and finally to find salvation through faith in Jesus Christ. In a very real sense, therefore, "infants and nursing babes" declare God's power and majesty. It is in His love for the powerless that we see living proof of God's creative might. When we study the delicate tiny features of their newborn state, we marvel at His attention to detail. Verse 2 concludes with the reminder that even God's enemies are silenced when the heavens are observed . . . or when little ones are considered.

Infants may be small and the stellar spaces silent, but both convey a profound significance to the observer. So it is at those times in our lives when we may think we are no longer that valuable or necessary. While God honors us by accomplishing His work through us, that is not the basis of our value. To put it another way, we are not valuable to God because of our usefulness. He values us whether we are productive or not.

There is an overwhelming comfort in that message. Human power or ability does not earn our Creator's love. He loves us regardless. We are special to Him no matter what happens, even if we become as weak as a newborn.

Making It Strong in Your Soul

If God loves you and values you regardless of your personal attributes—strength, power, wealth, talent, appearance, intelligence, or even morality—how does that affect your sense of self-worth? How does that affect your everyday decisions?

Day 4: *Psalm 8*
A Message from God

As though David continues his worship service, He opens his mouth and shares a message from God, which is the major theme of this composition. We can imagine his standing before the people and preaching about the needs of humanity and the grace of God.

First, he considers the pitiful inadequacy of humanity. Read verses 3–4 slowly. Think them over and enter into the mental picture David has in mind.

When I consider Your heavens, the work of Your fingers,
The moon and the stars, which You have ordained;
What is man that You take thought of him,
And the son of man that You care for him? (Ps. 8:3–4)

The Hebrew word translated "consider" is the common verb meaning "to see, behold, take a look." David was out among the splendor of natural phenomena. As he looked about him he was gripped with the startling realization of God's greatness. Every one of us has had that experience. When we glance heavenward, we are struck with awe. We "take a look" at the expanse, and invariably, we are overwhelmed!

David refers to God's creation as "the work of Your fingers." Creating the universe was nothing more than "finger work" for God; salvation, however, represents His "arm work" (Isa. 52:10; 53:1; 59:16; Ps. 77:15, KJV).

In asking the question, "What is man?" David uses a rather uncommon term for man. *Enosh* comes from a Hebrew verb that means "to be weak, sick, frail." In other words: "In comparison to your splendor and majesty, O Lord, what is puny, weak, frail humanity?" According to David, God overlooks our lowly status and acts on behalf of humanity in two significant ways: He takes thought of him and takes care of him.

What do these things mean? The first statement—"take thought of"—means that God remembers us, while the second phrase—"care for"—means He pays attention to us. What an amazing truth! If the daily grind of feeling overlooked has you in its grip, here is a thought worth massaging: the God who created all the magnificent surroundings of the universe actually remembers and pays attention to puny individuals like you and me. It is easy to believe that God has too many other things to concern Himself with than to care about us. Peter reminds us, however, that "[God] cares for you" (1 Peter 5:7). God never overlooks His own!

This prompts David to reflect on the grace of God.

Yet You have made him a little lower than God,
And You crown him with glory and majesty!
You make him to rule over the works of Your hands;
You have put all things under his feet,
All sheep and oxen,
And also the beasts of the field,
The birds of the heavens and the fish of the sea,
Whatever passes through the paths of the seas. (Psalm 8:5–8)

In spite of the vast difference between God and man, David declares that the Lord has set His love upon us and has given humanity a place of dignity and importance in this world. We are made lesser than angels in terms of power, but we are, nevertheless, crowned with glory and majesty. Moreover, He gave us the responsibility and privilege of ruling over the world as His vice-regents (Gen. 1:28–30). Hebrews 2:6–9 applies these verses to Jesus Christ, making this section of Psalm 8 messianic and prophetic. Historically, however, it is applicable to all humans. While Jesus is the Son of God, we share this honor and responsibility with Him. *Amazing!*

Making It Strong in Your Soul

Take the time tonight to walk out under the stars, lie on your back, and look up. As you study the vast stellar spaces, remember that God loves you, individually, more than He loves the universe. Then, examine your habits and choices. Are they driven by a desire to earn love and respect from others, or from God?

Day 5: *Psalm 8*

Front and Center in the Mind of God

It's humbling to think that the Creator of the universe, whose power, knowledge, and goodness know no limits, actually cares about us and loves us individually and personally. Think about how difficult it would be to reach the CEO of a major corporation to discuss your problems with a product. Or imagine trying to get a few moments alone with the President of the United States to talk about your foreign policy concerns. We all know how poorly that would turn out. It's not their fault; with limited time and energy, they have to prioritize. Furthermore, we who have large families sometimes find it difficult to stay current with all our little ones. Keeping up with the daily lives of our ten grandchildren could turn into a full-time job; almost impossible for mere man. So, the fact that the Ruler of the universe takes personal care of me is more than I can fathom. He takes a personal interest in each one who trusts in Him. He adds oil to our grind of feeling overlooked by reminding us of His personal interest.

Perhaps as you read this you feel alone, deserted. What a distressing, barren valley is loneliness! But listen! If you have the Lord Jesus Christ as your personal Savior, you have a constant Companion and Friend. He never leaves you in the lurch. This psalm is proof positive that He does not consider you unimportant or overlook you. He isn't irritated by your coming to Him with your needs. He never looks upon your prayers or requests as interruptions. Even as James reminds us: He gives "generously and without reproach" (1:5). He provides good gifts without "variation or shifting shadow" (1:17).

Do you know why? The answer is Grace—sheer, undeserved, unmerited, unearned favor. Therefore, right now, cast your feeling of insignificance and despair on Him. Tell Him that you are claiming this Eighth Psalm as a promise of His personal grace, concern, and love for you.

Remember, this is a psalm "on the Gittith." David composed it perhaps as a victory hymn after defeating the giant, Goliath. I challenge you to take that personal "giant" of feeling overlooked and ask God to give you victory over it today. Who knows? Another Goliath could fall by sundown.

David concludes his song with a benediction, the same words he used in the doxology: "O LORD, our Lord, how majestic is Your name in all the earth" (v. 9). We add to David's benediction our own affirming response: Amen.

Making It Strong in Your Soul

Toward the end of the week, call to mind several recent occasions when the Lord came to your rescue or gave you assistance or perhaps granted a request. Pause to thank Him because He cares for you. Tell Him how grateful you are for His attention to detail in every area of your life. Then use those recollections to salve your emotional wounds. While circumstances may place you on the sidelines, you remain front-and-center in the mind of God!

THE GRIND OF DESPONDENCY

For the choir director. A Psalm of David.

How long, O LORD? Will You forget me forever?
How long will You hide Your face from me?
How long shall I take counsel in my soul,
Having sorrow in my heart all the day?
How long will my enemy be exalted over me?
Consider and answer me, O LORD my God;
Enlighten my eyes, or I will sleep the sleep of death,
And my enemy will say, "I have overcome him,"
And my adversaries will rejoice when I am shaken.
But I have trusted in Your lovingkindness;
My heart shall rejoice in Your salvation.
I will sing to the LORD,
Because He has dealt bountifully with me.

(Psalm 13)

Day 1: *Psalm 13*

The Heartbreak of Hopelessness

Many years ago when I was living in Dallas attending seminary, I received a phone call that led me to a tiny, dirty garage apartment. I was met at the screen door by a man with a 12-gauge shotgun. He invited me in. We sat for over an hour at a tiny kitchen table with a naked light bulb hanging above it. He poured out a heartbreaking story. He had just been released from the hospital, recovering from back surgery. He was alone, having lost contact with his wife (and their only son) when his marriage failed many years before. As we talked of the man's intense struggles, I noticed that his small apartment was full of pictures—all of them of his son at various stages of growth.

There were photos taken of the boy when he was still in diapers. Others were with his dad when the lad was graduating from kindergarten. Still others showed him in his Little League uniform with a bat over his shoulder . . . on and on, right up through high school. The man's entire focus centered upon a marriage that had failed and a boy he no longer was able to enjoy. Those nostalgic "misty, water-colored memories of the way we were" held him captive in a prison-house of regret and despondency. Unfortunately, my attempts to help him see beyond the walls of his anguish proved futile. In less than a week, he shot himself to death in his car, which he had driven deep into the woods in East Texas. To him, life was no longer worth the fight.

It's normal to grieve after a significant loss. Grief is the painful process of adjusting to a new set of circumstances. As acceptance takes place, grief subsides, giving way to joy again. Sometimes, however, grief can lead to hopelessness instead of acceptance. That's despondency. Perpetual, downward-spiraling hopelessness.

It is not necessary to read Psalm 13 many times to detect some despondency in David. Like my lonely friend in the apartment, the psalmist feels down. Forgotten. It is that age-old "nobody seems to care" syndrome. Despair may not be too strong a description of his emotional temperature. My grandfather would have said "he's under the pile." We understand! I'm convinced it is these mutual feelings that cause us to be drawn to the Psalms on our blue days. David feels miserable. No one knows the reason for certain; the background of many of the psalms remains a mystery. Nevertheless, his words resonate with our own painful feelings when we're "under the pile."

If you or someone you know is growing despondent, what is the issue at hand? What circumstance triggered this grief? Take a few moments to describe it in writing, in the third person, as though telling a story about a fictional character.

❦

Day 2: *Psalm 13*

From Despondency to Ecstasy

David's struggle with despondency grew very intense, perhaps prompting him to write the song we know today as Psalm 13. We can't be certain of the issue plaguing the poet-king. We do know, however, that some of David's darkest days came before he was officially promoted to the throne of Israel. God was preparing him for an immense task, and He used the trials to shape him into a man of maturity and inner strength. It may help us to look back into 1 Samuel for what might have been the circumstances that led David to write this song. (See 1 Sam. 18:9–15, 28–29; 20:30–33.)

He had just slain Goliath of Gath. The Philistines, therefore, had become a defeated foe of Israel, and David had become the most famous (though still youthful) hero in the land. As a result, the people sang his praises, which, in the process, aroused King Saul's jealousy. How he hated David's popularity! As a result, Saul fell into such a fit of hostility he became focused on murdering David. Exit harmony. Enter despondency.

Think of it! From that time on, David became the object of Saul's diabolical plan. Though innocent before God and loyal to King Saul, David literally ran for his life and lived as an escaped fugitive in the hills of Judea for more than a dozen years. Think of that!

Hunted and haunted by madman Saul, David must have entertained doubts at times. He often had no one but the Lord to turn to in his despondent moments. There he was, the anointed king-elect, existing like a beast in the wilderness, running for his life. (That would disillusion anyone!) I can imagine David slumped beside several large bushes or hidden beneath a boulder alongside some mountain—dirty and despondent, wondering if the chase would ever end.

With that as a backdrop, Psalm 13 makes a lot of sense. Like many of the "lament psalms," this is a song addressed to God, a prayer consisting of six verses that build toward a climax. It begins in the pit of despondency and concludes on the mountain peaks of ecstasy. Here is how I would outline David's song of despondency:

I. *David is on his face*—flat on the ground, focused on his misery and complaints (vv. 1–2).
   A. He focuses on the depth of the trial.
   B. He focuses on the length of the trial.
II. *David is on his knees*—taking his burden to the Lord and admitting his own dependence upon Him (vv. 3–4).
III. *David is on his feet*—rejoicing and singing (vv. 5–6).

Making It Strong in Your Soul

As you review the stages of David's sorrow expressed in song, at which stage do you find yourself now? "On your face," "on your knees," or "on your feet"? Based on your answer, what would you say to someone at another stage?

Day 3: *Psalm 13*
Going It Alone

Psalm 13 begins where the despondent person spends most of his or her time: flat on the ground, crushed under the weight of sorrow. In the first section of the song, we see . . .

David on His Face

How long, O LORD? Will You forget me forever?
How long will You hide Your face from me?
How long shall I take counsel in my soul,
Having sorrow in my heart all the day?
How long will my enemy be exalted over me? (vv. 1–2)

Swamped by the overwhelming trials of life, David resorts to four common and human ways to handle despondency. In these two verses he reminds us of ourselves and four mental escape routes we often take under pressure.

1. God has forgotten me—forever. Remember the last time you felt abandoned? "How long, O Lord? Will You forget me forever?" Since the testing had continued so long without hope of relief, David finally became emotionally crushed beneath the load. He wondered if God had abandoned him.

2. God doesn't care about me. This is nothing short of gross self-pity. "How long will You hide Your face from me?" This inevitably accompanies feelings of abandonment, which whisper lies: "God has simply lost interest. He said He would take care of me and bear my burdens and lift my load, but that isn't the case!" (Sound a little familiar?) God's Word is painfully honest. How often we see ourselves reflected on the pages of the Bible.

3. I'm going to have to work things out for myself. This is doubting God's promises, suggesting He is not trustworthy. "How long shall I take counsel in my soul?" The Hebrew term translated "take counsel" means to "plan." David had begun to plan a way out, adjust matters himself. "After all," he might have said, "God gave me a mind and He expects me to use it. God helps those who help themselves!"

Hold it! Is that true? You may be surprised to know that statement never appears in Scripture! Let's pause and remind ourselves of several of Solomon's sayings:

Trust in the LORD with all your heart
And do not lean on your own understanding.
In all your ways acknowledge Him,
And He will make your paths straight. (Proverbs 3:5–6)

Commit your works to the LORD,
And your plans will be established. (Proverbs 16:3)

When a man's ways are pleasing to the LORD,
He makes even his enemies to be at peace with him.
(Proverbs 16:7)

The lot is cast into the lap,
But its every decision is from the LORD. (Proverbs 16:33)

What happens when we try to work things out in our own flesh? Exactly what happened to David. And what was that? Look at the next part of Psalm 13:2, "Having sorrow in my heart all the day."

Sorrow, strain, frustration, and worry became his constant companions. Such are the byproducts of do-it-yourself activities. When will we ever learn to leave our burdens with the Lord and let Him work out the details?

4. I resent this trial! It's humiliating to endure being stepped on. Pride has now been wounded, so it retaliates. "How long will my enemy be exalted over me?"

Isn't this a typical complaint? Again, I remind you, it comes from pride. It says, in effect, that I have the right to defend the truth, especially when it comes to some enemy taking advantage of me. How we fight to maintain our pride! How we long to be appreciated and well thought of! David was having to learn that the truth will defend itself. It will emerge as the champion in God's own time.

Making It Strong in Your Soul

Which of David's responses resonates most deeply with you right now?

1. *God has forgotten me—forever.*
2. *God doesn't care about me.*
3. *I'm going to have to work things out for myself.*
4. *I resent this trial!*

What has been your response? How has this response been working for you?

Day 4: *Psalm 13*

Looking to God

As I read Psalm 13 and reflect on the section describing David on his face, overwhelmed with grief and hopelessness, I see two practical areas of application:

1. It was the length of the test that began to weary David. "How long" occurs four times in two brief verses. Let us remember that God not only designs the depth of our trials but also their length. Sometime soon, read the words of the ancient prophet Habakkuk, chapter 1. He too asked, "How long?"

2. In the first two verses of Psalm 13 David turns against everyone and everything except himself. What I learn from this is that when I try to handle a test in the flesh, I turn against God, my enemy, or my circumstance rather than first asking the Lord what He is trying to teach me in this situation. What wonderful lessons God wishes to teach us if our proud hearts would only be willing to melt in the furnace of affliction.

In the midst of his grief and sorrow, David makes a critical choice. Rather than continue the downward spiral of sorrow, he changed his posture. This brings us to the second section of the song.

David on His Knees

Consider and answer me, O LORD, my God;
Enlighten my eyes, or I will sleep the sleep of death,
And my enemy will say, "I have overcome him,"
And my adversaries will rejoice when I am shaken. (vv. 3–4)

Something happened to David between stanzas 2 and 3 of his hymn. Perhaps he listened to his own complaints and realized it was self-pity. I've done that, haven't you? Maybe he paused in his composition and looked back over what he had just written . . . and became alarmed at the unbelief that began to surface before his eyes. We observe a genuine and marked difference now. He is up off his face. His despondency is beginning to lift. We find him, at last, on his knees—the place of victory. The martyred missionary, Jim Elliot, once wrote: "The saint who advances on his knees never retreats."

Please observe how closely verses 3 and 4 are connected with verses 1 and 2. David seems to recollect and redirect his complaints as he talks to the Lord about them. Three changes become apparent.

First, instead of viewing the Lord as being removed and unconcerned (v. 1), David requests that He "consider and answer" him (v. 3). And don't miss what he calls the Lord in verse 3—"my God!" The distance is now gone in David's mind. He is embracing an altogether different outlook.

Second, instead of the despondency and distress that had become his heart attitude due to his attempts to work things out (v. 2), he now asks the Lord to "enlighten my eyes."

Again, the Hebrew gives us a clearer understanding of this. The word translated "enlighten" in verse 3 is in the causative stem, meaning literally "to cause to shine." In Numbers 6:24–26 the identical term occurs in a benediction we've heard many times:

The Lord bless you, and keep you;
The Lord *make His face* shine on you,
And be gracious to you;
The Lord lift up His countenance on you,
And give you peace.
(Emphasis is mine.)

David's countenance had lost its "shine." His face, and especially his eyes, had become hard, flat, and dull. He longed for God's brightness to reflect itself once again from his eyes—his face had fallen.

I want to state once again that when trials are dealt with in the flesh, the eyes bear the marks of that fact. We cannot hide it. Our entire countenance becomes rigid and inflexible, lacking the "sparkle" and the "light" that once manifested itself from our hearts. When inner joy leaves, so does the "shine" from our eyes.

Third, instead of worrying about his exalted enemy (v. 2), David now mentally releases his enemy to the Lord and lets Him take care of the results (vv. 3–4).

I notice this marked change in David occurred when he decided to lay it all out before God in prayer. Although it sounds like a cliché, our fervent petition is still the most effective oil to reduce the friction from the daily grind of despondency.

Making It Strong in Your Soul

If you stopped asking God to change your external circumstances and prayed instead a prayer of surrender, asking Him to change *you*, what do you think would happen? What keeps you from praying this kind of prayer?

Day 5: *Psalm 13*
A Song of New Hope

As David's song—preserved for us as Psalm 13—reaches its climax, David's posture has changed once again.

David on His Feet

> But I have trusted in Your lovingkindness;
> My heart shall rejoice in Your salvation.
> I will sing to the LORD,
> Because He has dealt bountifully with me. (vv. 5–6)

The first word in verse 5 is "but." That little word usually introduces a contrast to the reader. It's as if David is saying, "In contrast to my earlier complaints and fears, my dull eyes and proud heart . . . I have trusted! . . . My heart shall rejoice! . . . I will sing!"

Notice his exclamations of praise? What a delightful difference! This sounds more like the David we know, doesn't it? We dare not overlook the last part of the final verse: "Because He has dealt bountifully with me."

How significant! Read it again, then stop and think. David's circumstances had not changed. Saul still hunted him. The barren slopes of Judea were still barren. His hunger, if present before he wrote the psalm, continued to gnaw at his stomach. His outward circumstances had not changed, yet David's conclusions had spun a 180-degree turn from his original thoughts. Why? Because *David* had changed. God had "dealt bountifully" with him.

So, what does this mean for us? What encouragement can we draw from David's song? How can we emulate David and rise above our own sorrowful circumstances?

First, we must recognize that God uses trials to transform *us*, not our surroundings. God wishes to train us, to mold us. He uses the distressing circumstances brought on by evil to benefit us rather than destroy us. The evils intended by the world become His tools.

In doing so, He deals bountifully with us . . . deep within where no one else can see or touch.

We have not learned the most basic and essential lessons God has designed for us in any given trial until we can say, "He has dealt bountifully with me."

In the magnificent Psalm 119, David declares this same conclusion in verses 71 and 75. In fact, he says such trials are good for us!

It is good for me that I was afflicted,
That I may learn Your statutes. . . .
I know, O Lord, that Your judgments are righteous,
And that in faithfulness You have afflicted me.

This is what the apostle Paul came to realize from his "thorn in the flesh" as he wrote in 2 Corinthians 12:9:

And He has said to me, "My grace is sufficient for you, for power is perfected in weakness." Most gladly, therefore, I will rather boast about my weaknesses, so that the power of Christ may dwell in me.

Weakness is not a symptom of a terminal disease. It is simply tangible proof of our humanity. Better still, it is the platform upon which God does some of His most magnificent work. If the daily grind of despondency has begun to wrap its clammy fingers around you and drag you under, let me encourage you to get better acquainted with this unique song of new hope. It can be not only a comfort to your soul; very likely, it will lift you off your face and put you back on your feet.

Making It Strong in Your Soul

This kind of prayer requires incredible trust in God and His character. It demands more faith than believing He can or will change your circumstances. Are you willing to exercise this kind of trust? Explain your answer to a friend.

THE GRIND OF WEAKENED INTEGRITY

A Psalm of David.

O LORD, who may abide in Your tent?
Who may dwell on Your holy hill?
He who walks with integrity, and works righteousness,
And speaks truth in his heart.
He does not slander with his tongue,
Nor does evil to his neighbor,
Nor takes up a reproach against his friend;
In whose eyes a reprobate is despised,
But who honors those who fear the LORD;
He swears to his own hurt and does not change;
He does not put out his money at interest,
Nor does he take a bribe against the innocent.
He who does these things will never be shaken.

(Psalm 15)

Day 1: *Psalm 15*
God's Standard of Living

Benjamin Franklin once called David's Psalm 15 the "Gentleman's Psalm." To him, it represented the standard of life after which a gentleman should pattern his walk. As fine a description as that may be, David's song goes even deeper than that—it is indeed the "Christian's Psalm." It sets forth not so much the way a person finds the Lord as the way we are to live after the Lord has entered our life. In other words, it doesn't deal with how someone becomes a Christian, but rather how a Christian should maintain a life of integrity. It sets forth many of the moral and ethical characteristics God desires in His children's day-to-day lifestyle, both in public and in private.

It should come as a surprise to no one that ours is a day of weakened integrity. Pause for a moment and call to mind a few of the more prominent examples:

- Military officers stationed at an overseas embassy, given the responsibility to protect confidential documents, traded our secrets for sexual gratification.
- Sex scandals in politics have become commonplace, even among those championing "family values."
- The men and women running our largest financial institutions have victimized their customers and even the United States government for their own financial gain.
- Even the religious world has not escaped a breakdown in integrity. Sex scandals and the misuse of ministry funds have put a black eye on the face of several televangelists, which cannot help but bruise the testimony of other media ministries even though they may be squeaky clean. When a cloud of suspicion appears over several well-knowns, even the obscure are affected by the shadow.

Like many of David's songs, we cannot determine from the lyrics what prompted him to write. Perhaps that's intentional. By leaving out his own personal details, he allows us to write in our own. His words then become our words as we lament the daily grind of weakened integrity.

Aside from David's specific concerns, and ours, there is a broader biblical context that gives the psalm real significance. Let me explain.

The moment a believing sinner gives his heart to Jesus Christ, he is declared to be the recipient of numerous spiritual blessings.

These make up our eternal inheritance, which never changes. We become a child of God (John 1:12), adopted into His family forever (Rom. 8:14–17), sealed and secure (Eph. 1:13), delivered from darkness into God's love (Col. 1:13), a member of a priesthood (1 Peter 2:9), and on and on! These things *never* change, regardless of our walk. They become our permanent inheritance. In that way, they represent our unchanged eternal position in God's eyes.

But something else is also true: We have *temporal* fellowship with our Lord. From salvation onward, the child of God has the privilege of living under the control of the Holy Spirit. The flip side of that arrangement introduces a possibility: he may, instead, choose to sin and walk in the energy of his own flesh, and thus break this temporal fellowship that is ours to claim. When he or she does, the individual chooses to reject God's power and blessing, and then moves immediately out of the realm of fellowship into the realm of divine discipline. Let me hasten to add that his tragic loss of temporal fellowship need not be extended. If the believer will confess his sins (1 John 1:9) and begin to walk in dependence upon the Holy Spirit (Gal. 5:16; Eph. 5:18), temporal fellowship will immediately be restored.

Let me put this another way, just to be clear. If you have trusted in Christ, your eternal destiny is secure, despite your personal failures. However, you can be cut off from the benefits of fellowship in this life. You can excuse yourself from God's banquet table of fellowship and choose to eat the husks of sin. And you will reap the consequences of your choices while in this life: malnourishment, loneliness, sorrow, regrets . . .

How does all this tie in with Psalm 15? Simply that this divine song has to do with our walking in the realm of temporal fellowship. In fact, it mentions some of the things we should be doing within the framework of that fellowship. It deals with those works of righteousness that are prompted by the Holy Spirit while we are walking in dependence upon our God. When these things begin to fade from our lives, our integrity is inevitably weakened—and ultimately, our testimony is hurt.

Making It Strong in Your Soul

Weakened integrity is a process like erosion, so gradual it often eludes detection until it causes catastrophic damage. No one is immune; everyone must be on guard. Where do you notice your own standards starting to soften? Is this the result of becoming a more grace-filled person, or the telltale sign of becoming lax?

Day 2: Psalm 15
Fellowship with God

If you read Psalm 15 carefully, you will discover the entire song all hangs upon the first verse. Verse 1 is crucial in that it asks a probing question. David's answer forms the rest of the psalm. He then arrives at a wonderful promise. A simple outline could be:

    I. Question: "Who may abide in Your tent?" (v. 1)

    II. Answer: "He who walks with integrity." (vv. 2–5)

    III. Promise: "He will never be shaken." (v. 5)

The Question

David's Psalm opens with a probing question, put in the form of a metaphor.

> O Lord, who may abide in Your tent?
> Who may dwell on Your holy hill? (v. 1)

The song is a prayer directed to God, whose name appears in Hebrew as the four consonant letters YHWH. Using the Lord's sacred name, David asks two questions that appear different, but they actually seek a single answer. Hebrew poetry, as we saw earlier, often uses a grammatical device called "synonymous parallelism," in which two lines express the same thought using different words or phrases. Literally, they read: "YHWH, who shall dwell in your tent? Who shall settle down on your holy mountain?"

The references to "tent" and "holy mountain" are both symbols of God's presence—descriptive expressions of intimate fellowship. At the time, the temple had not yet been built; the Israelites worshiped God in the tabernacle, a large tent structure. The ark of the covenant was kept in the center of the tabernacle, in the Most Holy Place, and that's where God's *shekinah* glory could be found. The otherworldly light of the *shekinah* represented God's special presence among the Israelites, establishing them as a nation, protecting them from harm, and blessing their faithfulness.

The expression "Your holy hill (mountain)" recalls the event in Exodus when Moses met God on Mount Sinai to receive His law (Exod. 24:12–18). On that occasion, a fiery, glowing cloud covered the summit. The expression also refers to the summit of Jerusalem, the future home of the temple, where God's presence would abide and where all people were invited to worship Him.

David asked, "What kind of an individual does it take to maintain and enjoy intimate fellowship with You, Lord?"

Making It Strong in Your Soul

Remember, this has to do with our relationship with God in the here and now, not the hereafter. What kind of person is able to have joyous fellowship with God? How does unrepentant or ongoing sin affect one's experience of fellowship with God? Do you currently have this kind of experience with Him?

Day 3: *Psalm 15*
Facets of Integrity

avid's song, Psalm 15, opens with a probing question about our experience of fellowship with God in the temporal realm, our relationship with Him in daily life. He wanted to know what characteristics mark the person who is able to enjoy unencumbered, uninhibited association with the almighty Creator of the universe. Inspired by the Holy Spirit in his writing, David received and then recorded the Lord's reply.

The Answer

> He who walks with integrity, and works righteousness,
> And speaks truth in his heart.
> He does not slander with his tongue,
> Nor does evil to his neighbor,
> Nor takes up a reproach against his friend;
> In whose eyes a reprobate is despised,
> But who honors those who fear the LORD;
> He swears to his own hurt and does not change;
> He does not put out his money at interest,
> Nor does he take a bribe against the innocent. (vv. 2–5)

David's answer describes several facets of the same gem called integrity (v. 1). He envisions a man who "walks with integrity." The Hebrew word means "to be solid, wholesome, complete." The believer who is interested in maintaining temporal fellowship is careful about how he or she lives, where he or she goes, and what he or she says. The "solid" person walks in the realm of truth, refusing to live a lie.

I count ten specific characteristics of integrity, each deserving our attention.

1. *He who works righteousness.* This has to do with what we do. Righteousness is to be the habit of our conscious life. Our dealings

are to be honest, our activities clear of compromise. We are to obey the laws of the land and to let the Law of God guide our every decision. Not merely law-abiding and moral, but above reproach. To do less is to weaken our integrity.

2. He who speaks truth in his heart. This has to do with how we think. Notice that the truth mentioned here is spoken "in the heart"—attitudes, reactions, plans, and motives are in David's mind. The source of these things (the heart—Prov. 23:7 KJV) is to be a bedrock of truth, no place for deception or lies or a hidden agenda!

3. He who does not slander with his tongue. This and the next two characteristics have to do with what we say. The Hebrew word translated "slander" literally means "to go about, to foot it"—we might even say "to hoof it." This would include one who walks here and there spreading malicious slander, pouring out verbal venom, and poisoning others' reputations behind their backs.

This is an excellent time for me to pose a direct question. Does this describe you? Are you a gossip? Do you inwardly enjoy hearing or passing on some juicy tale that colors another's reputation? It is interesting that in the list of seven things God hates (Prov. 6:16–19) three have to do with the tongue.

Several years ago I was given wise counsel regarding the use of my tongue. I hope it will help you as much as it has helped me. Before you pass along information or comments about someone else, let it first pass through four gates for approval. If all four give you a green light, share it without hesitation:

Gate 1: Is it confidential? If so, never mention it.

Gate 2: Is it true? This may take some investigation.

Gate 3: Is it necessary? So many words are useless.

Gate 4: Is it kind? Does it serve a wholesome purpose?

Here's another good piece of advice: If you ever have to say, "I hate to say this, but . . ." or "I really shouldn't say this, but . . ." then don't! Few statements from Scripture are more pointed on this subject than Ephesians 4:29. Look at it as it is recorded in Eugene Peterson's paraphrase (MSG):

Watch the way you talk. Let nothing foul or dirty come out of your mouth. Say only what helps, each word a gift.

Making It Strong in Your Soul

Two of these first three facets of integrity involve the tongue. How have you been harmed by irresponsible or malicious talk? How have you harmed others with your speech? What can you do to help repair the damage you have done?

Day 4: *Psalm 15*

Integrity in Relationships

D avid's song explores the characteristics of a person who enjoys fellowship with the Lord in this life with seven more facets of integrity. As you consider each one, take note of the Lord's emphasis on relationships.

Who enjoys fellowship with God?

4. *He who does not do evil to his neighbor.* The Spirit-filled believer is loyal and consistent—not fickle, not erratic. He does not consciously bring difficulty upon others.

5. *Nor takes up a reproach against his friend.* The Hebrew word translated "reproach" refers to sharp, cutting, and scornful speech about others, either behind their backs or to their faces. When others begin this kind of talk, the person of integrity refuses to join in. There is honesty yet gentleness (Gal. 5:22–23) in his or her character.

6. *In whose eyes a reprobate is despised.* A reprobate mentioned here is literally a "worthless reprobate," someone who is totally disinterested in spiritual things. The genuine believer with strong integrity will discern the impact such a person can have on his own walk with the Lord, and will be wary of cultivating a close association with him or her. "Do not be deceived: 'Bad company

corrupts good morals'" (1 Cor. 15:33). If a friendship is cultivated, let it be for the sake of evangelism.

7. *He honors those who fear the Lord.* Like the preceding phrase, this refers to our choice of friends; only this phrase addresses those with whom we *should* keep company. The believer who walks with the Lord has a scale of values that is determined by biblical principles. Because we tend to emulate those with whom we spend time, we need Christlike friends.

8. *He swears to his own hurt, and does not change.* This means that we perform what we promise, even when keeping our word is difficult to achieve. Our word should be our bond. The Christian with integrity makes it his or her aim to follow through on commitments, even when it's no longer convenient . . . even when it hurts.

9. *He does not put out his money at interest.* According to Deuteronomy 23:19–20 and Leviticus 25:35–38, the Jew was commanded not to loan money to a needy Jewish brother with interest. He was to assist generously and unselfishly. The believer in Christ who offers to extend personal financial assistance to his brother in Christ should do so without interest—love being his only motive. (Needless to say, discernment must accompany love . . . or we will have more love than money!) Not every financial need among believers is a "need." Some "needs" stem from careless spending.

10. *Nor does he take a bribe against the innocent.* My Webster's dictionary defines a bribe as "money or favor bestowed on or promised to a person in a position of trust to pervert his judgment or corrupt his conduct." We have all read about what has come to be known as "influence peddling." Not even Wall Street has been protected from such schemes. The psalmist's point is clear: one with integrity won't stoop to that level.

Making It Strong in Your Soul

Did you notice the consistent emphasis on relationships? Arguably, all ten characteristics are relational. What does this suggest is the correlation between our treatment of others and our fellowship with God?

✦

Day 5: *Psalm 15*

Secure in God

While salvation is entirely a work of God—an unconditional commitment on His part to preserve those He has saved (John 10:28–29; Rom. 8:28–39; 2 Tim. 1:12)—He gives us a genuine stake in maintaining the quality of our spiritual lives. Those who lead lives of integrity receive something valuable for their faithfulness.

The Promise

. . . he who does these things will never be shaken (v. 5).

The Hebrew term rendered "shaken" is a figure of speech describing great insecurity. Think of a pole used by two people to carry something heavy, wobbling and bobbing up and down with each step. That's the word picture of instability.

Those who bring these areas under the control of the Holy Spirit will enjoy a sense of stability despite the shaky, chaotic world around them. They live stable, solid, dependable lives. They don't wonder if God is angry with them when bad things happen. They don't question the goodness of God or suspect His absence during sorrowful times. They aren't tossed about by the winds and waves of circumstance. Their thinking remains solidly anchored in God's Word, which they obey with consistency.

Perhaps that's why Ben Franklin thought of this person as a gentleman. Such people are rare, indeed. No wonder they aren't easily shaken! Integrity reinforces a life with steel.

Making It Strong in Your Soul

How does leading a life of integrity affect your feeling of security in your relationship with God? How does feeling secure in your relationship with God affect your relationships with others? If you feel solid in your fellowship with God, how will that influence the choices you make in moral dilemmas?

THE GRIND OF DIVINE SILENCE

For the choir director. A Psalm of David.

The heavens are telling of the glory of God;
And their expanse is declaring the work of His hands.
Day to day pours forth speech,
And night to night reveals knowledge.
There is no speech, nor are there words;
Their voice is not heard.
Their line has gone out through all the earth,
And their utterances to the end of the world.
In them He has placed a tent for the sun,
Which is as a bridegroom coming out of his chamber;
It rejoices as a strong man to run his course.
Its rising is from one end of the heavens,
And its circuit to the other end of them;
And there is nothing hidden from its heat.
The law of the LORD is perfect, restoring the soul;
The testimony of the LORD is sure, making wise the simple.
The precepts of the LORD are right, rejoicing the heart;
The commandment of the LORD is pure,
     enlightening the eyes.
The fear of the LORD is clean, enduring forever;
The judgments of the LORD are true;
     they are righteous altogether.
They are more desirable than gold, yes, than much fine gold;
Sweeter also than honey and the drippings of the honeycomb.
Moreover, by them Your servant is warned;
In keeping them there is great reward.
Who can discern his errors? Acquit me of hidden faults.

Also keep back Your servant from presumptuous sins;
Let them not rule over me;
Then I will be blameless,
And I shall be acquitted of great transgression.
Let the words of my mouth and the meditation of my heart
Be acceptable in Your sight,
O LORD, my rock and my Redeemer.

(Psalm 19)

Day 1: *Psalm 19*
A Deafening Silence

Ever felt completely removed from God's awareness? It's almost like you're standing at the bottom of a long stairway looking up, isn't it? The light is off, and even though you knock or call out for a response, nothing happens. No answer is heard. Not even a stir.

You're not alone. Many a soul struggles at this very moment with divine silence. And to make matters worse, it can grind on for days, weeks, even months. Following a calamity, the victim crawls out, cries out, and expects overnight relief . . . it doesn't come. A mate who has been there for years suddenly packs up and walks out. The one who is left alone to face what seem to be endless responsibilities turns to God for divine intervention, for His comforting reassurance, for His miraculous provision, only to be met with silence. That awful silence! Equally difficult is a lingering illness. No prayer seems to change anything. As the deafening silence continues from above, fever increases and pain intensifies below.

Believe it or not, Psalm 19—a grand song that directs our attention to the skies—has something to say about those anguishing times of silence on earth. The lyrics to this psalm of David fall naturally into two sections with a sharp line of division in the middle. So obvious is the dividing line that some have suggested the song was composed by two different people, each emphasizing a particular subject. I have confidence, however, that David composed the entire song and that his sudden shift in emphasis is deliberate.

The dividing line falls between verses 6 and 7. The first section (vv. 1–6) deals with *the world God has created*. It describes in vivid fashion the fact that His creative work displays His power and His glory. The second section (vv. 7–13) deals with *the truth God has communicated*. It describes some of the benefits derived from the Scriptures as well as the discernment it can bring to one's personal life. The song concludes with a prayer (v. 14). The composition as a whole brought David much-needed relief during the Lord's long silence and has given hope to many generations of people who have struggled through the grind of divine silence. Throughout the song, David reminds us that the Lord is not only close to His creatures, He cares for us as well. Here is an outline of the psalm.

I. The World God Has Created (vv. 1–6)
   A. Overall Declaration (vv. 1–4)
      1. Consistent (vv. 1–2)
      2. Silent (v. 3)
      3. Universal (v. 4)
   B. Specific Illustration—the Sun (vv. 4–6)
      1. Appearance Described (vv. 4–5)
         a. "tent"
         b. "bridegroom"
         c. "strong man"
      2. Activity Described (v. 6)
         a. "its rising"
         b. "its circuit"
         c. "its heat"
II. The Truth God Has Communicated (vv. 7–13)
   A. Its Presence among Us (vv. 7–9)

1. Titles (five are given)
2. Characteristics (six are given)
3. Benefits (four are given)
B. Its Value to Us (v. 10)
1. Gold . . . fine gold
2. Honey . . . honeycomb
C. Its Work within Us (vv. 11–13)
1. Warning
2. Rewarding
3. Discerning
4. Revealing
III. Closing prayer (v. 14)

Making It Strong in Your Soul

Think of a time in the past when it seemed like God had withdrawn Himself from you, leaving you to suffer through divine silence. What were the circumstances? What advice or reassurance did people offer? As you reflect on that earlier time, how has your perspective of that difficult season changed?

Day 2: *Psalm 19*
God Speaks through His Creation

David has packed a lot of great theology into a short space in Psalm 19. Unfortunately, we can hit only the highlights of these fourteen verses because neither time nor space permits us to dig into the depths of each one. However, I urge you to take the outline and use it as a guide in your own, personal study of this magnificent composition. It is a veritable treasure house of truth.

For six verses, David looks heavenward. He ponders the vast universe surrounding our little globe, that realm we call deep space.

The World God Has Created

The heavens are telling of the glory of God;
And their expanse is declaring the work of His hands.
Day to day pours forth speech,
And night to night reveals knowledge.
There is no speech, nor are there words;
Their voice is not heard.
Their line has gone out through all the earth,
And their utterances to the end of the world.
In them He has placed a tent for the sun,
Which is as a bridegroom coming out of his chamber;
It rejoices as a strong man to run his course.
Its rising is from one end of the heavens,
And its circuit to the other end of them;
And there is nothing hidden from its heat. (vv. 1–6)

David celebrates the power and majesty of God, saying He uses "the heavens" and "their expanse" to declare His greatness (v. 1). Then, the poet-king reminds us that this declaration is (1) *consistent*—"day to day . . . night to night"; (2) *silent*—"no speech, nor . . . words . . . Their voice is not heard"; and (3) *universal*—"all the earth . . . to the end of the world." According to this song, God's majestic universe contains a message. It is, in fact, a bold announcement! Regardless of the time of day, location, or our native language, if we look up, we are able to "hear" His message! We have a Creator whose power supersedes all human kings and governments. Because authority implies accountability, we can be reasonably sure this ultimate ruler will require everyone to stand before Him to be judged.

As the apostle Paul wrote,

For the wrath of God is revealed from heaven against all ungodliness and unrighteousness of men who suppress the truth in unrighteousness, because that which is known about God is evident within them; for God made it evident to them. For since the creation of the world His invisible attributes, His eternal power and divine nature, have been clearly seen, being understood through what has been made, so that they are without excuse. (Romans 1:18–20)

Did you grasp that? God reveals "His eternal power and divine nature" so clearly that everyone is left "without excuse." Don't let anyone tell you that God has hidden Himself from the world! Every intelligent being lives every waking moment under the constant reminder of God's presence, sovereignty, and power. Stubborn unbelief causes humanity to miss God's persistent message. Anyone who struggles with the mystery of divine silence—whether it's while picking up the pieces after a disaster, or recovering from the loss of a loved one, or trying to find a burst of hope to go on beyond a divorce—needs only to look up. God is speaking!

More specifically, consider the sun's symbolism in Psalm 19:4–6: both its appearance and activity provide ample information to anyone who asks: "Is there a God?" No one other than our God could create, sustain, and employ such a heavenly body as the sun. Its size, temperature, and distance from us (thanks to the perfect filter system of our atmosphere) provide us with just the right level of heat and light.

Making It Strong in Your Soul

What part of nature do you find most awe-inspiring? Because every created thing in the universe testifies to its Creator, perhaps it would be a good idea to spend some time observing or learning about His handiwork. How and when can you begin?

Day 3: *Psalm 19*
God Is Not Silent

The heavens may declare God's power and glory, but they do not declare His will or His plan and promise of salvation. God has communicated those marvelous truths only in His Word—the living Scriptures, the Bible. In a sudden shift in perspective, David turns from the general evidence of God's creative power to the specific evidence of God's desire for a relationship with people.

The Truth God has Communicated

The law of the LORD is perfect, restoring the soul;
The testimony of the LORD is sure, making wise the simple.
The precepts of the LORD are right, rejoicing the heart;
The commandment of the LORD is pure, enlightening the eyes.
The fear of the LORD is clean, enduring forever;
The judgments of the LORD are true; they are righteous altogether.
They are more desirable than gold, yes, than much fine gold;
Sweeter also than honey and the drippings of the honeycomb.
Moreover, by them Your servant is warned;
In keeping them there is great reward.
Who can discern his errors? Acquit me of hidden faults.
Also keep back Your servant from presumptuous sins;
Let them not rule over me;
Then I will be blameless,
And I shall be acquitted of great transgression. (Psalm 19:7–13)

Notice the change from "God" (vv. 1–6) to "LORD" (vv. 7–14). In the first section of the Psalm, David uses the Hebrew word *El*, which is God's generic title. It means "God, mighty one, strength." In the second section, however, David uses God's name, represented by the four consonants, YHWH, and typically translated "LORD" in the Old Testament. God is not merely a powerful creative force; He is a person with whom we're able to have a relationship.

Therefore, David includes in this second part of the song a more personal example of God's presence.

Observe first the titles God gives His Word—"law . . . testimony . . . precepts . . . commandments . . . judgments." Next, observe the characteristics of Scripture—"perfect . . . sure . . . right . . . pure . . . true . . . righteous." Then, observe the benefits it provides— "restoring the soul . . . making wise the simple . . . rejoicing the heart . . . enlightening the eyes." Talk about communicating something with effectiveness! No one could name another book or any other piece of literature that can do such an effective job in the life of mankind. While the Lord isn't likely to speak audibly to you, He is *not* silent! He has said—and continues to say—more than we can absorb and apply.

Making It Strong in Your Soul

How much time do you devote each week to reading God's message to you? How does this amount of time compare to the time you give other activities, such as watching television, enjoying a hobby, or being involved in other forms of entertainment? Have you considered listening to an audio version of the Bible in your car or on your MP3 player?

Day 4: *Psalm 19*
God's Incomparable Word

As David considers the impact of God's written communication in the second section of Psalm 19, he's prompted to appraise the value of Scripture. He uses two illustrations for the purpose of comparison:

1. Gold . . . fine gold (v. 10). As the king of Israel, David knew the value of gold. He had plenty of it! And, like today, it was considered among the most precious of possessions. A king's power—his ability to rule and to get things done—was partly measured by the amount of gold in his treasury. The phrase "fine gold" refers to purified gold as opposed to random pieces of jewelry, coins, or powder. Throughout history, this precious metal has been melted down to remove any impurities, including other metals. The result was concentrated, unadulterated wealth and power in the form of gold bullion.

2. *Honey . . . honeycomb (v. 10).* David declares God's Word to be sweeter than the most delectable of foods. Note that it is not just honey, but honey flowing from the combs. For much of his early life, David lived in the wilderness and learned how to live off the land. Ask any survival expert today, and he'll tell you that finding a honeycomb is like finding treasure. Pure calories in the most delectable form. (Makes my mouth water!) Moreover, there are several metaphors to consider:

- It is provided through the work of someone other than ourselves; the bee virtually lays it on our platter.
- It is a natural food that doesn't need a lengthy time of digestion before it goes to work. Honey provides instant energy.
- It is a flavor like no other. Nothing has sweetness like the rich taste of honey.

Honey—what a fitting analogy!

Read those three things again with God's Word in mind. Through the efforts of another, we have His Word. It goes to work immediately upon entering our spiritual system. And no other piece of literature can even compare with its uniqueness.

Finally, verses 11–13 tell us of specific ways God's truth works within us. Through the Scriptures we are warned of evil and potential dangers. The individual who really knows (and applies!) his Bible is kept from numerous sins simply because he believes God's warning signals. Then, biblical truths assure us of personal reward—"great reward." Furthermore, they provide us with discernment—the ability to know right from wrong. Simple though that may sound, it is one of the most reliable signs of maturity, according to Hebrews 5:14. "But solid food is for the mature, who because of practice have their senses trained to discern good and evil."

God's Word also reveals error, sin, presumption, and transgression to those who ponder the pages of Scripture.

Making It Strong in Your Soul

How have you benefited from your knowledge of the Bible? Think in practical terms, such as marriage, family, career, ethics, and decision-making. Review Psalm 19 to consider "errors" and "hidden faults" (v. 12) as well as "presumptuous sins" (v. 13). Ask the Lord to reveal them to you this week.

Day 5: *Psalm 19*

Listening with Retuned Ears

D avid sums up his feelings in Psalm 19 with a brief prayer. In fact, these three lines are some of the most familiar in the entire book of Psalms.

> Let the words of my mouth and the meditation of my heart
> Be acceptable in Your sight,
> O LORD, my rock and my Redeemer. (v. 14)

While God may seem silent at times, the problem is not that He isn't communicating; it's that we aren't hearing Him. Withdrawing from the pain of life may have cut us off from the many ways God expresses His love: through the inner transformation of the Holy Spirit, through nature, through caring family and friends, through opportunities to serve. Or, our ears may be clogged with self-pity. Or, because of faltering faith, we may refuse to believe God cares or continues to demonstrate His love.

The fact is, God has revealed Himself so thoroughly through His creation and through the Scriptures, He need not ever speak again. Nevertheless, He remains consistently involved with His world and the people He made. When we take this at face value, choosing to believe He is not silent, our ears become attuned to His constant communication. I know this to be true from personal experience. When I find myself falling prey to the lie that God is silent, I immediately turn to where I know for certain God speaks: His Word. I respond to the world's lie by taking in truth. Then, with my ear retuned to hear God's voice, I find Him communicating in more ways than I realized.

Stay in the Word this week, my friend. Claim His blessings— dare Him to fulfill His promises. The "words of your mouth" and "meditation of your heart" will take on a whole new pattern of godliness and power. Furthermore, He will no longer seem distant from you or silent to you.

Making It Strong in Your Soul

Throughout this week, look for examples of God's nonverbal communication. The Holy Spirit creates clarity within, always in conformity with Scripture. Nature bears the fingerprints of its Maker. Faithful followers of Christ bring "love, joy, peace, patience, kindness, goodness, faithfulness, gentleness, and self-control (Gal. 5:22–23), the personal attributes of God. Keep an open mind. Stay alert to what the Lord wants to show you.

THE GRIND OF UNCERTAINTY

A Psalm of David.

*The L*ORD* is my shepherd,*
I shall not want.
He makes me lie down in green pastures;
He leads me beside quiet waters.
He restores my soul;
He guides me in the paths of righteousness
For His name's sake.
Even though I walk through the valley of the
*   shadow of death,*
I fear no evil, for You are with me;
Your rod and Your staff, they comfort me.
You prepare a table before me in the presence of my enemies;
You have anointed my head with oil;
My cup overflows.
Surely goodness and lovingkindness will follow me
*   all the days of my life,*
*And I will dwell in the house of the L*ORD* forever.*

(Psalm 23)

Day 1: *Psalm 23*
The Woeful Song of Frightened Sheep

I have observed that few inner battles are more fierce than the daily grind of uncertainty. No doubt you too have encountered one or more of its many faces as you have struggled with a career choice, new direction in life, purpose in pain, job security, financial pressures, physical handicaps, relational snags, and a dozen other confusing puzzles not quickly or easily solved. It is for the dark hours of uncertainty that David penned a song we know as Psalm 23. This brief song composed by a former shepherd has endeared itself to people in every circumstance of life:

- The soldier in battle, fearing injury and possible death
- The grieving widow standing before a fresh grave,
  wondering how she can go on with her life
- The guilty wanderer seeking forgiveness and direction
- The lonely stranger longing for love and companionship
- The suffering saint strapped to a bed of pain
- The destitute and the forgotten
- The depressed and the jobless
- The prison inmate and the persecuted
- The prodigal and the orphaned

All have endured the daily grind of uncertainty. When the trials of life push us to the limit and our hearts are heaviest, this magnificent "Psalm of the Shepherd" offers comfort and assurance, especially for those who lack the secure feeling of God's perpetual presence.

Because of the popularity of this song and the numerous truths that are hidden in it, we will want to spend more time on it than we have on the others. Therefore, I've chosen not to give a formal outline. Instead, we will consider the analogy of sheep to the children of God, the theme of constant provision by our Shepherd-Lord, and an explanation of each verse.

So, then, let's begin with the analogy at the center of David's song. Psalm 23 is the woeful song of a frightened sheep, as though it were considering its life with its shepherd and recording its experiences. Consider some of the similarities between helpless sheep and God's feeble children:

1. *Sheep lack a sense of direction.* Unlike cats and dogs, sheep can get lost easily—even in the familiar environment of their own territory. So it is with believers—we cannot guide ourselves. We must rely completely on the Word of God and the voice of our Shepherd-Savior.

2. *Sheep are virtually defenseless.* Most animals have a rather effective means of defense—sharp claws; teeth; speed; ability to hide; keenness of smell, sight, and hearing; great strength; ferocity. But sheep are awkward, weak, and ignorant; they have spindle legs and tiny hoofs, and are pitifully slow, even devoid of an angry growl. Defenseless! The only sure protection for the sheep is the ever-watchful shepherd. So it is with the believer, who is admonished to be strong—"in the Lord" (Eph. 6:10).

3. *Sheep are easily frightened.* Being ignorant, unimpressive in stature, and very much aware of their weakness, sheep find comfort only in their shepherd's presence, including his reassuring songs in the night. Psalm 27:1 also refers to this type of Shepherd-Lord relationship that we have with God.

4. *Sheep are, by nature, unclean.* Other animals lick, scrape, and roll in the grass to cleanse themselves—but not sheep. They will remain filthy indefinitely unless the shepherd cleanses them. We too by nature are unclean and filthy. Apart from our tender Shepherd's cleansing (1 John 1:7–9) we would remain perpetually dirty.

5. *Sheep cannot find food or water.* While most animals have a keen sense of smell, sheep depend upon their shepherd completely. If left to themselves, sheep will eat poisonous weeds and die—and when one does it, the others will follow the leader. Again, as children of God, we are equally dependent.

6. *The sheep's wool does not belong to the sheep.* While sheep may produce wool, the shepherd owns their wool. All bona fide spiritual production in the life of the Christian belongs to the Lord. The Lord, by means of the Holy Spirit, provides for all such production. In every way, you see, we are indeed "His people and the sheep of His pasture" (Ps. 100:3).

Making It Strong in Your Soul

Very few of us in twenty-first-century urban cultures have any experience with sheep. To make the most of God's word picture, locate some educational material—books, videos, Internet resources, etc.—and learn all you can about caring for sheep. I will warn you, however, the analogy is not flattering!

Day 2: *Psalm 23*
In the Shepherd's Care

Like many of the songs found in the Bible, Psalm 23 states its case in the first verse and simply verifies it in the remainder of the song. The key thought is this: Because the Lord is my Shepherd, I shall lack nothing! No uncertainty should frighten me. Here is the way the theme of Psalm 23 is played out in the balance of David's famous song:

> I shall not lack rest or provision—why? He makes me
>   lie down in green pastures.
> I shall not lack peace—why? He leads me beside
>   quiet waters.
> I shall not lack restoration or encouragement when I faint,
>   fail, or fall—why? He restores my soul.
> I shall not lack guidance or fellowship—why? He guides me
>   in the paths of righteousness.
> I shall not lack courage when my way is dark—why?
>   Even though I walk through the valley of the shadow
>   of death, I fear no evil.
> I shall not lack companionship—why? You are with me.
> I shall not lack constant comfort—why? Your rod and
>   Your staff, they comfort me.
> I shall not lack protection or honor—why? You prepare a

table before me in the presence of my enemies.

I shall not lack power—why? You have anointed
  my head with oil.

I shall not lack abundance—why? My cup overflows.

I shall not lack God's perpetual presence—why?
  Surely goodness and mercy shall follow me
  all the days of my life.

I shall not lack security—why? I will dwell in the house of
  the Lord forever.

Verse 1

The first verse establishes the theme of the song. But for now I call
your attention to two things in this sentence:

1. David refers to God as "the LORD." This divine name is based
on the Hebrew verb "to be" and stems from God's identification
of Himself to Moses. He said, "I AM WHO I AM" and "Thus you
shall say to the sons of Israel, 'I AM has sent me to you'" (Exod.
3:14). The idea being, YHWH is the self-existent Being, the God
who actually exists, as opposed to all those that do not exist.

2. David calls YHWH "my Shepherd." To David (the sheep),
God was his own personal Shepherd. Not merely the shepherd of
the great flock of all humanity, but the shepherd who calls him by
name and cares for him as an individual.

Verse 2

Having established the theme, the composer begins to develop the
word picture. He starts with the pastoral picture of sheep under
a shepherd's care. I am told that sheep, being stupid animals,
frequently are alarmed and actually run over each other, racing
away from something that startles them. The shepherd corrects
the problem by catching a sheep and gently, yet firmly, forcing it
to lie down and feed quietly on the grass beneath its feet. David
remembers such an occasion as he writes, "He makes me lie down."

In our hectic, hurried, harassed age in which headache and

tranquilizer medications have become the best-selling national products, we must occasionally be made to lie down by our Shepherd-Savior. When He steps into our helter-skelter world, He must often force us to rest. If that has occurred, give thanks—the pastures are green!

This verse concludes with another pleasant picture: "He leads me beside quiet waters." Look at that phrase. Literally, it refers to waters that have been stilled. Mentally capture the peaceful scene. The sheep are weary and worn. They need a long, refreshing drink from the rapid stream nearby. But sheep are instinctively afraid of rapidly running water. Perhaps they think that if water should get on their heavy coats of wool, they would become waterlogged and sink beneath the surface of a stream. As a result, even though tired and hot from a blistering day, thirsty sheep will only stand and stare at the fast-flowing stream but never drink. Uncertainty keeps them from needed refreshment. The shepherd leads them to quiet, peaceful waters, where they may drink without fear.

Making It Strong in Your Soul

Who is your shepherd? In whom do you trust when you are feeling caught in the daily grind of uncertainty? To whom do you turn for direction? A pastor? A psychologist? A close friend? Your coach? A priest, teacher, or small group leader? Have you considered that these people are merely sheep, just like you?

Day 3: *Psalm 23*
The Shepherd Restores

As a former shepherd keeping watch over flocks in the wilderness, the composer of Psalm 23 understood the nature of sheep, including their bad habit of wandering. When one is attracted to a clump of grass away from the flock, off he goes, and sometimes he's followed by several other woolly wanderers. Soon, night falls. Lurking in the darkness are hungry wolves, four-legged savages, looking for a supper of mutton! The shepherd counts his sheep, calling them by name.

Verse 3

The song includes this line: "He restores my soul." It's about restoration. The term is loosely based on the idea of repentance— a "turning back"—only it's not accomplished by the sheep, but the Shepherd. Realizing he has a wanderer missing, the shepherd sets out to "restore" or "return" that wandering member of his flock, calling its name and awaiting an answering bleat out in the wilderness. The wanderer is restored to fellowship despite himself.

Occasionally, one particular young sheep will get into a habit of wandering. Again and again the shepherd will have to go and find the wandering lamb. When such occurs too often, the shepherd will lift the lamb from the thistles and cactus, hold it close, and abruptly break its leg. He will make a splint for the shattered leg and then carry that once-wayward lamb over his shoulders. Hopefully, during this period of restoration, the sheep learns not to wander off and to depend completely upon its shepherd.

Finally, verse 3 promises guidance. Look at the last part of this verse. Literally, it means: "He guides me in the right tracks for His name's sake."

The Palestinian shepherd was a master at reading tracks. Many marks and paths sprawled across the rugged terrain. Some were made by wilderness beasts; others by robbers lying in wait. The wind also etched its subtle "track" in the sand. To the untrained, dull eye of the sheep, they all looked alike—like real paths. But they led nowhere. The sheep were wise to follow only their shepherd, who always led them along the "right track." After all, it was the shepherd's reputation that was at stake: "for His name's sake."

Verse 4

The tone changes in the latter half of Psalm 23, but not the Shepherd! From the verdant, fertile slopes and bubbling brooks of verses 2 and 3, we are plunged immediately down into the "valley of the shadow of death"—literally translated the "valley of deep darkness." How does this tie in with verse 3? You'll observe that verse 3 promises that our Shepherd-Savior guides us along "right tracks." Verse 4 is simply saying that one of these tracks or paths winds along the steep, downward valley below. There is a reason for this.

Early in the year, the flocks graze leisurely in the lowlands, but as summer's sun begins to melt the high mountain snow, the shepherd leads his flock to better grazing land above. This trip inevitably includes some dangerous paths filled with uncertainties and fearful sights. The way is dark, unfamiliar, difficult. The trees periodically blot out the sunlight, and there are serpents coiled to strike as well as hungry wolves lurking in the shadows. But the sheep walking beside his shepherd is secure because the shepherd is near, leading the way, fully aware of the valley's path. Such a scene was as familiar to David as a sheet of music is to an orchestra conductor. The ancient shepherd-made-king mentally sifts through those earlier days as a lad in the wilderness with his father's flock and pictures himself as a sheep: "Even though I walk through the valley of deep darkness . . . "

As God's sheep, we are sometimes led by Him into the valley of darkness, where there is fear, danger, uncertainty, and the unexpected . . . even death. He knows that the only way we can reach the higher places of Christian experience and maturity is not on the playground of prosperity but in the schoolroom of suffering. Along those dark, narrow, pinching, uncomfortable valleys of difficulty we learn volumes! We keep our courage simply because our Shepherd is leading the way. Perhaps that is what the writer had in mind when he exhorted us to keep ". . . fixing our eyes on Jesus. . . . For consider Him . . . so that you may not grow weary and lose heart" (Heb. 12:2–3).

Notice the psalmist says that because "You are with me," he is kept from being afraid. Mark it down, my friend. There is no experience, no valley (no matter how severe or uncertain) that we must journey alone.

Take note of what gives David comfort. He recalled the tools of his former trade: the rod and staff. The shepherd's rod was a symbol of his power. Actually, it was an oak club about two feet in length. It was used to defend the flock against wild beasts. The head of this rod was round, usually whittled from the knot of a tree—in which the shepherd had pounded sharp bits of metal. This heavy club could easily kill a lion or bear or stealthy thief threatening the safety of the sheep.

The shepherd's staff was his crook, which was bent or hooked at one end. It provided the shepherd with an instrument for prying a sheep loose from a thicket, pushing branches aside along the narrow path, and pulling wandering sheep out of holes into which they had fallen. He also used it to beat down high grass to drive out snakes and wild beasts. Like the rod, the staff was a symbol of the shepherd's power and strength. The sheep took comfort in the strength of its shepherd.

Making It Strong in Your Soul

In what ways do you "wander" from a faithful relationship with God? Describe the kind of relationship you would have with the Lord if He did not continually restore you. Why do you think God does this for His people?

🎵

Day 4: *Psalm 23*

The Shepherd Provides Abundantly

As David's song of the sheep concludes, he suddenly drops the analogy to consider his own experience of God, both as a simple man in need of a Savior and as a king in need of divine guidance.

Verse 5

No sheep ever ate at a literal "table" prepared for it. Abruptly, we are transported from the green pastures, the valley, and the rugged mountainside to "a table" in the enemy's presence. While the setting has shifted, David still has the analogy in mind. The common experience of a shepherd with his flock will help us understand. I have Charles W. Slemming to thank for help with this verse. He has done a masterful piece of work in his writings concerning shepherds in the Middle East.

In this case he tells of the shepherd who comes to a new field in which he plans to graze his flock. The shepherd doesn't just turn them loose; he inspects the field for vipers—small brown adders that live underground. They frequently pop up out of their tiny holes and nip the sheep on their noses. The bite from these natural enemies sometimes causes an inflammation that can, on occasion, kill the stricken sheep.

Knowing this danger, the shepherd restrains his sheep from a new field (which may be infested) until he can inspect it. He walks up and down, looking for the small holes. Upon finding these holes, he takes a bottle of thick oil from his girdle. Then, raking down the long grass with his staff, he pours a circle of oil at the top of each viper's hole. Before he leads the sheep into the new, green field, he also spreads the oil over each sheep's head—in that sense he "anoints" them (rubbing their heads) with his oil. When the vipers beneath the surface sense the presence of sheep and attempt to attack from their holes, they are unable to do so. Their smooth bodies cannot pass over the slippery oil—they become prisoners inside their own holes. The oil on the sheep's head also acts as a repellent, so if a viper does manage to come near, the smell drives the serpent away. Therefore, in a very literal sense, by oiling the vipers' burrows, the shepherd has prepared the table—the meadow—and the sheep are able to graze in abundance right in the enemy's presence.

We dare not overlook "My cup overflows." This refers not to oil, but to water. Again, David recalls his experience in the wilderness providing cool well water for his flock. When there were no streams, a shepherd quenched his flock's thirst beside a well—rather rare in the wilderness. Some wells were deep—as much as a hundred feet down to the water. To draw the water, the shepherd used a long rope with a leather bucket at the end. Since the bucket held less than a gallon and had to be drawn by hand, then poured into a stone basin beside the well, the process was long and laborious. If the flock numbered a hundred, the shepherd could easily spend two hours or more if he allowed them to drink all they wished. Only a kind, considerate shepherd satisfied his thirsty sheep with an overflowing basin.

How lavishly our Father provides! What bounty! What abundance! Ephesians 3:20 describes our Shepherd-God as One who does "abundantly beyond all that we ask or think." Not just barely, but abundantly!

I like the way Haddon Robinson expresses this thought:

With Him the calf is always the fatted calf; the robe is always the best robe; the joy is unspeakable; and the peace passes understanding. There is no grudging in God's goodness. He does not measure His goodness by drops like a druggist filling a prescription. It comes to us in floods. If only we recognized the lavish abundance of His gifts, what a difference it would make in our lives! If every meal were taken as a gift from His hand, it would be almost a sacrament.[2]

May God give us a fresh realization of the overwhelming abundance He provides. Indeed, our cup overflows. Grace super-abounds!

---

2 Haddon W. Robinson, *Psalm Twenty-Three: A Devotional* (Chicago: Moody Press, 1968), 52.

As you reflect on your faithfulness as a member of God's flock, what do you deserve? Now do a mental inventory of your blessings, including relationships, money, possessions, your standard of living—everything. Take a few moments to express your response to God in prayer.

Day 5: *Psalm 23*

The Shepherd Secures the Future

As David brings his song of the sheep to a close, having reflected on the Lord's faithful care throughout his life, he then considers his future.

Verse 6

In his book *The Shepherd Psalm*, F. B. Meyer refers to "goodness and lovingkindness" as our "celestial escort."[3] Another commentator suggests that these are "God's sheepdogs," ever near His flock, ever nipping at our heels, always available.[4] Perhaps that is a fitting analogy, especially when we consider that they "follow" us. Because we are "prone to wander, prone to leave the God we love," He sends His faithful companions out after us—goodness and mercy—kindness and lovingkindness. Our Lord deals with us so kindly, so graciously. What a difference between God and man! Let man go on a search for a wayward soul and there is often bitterness and revenge and impatience in his steps, especially if the search is lengthy. But with God, there is goodness and lovingkindness.

I am convinced that one of the reasons the prodigal son "came to himself" and finally returned home was because of the kind of father he had. There is no magnet with a stronger pull than genuine

---

3 F. B. Meyer, *The Shepherd Psalm* (New York: Fleming H. Revell Company, 1895), 162.
4 Haddon W. Robinson, *Psalm Twenty-Three: A Devotional* (Chicago: Moody Press, 1968), 59.

love. Love has drawn back more wanderers and softened more hard hearts than this world will ever know. It is fitting, then, that you and I are followed "all the days" of our lives by goodness and lovingkindness. God knows what will best do the job! How varied are our Lord's methods.

Mark it down, my friend, God knows how to deal with His children. More specifically, He knows how to deal with you. His dealings follow you all the days of your life. Your circumstances right now are part of His plan for you.

This wonderful song concludes with a familiar and comforting thought: "I will dwell in the house of the LORD forever." The psalmist is not referring to a place as much as he is to a Person. Notice that the Twenty-third Psalm begins and ends with "the LORD." David longed to be in his Lord's house, because he could then be in his Lord's presence.

You see, the ultimate goal in David's heart was a face-to-face relationship with His Lord forever. Instead of vague uncertainty, he had confidence. We Christians will enjoy a never-ending fellowship with God the moment we draw our last earthly breath. What assurance!

That is exactly what Jesus Christ promises those who believe in Him . . . not merely "I hope so" but "I know!" In Him we truly have everything we need.

Making It Strong in Your Soul

Have you felt uncertain lately, perhaps a little insecure about the future? Do you know someone who might feel the same way? Review the Twenty-third Psalm, then pick up the phone and encourage him or her with what you have discovered in this song of the sheep. You may be surprised by the encouragement *you* receive.

THE GRIND OF MISTREATMENT

A Psalm of David.

Vindicate me, O LORD, for I have walked in my integrity,
And I have trusted in the LORD without wavering.
Examine me, O LORD, and try me;
Test my mind and my heart.
For Your lovingkindness is before my eyes,
And I have walked in Your truth.
I do not sit with deceitful men,
Nor will I go with pretenders.
I hate the assembly of evildoers,
And I will not sit with the wicked.
I shall wash my hands in innocence,
And I will go about Your altar, O LORD,
That I may proclaim with the voice of thanksgiving
And declare all Your wonders.
O LORD, I love the habitation of Your house
And the place where Your glory dwells.
Do not take my soul away along with sinners,
Nor my life with men of bloodshed,
In whose hands is a wicked scheme,
And whose right hand is full of bribes.
But as for me, I shall walk in my integrity;
Redeem me, and be gracious to me.
My foot stands on a level place;
In the congregations I shall bless the LORD.

(Psalm 26)

Day 1: *Psalm 26*
Mistreated, Misjudged, and Maligned

If I were asked to give a popular title to this song, it would be: "How to Do Right When You've Been Done Wrong."

We have all been "done wrong," haven't we? Maybe that describes your circumstance right now: an intolerable working situation; a husband, wife, parent, or child who takes unfair advantage of you even when you have treated him or her kindly; a friend who has turned against you due to a misunderstanding of something you did with only the purest of motives. Such feelings grind away at our peace so severely we wonder if we can continue. Whatever the mistreatment you are having to endure, please accept this dual warning: DON'T BECOME BITTER . . . DON'T LET IT UNDERMINE YOUR RELATIONSHIP WITH GOD!

David states in the opening lines of his ancient composition that he has been the victim of some undeserved wrong—followed by his determination to trust in his Lord "without wavering." Read the first verse again, only this time more slowly, to sense the feeling behind it:

Vindicate me, O LORD, for I have walked in my integrity,
And I have trusted in the LORD without wavering.

Descriptive phrase, "without wavering." The Hebrew verb means "to slip, slide, totter, shake." David says that in spite of the painful grind of mistreatment he endured, he determined to trust in his Lord and not to slip or slide under the load! That explains why he begins the psalm with such an emotional plea: "Vindicate me, O LORD." You see, by his own honest admission, he had not done something to deserve the mistreatment; though not perfect, he was still walking in integrity. That was not pride; he was stating a fact to his Lord. As he continues, he reviews the specific resolutions that kept him upright while enduring unjust attacks.

Making It Strong in Your Soul

Think of the last time you were mistreated, misjudged, or maligned due to no wrongdoing on your part. How did you respond? Did your response make the problem better or worse? How did it affect your relationship with God?

♍

Day 2: Psalm 26
Open before the Lord

As David endured unfair treatment despite his doing what was right, He cried out to God in the verses of Psalm 26. As we read his anguished lyrics, we will uncover six resolutions David made which kept him (and will keep us) from slipping into bitterness and resentment during times of mistreatment.

1. Resolved: I will be open before the Lord (v. 2). In three different ways David invites the Lord to assess his inner being: "Examine . . . try . . . test." These three English terms represent three different Hebrew terms. The first one is *bachan*, meaning "to examine, prove, scrutinize." It is clearly portrayed in Psalm 139:23–24 by the word "search."

> Search me, O God, and know my heart;
> Try me and know my anxious thoughts;
> And see if there be any hurtful way in me,
> And lead me in the everlasting way.

The psalmist is asking God to "make an examination" of his inner being, to "scrutinize" him through and through.

The next term, translated "try" in verse 2, is the Hebrew *nasah*, which means to "test, try, prove." Deuteronomy 8:2 uses an emphatic form of the verb term to denote "an intensive test":

> You shall remember all the way which the LORD your God has led you in the wilderness these forty years, that He might humble you, *testing* you, to know what was in your heart, whether you would keep His commandments or not. (Emphasis mine.)

God put the Israelites to an intensive forty-year test so that the real condition of their hearts might be exposed. The Lord didn't do this so *He* would know the condition of their hearts, but so *they* would be able to examine their own motives and intentions . . . and then repent!

The third term, rendered "test" in verse 2, is yet another Hebrew verb: *tzahraf*. This is such a vivid term! Literally, it means "to smelt, refine, test." Of the thirty-two times it is used in the Old Testament, it appears in verb form; twenty-two of those times it is linked with the activity of refining gold or silver to remove impurities.

Do you grasp the principle? When wrong comes your way, be open before the Lord. Invite Him (1) to make an internal search and examination of your life for the purpose of determining your character, (2) to undertake an intensive, in-depth process of revealing *to you* the real condition of your heart, and (3) to refine you, and in the process, to remove any impurities.

While you may not have brought on the mistreatment through sin, your response might become sinful. To maintain your close fellowship with God, openly welcome His divine surgery on your innermost being. Decide to accept the wrong that comes your way as an opportunity to become increasingly more transparent and pure before the Lord. Ask Him for insight—for a full disclosure of your inner person.

2. *Resolved: I will remember His love and continue to obey His word (v. 3).* David wrote, "For Your lovingkindness is before my eyes, and I have walked in Your truth" (Ps. 26:3). That statement implies two very subtle yet common temptations that occur when mistreatment comes our way: first, to doubt God's love; and second, to drift into disobedience.

David declares, "Your lovingkindness is before my eyes." He resolved to view anything that comes before him through the filter of God's lovingkindness. Then, lest he drift into the ugly yet common temptation to strike back, he resolves to walk in God's truth. Do you see this? Clearly, David's eyes are on the Lord's *love* for him . . . and his guide through the otherwise bewildering maze of mistreatment is the Lord's *truth*.

Are you aware of the best proof of love? It is obedience. Our Lord reminds us of that in John 14:15, 21, 23:

"If you love Me, you will keep My commandments." (v. 15)

"He who has My commandments and keeps them is the one who loves Me; and he who loves Me will be loved by My Father, and I will love him and will disclose Myself to him." (v. 21)

Jesus answered and said to him, "If anyone loves Me, he will keep My word; and My Father will love him, and We will come to him and make Our abode with him." (v. 23)

If you are confident that God really loves you, you will neither doubt nor drift in your response. Instead, you will find great delight in pleasing Him. There is nothing quite like love to motivate us from within.

Making It Strong in Your Soul

Why is "being open before the Lord" so difficult when you have been treated unjustly by others? What is your greatest challenge to "remembering His love and continuing to obey His Word" during times of mistreatment? Sometimes, the perspective of a friend can help us where we fail. Ask someone close to you to pray with you and keep you accountable as you embrace these resolutions.

Day 3: *Psalm 26*
An Attitude of Gratitude

King David knew the sting of unjust treatment as keenly as anyone in history. To keep mistreatment from undermining his relationship with God, he put six resolutions into a song. Having committed to remaining open before the Lord and to remembering His love, David committed to letting God be the judge of others' sin.

3. Resolved: I will refuse the temptation to get even (vv. 4–5).

> I do not sit with deceitful men,
> Nor will I go with pretenders.
> I hate the assembly of evildoers,
> And I will not sit with the wicked. (vv. 4–5)

This matter of getting involved with the wrong crowd is a by-product of doubting and drifting. We are especially vulnerable to this trap when we have been mistreated. You will always find a group of people who will take your side, encouraging compromise and rebellion—those who say, "Why put up with that? You deserve justice, so get even. Fight back!"

Consider David's plight. Perhaps it was when Saul hunted for him out of jealousy. David did not deserve such unfair treatment.

Surely he had well-meaning friends who encouraged him to retaliate, to "get back" at Saul. On more than one occasion he deliberately resisted getting even, though a few of his friends urged him to do so. David felt that if the Lord was able to protect him, He was able to handle his enemies as well. (This would be a good time to stop and read 1 Sam. 24:1–20 and 26:6–12).

Then again, David may have written this song while he was going through the torment of those days when his favored son Absalom conspired against him and unfairly took the throne of Israel away from him (2 Sam. 15:1–6). The result? David was forced to run for his life. Wisely, even though mistreated, David never attempted to "get back" at his son or yield to the vengeful rhetoric of men around him.

Perhaps you have fallen prey to the unwise counsel of wrong associates. In the words of Psalm 26, when this happens you "sit with deceitful (worthless) men" and "go with pretenders (hypocrites)." Stop and ponder the words of 1 Corinthians 15:33: "Do not be deceived: 'Bad company corrupts good morals.'" How very true! You cannot identify yourself with wrong associates and walk away unaffected. The point is clear: do not let mistreatment cause you to turn to the godless crowd or adopt their way of handling things. It may seem logical, but getting even often backfires, and it never glorifies God!

4. Resolved: Maintain a positive attitude (vv. 6–7).

I shall wash my hands in innocence,
And I will go about Your altar, O Lord,
That I may proclaim with the voice of thanksgiving
And declare all Your wonders.

David was concerned that his heart remain right. Therefore, in his song, he refers to "washing his hands" and staying near "Your altar." These are word pictures familiar to the Jews. In Exodus 30:17–21, the laver (basin) of bronze that belonged in the tabernacle is mentioned. It was used for the washing of the priests' hands and feet before they approached the altar to minister. If they failed to wash, they risked death!

David picks up that very important and serious principle in his song on mistreatment and applies it to his situation. He stayed very near his Lord at this time, making sure his sins were confessed and his heart attitude was clean. By doing so, he remained pure and positive. This did not guarantee, however, that the mistreatment suddenly ended. Consider Psalm 73:13–14. In it, the composer admits the internal danger caused by mistreatment.

> Surely in vain I have kept my heart pure
> And washed my hands in innocence;
> For I have been stricken all day long
> And chastened every morning.

Let's not think that a clean and clear life is immediately blessed with pleasant circumstances. But rest assured that maintaining the proper relationship with the Lord is still the very best way to endure mistreatment. Ultimately, it is rewarded.

Also note that Psalm 26:7 refers to an attitude of thanksgiving. David actually proclaimed words of thanksgiving to God for being mistreated. Is that remarkable, or what? Talk about a positive attitude! The crucial test of giving thanks in everything (1 Thess. 5:18) occurs when we suffer mistreatment. That is the supreme test on our attitude of gratitude. There is every temptation to forget to give God thanks for the privilege of being His example to others when we have been "done wrong." Learn to respond first with a genuine "Thanks, Lord," when some undeserved attack comes your way. If you do this, you will be unique. Furthermore, a positive attitude clears our minds of needless debris, mental garbage that never fails to counteract all scriptural counsel.

Making It Strong in Your Soul

Refusing to get even while maintaining a positive attitude is, literally, a superhuman feat. What are some practical ways someone can seek and receive God's help? How can godly friends help someone implement this resolution consistently?

♎

Day 4: Psalm 26

Staying Faithful Together

David's prayer for protection while enduring mistreatment didn't merely ask God for help; the king's song included several commitments on his part.

    5. *Resolved: I will be faithful in public worship (v. 8).*

O LORD, I love the habitation of Your house
And the place where Your glory dwells.

As we read this verse, we can see why David was known as "a man after God's own heart." Even while he was under the pile, feeling more like a punching bag than a child of the Lord, he remained faithful to the place where he could sense God's glory—the tabernacle (v. 8). You must pause and read three brief statements from three ancient Psalms: 27:4, 65:4, and 84:10. To him, worship was no religious habit, no ritualistic, boring process; it was something essential, something vital. When enduring mistreatment, David looked up in worship.

Unfortunately, we live in a day when the value and necessity of public worship is de-emphasized. I realize that some churches may fail to point the worshiper to the living Christ and to teach His marvelous Word. But this does not mean that all churches and all public worship gatherings are to be ignored! Hebrews 10:23–25 leaves us no option; we are to assemble together for the purpose of mutual stimulation toward the expression of love and good deeds . . . if nothing else, for personal encouragement! This is so important when undergoing mistreatment. We need each other. Christian friend, do not neglect this God-ordained, healthy expression of your faith.

Let me add one further thought: show me a believer who consistently neglects the regular services of a church that faithfully preaches and teaches the Word, and I'll show you one whose cutting edge on spiritual things is getting dull—one who is eroding, spiritually speaking. I detect from my reading of the book of Acts that the healthy yet persecuted believers absolutely craved every opportunity to meet and worship together—even in secret. What a healthy example to follow!

Making It Strong in Your Soul

Why do you think worshiping God is so encouraging when the trials of life intensify? Why is thinking about God, instead of self, so helpful? Why do you think it's important to worship along with other believers?

Day 5: *Psalm 26*

Waiting with Patience

As David concludes his song about the grinding pain of unjust treatment and his chosen responses, he then commits to patience.

6. Resolved: I will patiently stand and wait for relief (vv. 9–12).

Do not take my soul away along with sinners,
Nor my life with men of bloodshed,
In whose hands is a wicked scheme,
And whose right hand is full of bribes.

But as for me, I shall walk in my integrity;
Redeem me, and be gracious to me.
My foot stands on a level place;
In the congregations I shall bless the LORD.

There is something about human nature that prompts us to jump in with both feet and quickly work things out. In this section of his song, David implies that such was the activity of those around him. The majority said that they "wouldn't stand for such a thing." All sorts of "wicked schemes" and hands "full of bribes" were implemented by others. Not David! He set himself apart with the phrase "but as for me." In Hebrew, the pronoun is extremely emphatic: "But me . . . as for me!"

He wanted it known that, unlike the majority, he wasn't going to panic and get all involved in those carnal anxieties and ulcer-producing activities of self-vindication. No way! What does he say? "I shall walk in my integrity." And he calls upon God to act on his behalf.

There's a calmness, a quiet confidence in those words.

- As for my present course: "I . . . walk in integrity."
- As for my defense: "Redeem me . . . be gracious to me."
- As for my inner feelings: "My foot stands."

What stability! What admirable patience! What assurance and faith! No sleepless nights, no struggling doubts—just patient waiting.

Look back at that term "redeem." The Hebrew is *padah*, meaning "to ransom, deliver." It is a term of relief—as if in exile. It is the idea of delivering someone from terrible stress and even death. And don't miss that intriguing phrase in verse 12: "My foot stands on a level place." The phrase "level place" comes from a single Hebrew term, *mishore*, which can be traced back to the verb *yashar*, meaning "to be smooth, straight." The first term *mishore* means "level country, a plain." It conveys the idea of a place that has a high, commanding view, a broad range of vision in contrast to a place that is down in a deep gorge all shut in.

Do you get the picture? David is pleased to wait quietly on the Lord and remain objective. When he waits for God to deliver him, he maintains a panoramic perspective; he is able to look upon the entire process from God's viewpoint, not from his own limited human perspective. In brief, he is able to maintain wisdom.

You can anticipate the application. When we patiently wait on the Lord's deliverance, we are able to stay calm, objective, and wise in the midst of mistreatment. We can count on our Lord to be gracious and to deliver us at the right time. All the while, waiting enables us to maintain His perspective.

Look back over David's six resolutions that will help make mistreatment bearable:

1. I will be open before the Lord.
2. I will remember His love . . . continue to obey His Word.
3. I will refuse the temptation to get even.
4. I will maintain a positive attitude.
5. I will be faithful in public worship.
6. I will patiently stand, stay objective, and wait for relief.

Making It Strong in Your Soul

Are you at peace with each resolution, or do you need to come to terms with one or two? Do you know of someone right now who is enduring the grind of mistreatment? If so, why not write a note of encouragement? Or, even better, schedule a time to console him or her in person.

THE GRIND OF FEAR

A Psalm of David.

The LORD is my light and my salvation;
Whom shall I fear?
The LORD is the defense of my life;
Whom shall I dread?
When evildoers came upon me to devour my flesh,
My adversaries and my enemies, they stumbled and fell.
Though a host encamp against me,
My heart will not fear;
Though war arise against me,
In spite of this I shall be confident.
One thing I have asked from the LORD, that I shall seek:
That I may dwell in the house of the LORD *forever*
    all the days of my life,
To behold the beauty of the LORD
And to meditate in His temple.
For in the day of trouble He will conceal me in His tabernacle;
In the secret place of His tent He will hide me;
He will lift me up on a rock.
And now my head will be lifted up above
    my enemies around me,
And I will offer in His tent sacrifices with shouts of joy;
I will sing, yes, I will sing praises to the LORD.
Hear, O LORD, when I cry with my voice,
And be gracious to me and answer me.
When You said, "Seek My face," my heart said to You,
"Your face, O LORD, I shall seek."
Do not hide Your face from me,

Do not turn Your servant away in anger;
You have been my help;
Do not abandon me nor forsake me,
O God of my salvation!
For my father and my mother have forsaken me,
But the LORD *will take me up.*
Teach me Your way, O LORD,
And lead me in a level path
Because of my foes.
Do not deliver me over to the desire of my adversaries,
For false witnesses have risen against me,
And such as breathe out violence.
I would have despaired unless I had believed that I would
    see the goodness of the LORD
In the land of the living.
Wait for the LORD;
Be strong and let your heart take courage;
Yes, wait for the LORD.

(Psalm 27)

Day 1: *Psalm 27*
Frozen by Fear

One of the most paralyzing problems in all of life is fear. Our fears are directed in so many areas: fear of the unknown, fear of calamity, fear of sickness, disease, and death, fear of people, fear of losing our jobs, fear of enemy attacks, fear of being misunderstood . . . or rejected . . . or criticized . . . or forgotten . . . or (as we just considered) being mistreated. What makes matters worse is that the very thing we fear often occurs. Sometimes it is worse than we anticipated! I've known times when I felt virtually paralyzed with feelings of panic. As fear gets a firm grip on us, we become its victim.

This reminds me of a college friend of mine who worked several summers ago on a construction crew, building a large hospital in Dallas. He was assigned to the twelfth story and was given the job of helping a welder who was welding the flooring structure composed of huge, steel beams. So scared of falling, my friend literally shook with fear every day, though he admitted it to no one. One hot afternoon the welder looked up and noticed the man shaking in his boots. He yelled, "Are you scared, son?" The student stuttered "S-s-s-scared! I've been t-t-t-trying to tell you for t-t-t-two weeks that I q-q-q-quit!"

Frozen with fear!

If fear has become your daily grind, Psalm 27 should prove very helpful. It is a song intended to take the pain out of that dreadful grind.

The Passage and Its Pattern

A careful reading of King David's song will reveal a contrast between the first half (vv. 1–6) and the last half (vv. 7–14). The first six verses resound with praise, confidence, victory, and even singing, while the last eight verses are filled with needs—actually, a grocery list of requests. Look at the expressions David uses in his composition:

Verse 7: "Hear, O LORD . . . and answer me."

Verse 8: "Your face, O LORD, I shall seek."

Verse 9: "Do not hide. . . . Do not turn. . . . Do not abandon me nor forsake me."

Verse 11: "Teach me . . . O LORD."

These ancient lyrics seem to tremble in utter dependence.

As we begin our in-depth look at David's response to fear, let me point out the overall structure of the psalm.

Declaration of Praise (vv. 1–6)

Petition for Needs (vv. 7–13)

Exhortation to Wait (v. 14)

He first declared what he knew (vv. 1–6). He then expressed what he needed (vv. 7–13). And finally, he committed himself to waiting on God (v. 14).

Making It Strong in Your Soul

What is your customary response when fear grips you? Do you think your response is constructive for yourself and others? How would you change your response to fear if you could?

🎵

Day 2: Psalm 27

Facing Fear with Praise

As David faced his fears and expressed them to God in Psalm 27, he began with worship, celebrating the power and faithfulness of his God.

Declaration of Praise

The key to the entire song is verse 1. It consists of two similar sentences, each ending with a rhetorical question.

"The Lord is my light . . . my salvation . . . the defense of my life." Interestingly, David says God *is* all of this. The Lord doesn't simply *give* these things. In other words, the psalmist laid claim upon God Himself rather than His works. David knew Him personally. To David, the Lord was a very personal, ever-present Friend and Helper, not some distant Deity—an impersonal, abstract, theological Being who hid Himself high above the clouds. No, David saw the Lord as a faithful companion.

Because of the Lord's presence, which meant more to David than anything else, the composer asks: "Whom shall I fear . . . whom shall I dread?"

Here the Hebrew term for "fear" is a common one: *yarah*. But the term for "dread" *(pachad)*, meaning "to be in awe, to be filled with dread," is less common. The Lord God was so significant, so impressive, so overwhelmingly important to David that nothing and no one else inspired awe.

I find it encouraging that Psalm 23 declares, "I shall not want," and Psalm 26 states, "I shall not slide" (KJV). And now Psalm 27 says, I "will not fear." In each case, the composer finds what he lacks only in the presence and provisions of God.

Having considered the sufficiency of his God, David recalls the Lord's past victories over his enemies.

> When evildoers came upon me to devour my flesh,
> My adversaries and my enemies, they stumbled and fell.
> Though a host encamp against me,
> My heart will not fear;
> Though war arise against me,
> In spite of this I shall be confident. (vv. 2–3)

Note the specific occasions of potential fear: "evildoers . . . adversaries . . . enemies . . . a host . . . war." What a dark scene! And you'll notice that these things weren't mere possibilities; they were realities. He says, "when" not "if." He actually faced these dangers.

Take note of two observations. First, look at the intensity of the conflict: the evildoers came "to devour" (v. 2); the host had come to "encamp against me" (v. 3); war had risen "against me." This was no slight affliction. Second, look at the psalmist's response in the last phrase of verse 3. In spite of these dangers, both past and future, "I shall be confident." The Hebrew says, literally, "I *am* confident!" Dangers had come before and danger remained imminent. Pressure mounted. Severe days lay ahead. David had every reason to be shaking in his sandals . . . but he stood firm!

The Hebrew term used by David, translated "confident," does not mean self-reliant or brave, humanly speaking. In Hebrew it means "to trust, to be secure, to have assurance." Its Arabic counterpart is "picturesque": "to throw oneself down upon one's face, to lie upon the ground." The point I want to get across is that the source of David's confidence and stability was not his own strength—but God. His Lord was his only foundation for rocklike stability. What an unshakable foundation!

While living under intense pressure and difficulty, the courageous missionary to inland China, Hudson Taylor, once wrote: "It does not matter how great the pressure is. What really matters is where the pressure lies—whether it comes between you and God, or whether it presses you nearer His heart."[5]

Making It Strong in Your Soul

Why do you think praising God in the midst of fearful circumstances might be helpful? Think in both practical and theological terms. Can you recall times in your own past when God rescued you from danger? Did you record them in a journal? You might need them later!

Day 3: *Psalm 27*

Facing Fear with a Song of Faith

When fear has us in its icy grip, we quickly turn toward self-preservation. We hope to avoid loss, escape pain, or cheat death. Not David! His composition, preserved for us as Psalm 27, gives priority to eternal matters. Verses 4–6 revolve around the idea of David's desire to maintain constant, intimate fellowship with his Lord.

---

5 Dr. and Mrs. Hudson Taylor, *Hudson Taylor's Spiritual Secret* (Chicago: Moody Press, 1958), 107.

One thing I have asked from the LORD, that I shall seek:
That I may dwell in the house of the LORD all the days of my life,
To behold the beauty of the LORD
And to meditate in His temple.
For in the day of trouble He will conceal me in His tabernacle;
In the secret place of His tent He will hide me;
He will lift me up on a rock.
And now my head will be lifted up above
        my enemies around me,
And I will offer in His tent sacrifices with shouts of joy;
I will sing, yes, I will sing praises to the LORD.

Did you notice that the first-person singular pronoun is frequently used? It is woven through these verses—*I*, *me*, *my*. This is the testimony of David *alone*. This is a written account of a man's private life, his personal struggles with life's daily grinds. This is not David the public figure; it is David alone before his God.

I also observe that David says: "I will sing, yes, I will sing praises." This is the result of maintaining a close walk with the Lord. Ephesians 5:18 commands us to be "filled with the Spirit," to allow the Spirit of God to control us—our thinking, motives, attitudes, activity. This is vertical fellowship at its best! When we give the Holy Spirit complete control, He promises we will receive:

- a melodious heart—singing! (Ephesians 5:19)
- a thankful attitude—giving thanks! (Ephesians 5:20)
- a submissive spirit—be subject to one another!
  (Ephesians 5:21)

When was the last time you burst forth all alone in a song of worshipful trust? I think it is sad that the Christian's song is seldom heard outside the church building. Living in fellowship with the Lord should cause spontaneous melodies to burst forth throughout the day and night. How encouraging to *sing* our faith!

Making It Strong in Your Soul

When you feel fear growing within, how can music become a part of your response? David wrote a song; perhaps you could sing or play an instrument. At the very least, listening to uplifting, God-honoring music could be a very effective means of turning fear into praise.

🎵

Day 4: *Psalm 27*
Seeking God's Help

While David's first response to fear wasn't a panicked plea for help, he didn't live in denial. He merely chose to celebrate God's power and to recall His past triumphs. Eventually, however, David did ask the Lord for what he needed. No longer panicked, he expressed his desires with intense emotion.

Petition for Needs

Hear, O LORD, when I cry with my voice,
And be gracious to me and answer me.
When You said, "Seek My face," my heart said to You,
"Your face, O LORD, I shall seek."
Do not hide Your face from me,
Do not turn Your servant away in anger;
You have been my help;
Do not abandon me nor forsake me,
O God of my salvation!
For my father and my mother have forsaken me,
But the LORD will take me up.
Teach me Your way, O LORD,
And lead me in a level path
Because of my foes.
Do not deliver me over to the desire of my adversaries,

For false witnesses have risen against me,

And such as breathe out violence. (Psalm 27:7–12)

Rather than digging into these verses one by one, let's view them altogether. I want you to look back and take special note of the strong imperatives (the commands) in these verses.

Verse 7: "Hear . . . be gracious . . . answer me!"

Verse 9: "Do not hide Your face. . . . Do not turn. . . . Do not abandon . . . nor forsake me!"

Verse 11: "Teach me . . . lead me!"

Verse 12: "Do not deliver me over to . . . my adversaries!"

I don't find David taking it easy, yawning, and uttering a half-hearted request. I read boldness here—a determined, positive approach to God. He presents a respectful series of very practical commands. With unguarded, unrestrained fervency, the songwriter declares his requests, knowing they are in line with God's will. In other words, David didn't ask for anything God has not already promised. We would do well to imitate the fearful psalmist by offering this kind of prayer today. After all, the Lord already wants to fulfill these requests. Listen to three other verses on the same subject:

Therefore let us draw near with confidence to the throne of grace, so that we may receive mercy and may find grace to help in time of need. (Hebrews 4:16)

The effective prayer of a righteous man can accomplish much. (James 5:16)

Be anxious for nothing, but in everything by prayer and supplication with thanksgiving let your requests be made known to God. (Philippians 4:6)

As I read these statements, I am reproved by the hesitancy, the lack of fervency in too many of our prayers. We lack confident boldness in our prayers. We are to ask as though we mean it! Our Lord is pleased when we ask in boldness and without doubting.

Before turning to the final stanza of David's song, take special note of verse 10. "For my father and my mother have forsaken me, but the LORD will take me up." Nestled within the list of requests, we find a brief, candid admission from David's heart. His parents, for some unrevealed reason, had "forsaken" him. The original Hebrew term means "to leave, desert, abandon." I find it intriguing that David's own parents had turned their backs on their son, even though he was a godly man. Equally interesting is David's security as he declares, "But the LORD will take me up."

Do you remember the moving words of Isaiah 49:15–16? What hope they offer!

> Can a woman forget her nursing child
> And have no compassion on the son of her womb?
> Even these may forget, but I will not forget you.
> Behold, I have inscribed you on the palms of My hands.

The prophet, speaking for God, says that mothers may forget their infant babies, but the Lord does not forget one of His own. That, my friend, includes *you*.

Have you been forsaken? Have your parents turned against you? Even though you have tried to maintain a healthy relationship with them, have they misread your messages? Are they on a different wavelength? Refuse to become bitter. Claim the security your Lord promises you. You have nothing to fear because you have Him who has conquered fear. His care is more consistent than that of your parents.

Making It Strong in Your Soul

Do you live many of your days under pressure? (By the way, pressure is just another form of fear.) Plan a couple of times this week when you can pull away from your duties—alone—long enough to sing (or listen to music), praise God, and petition the Lord for your needs. Think of it as an investment in your spiritual productivity.

♬

Day 5: *Psalm 27*
Waiting on God

D avid's cry for help doesn't end with an account of God's sudden and miraculous provision. Instead, the songwriter commits to doing what comes least naturally to people in fear. He committed to doing *nothing*. He chose to wait on God. Read that again—aloud.

Exhortation to Wait

Wait for the LORD;
Be strong and let your heart take courage;
Yes, wait for the LORD. (Psalm 27:14)

It's a fitting conclusion, but completely unexpected. David levels an exhortation to himself to wait! He realized that the pressure would not suddenly leave. He knew his enemies would not do an about-face and depart immediately after he rose from his knees. He was realistic enough to know that anything worth having is worth waiting for. So, in the final lines of his song, he tells himself to relax, to enter into God's rest, to cease from his own works. (See Heb. 4:9–11). Strength and courage are developed *during* a trial, not after it is over. Waiting on God is essential.

The term "wait" is from the Hebrew verb *kawah*, which eventually carried the idea of eagerly looking for something. It originally meant "to twist, stretch." The noun form means "line, cord, thread." The literal definition became a word picture involving tension or eager anticipation. Isaiah 40:31 uses this same term: "Yet those who wait for the LORD will gain new strength."

If you are waiting for God to work this week, keep on waiting! In the wait there will come strength and courage. I urge you to review the truths in Psalm 27 each time you are tempted to be afraid. Don't become paralyzed and ineffective. Take yourself out of the grind of fear! Look upon each threatening circumstance as an opportunity to grow in your faith, rather than to retreat. How? Follow David's example.

First: Call to mind what you know to be true about God.

Second: Express what you need boldly.

Third: Wait. Let the fearful circumstance become God's opportunity to strengthen you.

Making It Strong in Your Soul

Waiting on God is a cultivated spiritual discipline. It requires patience and practice. Focus your attention on something you cannot fix—something causing you anxiety beyond your control. Each time the issue comes to mind, recall God's abilities and faithfulness, surrender the issue to His control, then choose to wait as you leave it in His hands. Repeat as necessary!

THE GRIND OF AN UNFORGIVEN CONSCIENCE

A Psalm of David. A Maskil.

How blessed is he whose transgression is forgiven,
Whose sin is covered!
How blessed is the man to whom the LORD
  does not impute iniquity,
And in whose spirit there is no deceit!
When I kept silent about my sin, my body wasted away
Through my groaning all day long.
For day and night Your hand was heavy upon me;
My vitality was drained away as with the
  fever heat of summer. Selah.
I acknowledged my sin to You,
And my iniquity I did not hide;
I said, "I will confess my transgressions to the LORD";
And You forgave the guilt of my sin. Selah.
Therefore, let everyone who is godly pray to You
  in a time when You may be found;
Surely in a flood of great waters they will not reach him.
You are my hiding place; You preserve me from trouble;
You surround me with songs of deliverance. Selah.
I will instruct you and teach you in the way
  which you should go;
I will counsel you with My eye upon you.
Do not be as the horse or as the mule
  which have no understanding,
Whose trappings include bit and bridle to hold them in check,
Otherwise they will not come near to you.

Many are the sorrows of the wicked,
But he who trusts in the LORD, lovingkindness shall
*   surround him.*
Be glad in the LORD and rejoice, you righteous ones;
And shout for joy, all you who are upright in heart.

(Psalm 32)

Day 1: *Psalm 32*
Living under the Cloud of Guilt

Your conscience may be invisible but it is certainly not inactive! Who hasn't been kept awake by its pleadings? With incredible regularity, an unforgiven conscience can rob us of an appetite, steal our sleep, and drive us to distraction.

Do you remember Edgar Allan Poe's haunting short story "The Tell-Tale Heart"? The main character has committed murder. Unable to escape the lingering guilt of his deed, he begins to hear the heartbeat of the victim he has buried under his floorboards. A cold sweat covers him as the *beat-beat-beat* goes on . . . relentlessly. It refuses to go away. Ultimately, it becomes clear that the pounding that drove the man mad was not in the grave down below but the pounding within his own chest. So it is with an unforgiven conscience.

The ancient songwriter David was no stranger to this maddening malady. As we shall soon discover, the longer he refused to come to terms with the enormity of his grinding guilt, the more he became physically ill and emotionally distraught. Only forgiveness can take away that grind.

As we begin to read through this song, two things catch the eye even before we get to verse one. First, we notice this is a Psalm of David. It is a song the man David was led to write under the inspiration of the Holy Spirit. So, at the outset let's remember that the song he writes describes some situation from David's personal experience. Second, we notice this is a *"maskil,"* a term that is unfamiliar to us. *Maskil* is a transliterated Hebrew word that appears before thirteen of the songs in this ancient hymnbook of the Hebrews. Most likely it is from *sakal*, a Hebrew verb meaning "to be prudent, circumspect, wise—to have insight;" it has to do with intelligent knowledge gained through reason. According to my English dictionary, "insight" means "the act or power to see into a situation." Putting all this together we understand that the Thirty-second Psalm is designed to give its readers wisdom and insight when dealing with certain situations.

The situation in this case is the grind that accompanies a guilt-ridden conscience. Psalm 51 should be considered along with Psalm 32. Both were written after David's adultery with Bathsheba and his attempt to cover up his sin by arranging her husband's death on the battlefield. Of the two, Psalm 51 was written first, during the anguish of guilt under which David suffered so severely. Psalm 32 was written after the anguish, after his forgiveness had been secured and his peace of mind restored. So, the theme of Psalm 32 could be "The Peace Following Forgiveness" and how it can be achieved. We learn right away that this song is incredibly relevant; we live in a world filled with people living under a thick cloud of guilt, a society in desperate need of forgiveness.

As you read the psalm, allow yourself to enter into the feelings of David. It is obvious that he is joyful at the outset, rejoicing in his present state of forgiveness (vv. 1–2). He then falls into a reflective mood as he thinks back to days past (vv. 3–5). Twice during this section of the song, he adds the word *selah*, which most scholars believe is a musical notation indicating a pause, most likely for reflection. When we come across this musical notation, it is best to pause and then read the section again, only this time more slowly and thoughtfully. The next three verses (vv. 6–8) look ahead to the future, directly addressing anyone who may read these words.

David's conclusion (vv. 9–11) exhorts his readers to live in an upright manner. Here, then, is an outline of the song.

   I. Expression of Present Joy (vv. 1–2)
  II. Reflection on Past Sins (vv. 3–5)
    A. Reluctance to confess (vv. 3–4)
    B. Willingness to confess (v. 5)
 III. Provision for Future Needs (vv. 6–8)
    A. Invitation (v. 6)
    B. Protection (v. 7)
    C. Guidance (v. 8)
  IV. Application to Every Believer (vv. 9–11)
    A. Don't be stubborn! (v. 9)
    B. Take your choice! (v. 10)
    C. Remain upright! (v. 11)

Making It Strong in Your Soul

Think of a time when your conscience has struggled with a shameful act (it may be now.) How did it affect your ability to eat, sleep, work, and concentrate? How did it affect your interaction with others? What did you do to find relief (if you indeed experienced relief)?

Day 2: *Psalm 32*
From Self-deception to Relief

I once asked my sister, Luci, to name the emotion she considered the most powerful and enjoyable of all. She surprised me with her answer: relief. After thinking for a moment, I had to agree. Relief is everyone's favorite feeling!

David's song about forgiveness begins with a celebration of relief, which he found in God's forgiveness of his transgression.

Expression of Joy

> How blessed is he whose transgression is forgiven,
> Whose sin is covered!
> How blessed is the man to whom the LORD
>   does not impute iniquity,
> And in whose spirit there is no deceit! (vv. 1–2)

In these two verses David expresses overjoyed, unrestrained, exuberant gratitude for the Lord's mercy. The two sentences begin just like Psalm 1 (in Hebrew, that is): "Oh, the happiness many times over!" The idea is that of multiplied, numberless blessings. He is rejoicing over the removal of sins that once pinned him to the mat of guilt and shame.

If you look closely, you'll find four specific terms for wrongdoing in the first two verses. They describe the downward steps that lead a person to the same condition in which David lived before he finally confessed his wrongdoing.

1. "Transgression." The word is from the Hebrew term *peshah*, meaning "to rebel, revolt." It describes a willful act of disobedience.

2. "Sin." This word is from the most common Hebrew term for wrongdoing: *khatah*, which means "to miss the mark, to miss the way, go wrong." It has to do with deviating from the path which pleases God, whether willfully or by error.

3. "Iniquity." This term, from the Hebrew *awōn*, paints a dark picture of sin as "infraction, crooked behavior, perversion," suggesting it comes from a corrupted nature.

4. "Deceit." *Remiah* is the original Hebrew term meaning "treachery, deception [and in some cases—as here], self-deception."

It appears the songwriter traces the downward spiral of wrongdoing, using increasingly strong terms for sin. It is a notorious tailspin with which, sadly, most of us are familiar. First, we rebel or revolt against God's revealed will. Next, we miss the way He marked out for us—the path of righteousness. Then, guilt grabs us and we go through the inner torment of severe, uncomfortable feelings. Without relief, the daily grind of an unforgiven conscience can drive a person mad. If he or she doesn't find relief in forgiveness, the only alternative is self-delusion through denial, minimizing, blame-shifting, making excuses, even redefining evil to make it appear good.

As self-deception sets in, as it did in David when he refused to deal with his wrong, the sinner's character becomes twisted. Because it happens slowly, many try to tolerate sin's consequences— those inner churnings and grinding turmoil. (We'll look at the daily grind of inner turmoil next.) If you have fallen into the torments of a guilty conscience through sin and you realize that self-deception is beginning to take over, I urge you to stop. Put a halt to your downward plunge and openly confess your wrong to your Lord. Do whatever is necessary, no matter how drastic, to prevent repeated failure. Read these next two statements from Scripture with great care:

> He who conceals his transgressions will not prosper,
> But he who confesses and forsakes them will find
> compassion. (Proverbs 28:13)

> If we confess our sins, He is faithful and righteous to forgive
> us our sins and to cleanse us from all unrighteousness.
> (1 John 1:9)

Making It Strong in Your Soul

Take a few moments to examine your attitude toward sin. Are you now "okay" with a specific behavior that used to torment your conscience? Have you learned to live with a sinful habit without confessing it? Do you have a secret life . . . an unrevealed routine you keep concealed from everyone? Beware! You are in danger! Find a trusted, godly friend and begin with a full acknowledgment of the whole sordid mess.

Day 3: *Psalm 32*
The Bitter Price of Secret Sin

David's celebration of God's forgiveness takes a dark turn as he recalls his anguished past. He remembers—perhaps accompanied by a gloomy minor key—the days of misery he spent in the isolation of secret sin.

Reflection on Past Sins

When I kept silent about my sin, my body wasted away
Through my groaning all day long.
For day and night Your hand was heavy upon me;
My vitality was drained away as with the fever heat
    of summer. Selah.
I acknowledged my sin to You,
And my iniquity I did not hide;
I said, "I will confess my transgressions to the LORD";
And You forgave the guilt of my sin. Selah. (vv. 3–5)

David takes us back to those tragic days when he refused to acknowledge his wrong (vv. 3–4). These amazing lyrics describe what went on inside the composer during his tormented days of unconfessed sin. He admits that "keeping silent" about his sin cost him dearly. He paid a bitter price to preserve his secret. The inner conflict brought on a psychosomatic illness. His tormented mind, wracked with mental and emotional conflict—his refusal to deal completely and honestly with sin—caused several physical ailments.

- His "body wasted away."
- He groaned "all day long."
- He endured this "day and night."
- His "vitality (literally 'sap, juices') drained away."
- He had a "fever heat" like the hot summer.

Abruptly, he adds *Selah*—pause and consider!

Obviously, during that miserable period of time, God's hand was heavy upon him. In the words of Proverbs 13:15, "The way of the treacherous is hard." Like a tree trying to survive without water from refreshing rains, David was utterly miserable and became spiritually barren in this sinful state.

Finally, David found relief through confession (Ps. 32:5). Without restraint he poured out his sinful condition. Don't miss the progression:

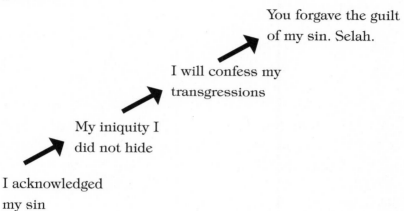

You forgave the guilt
of my sin. Selah.

I will confess my
transgressions

My iniquity I
did not hide

I acknowledged
my sin

Like a cool, cleansing shower on a hot, sweaty day, God's forgiveness washed away not only David's sins but also silenced his tormenting guilt. The Lord penetrated into the depths of the poet's inner being to provide that magnificent relief only He can bring: PEACE. God forgave completely because David confessed completely.

If you are harboring some sin, if you are keeping hidden a few secret regions of wrong, then don't expect to enjoy freedom from guilt. There is an unspoken principle that runs through the pages of Scripture like a scarlet thread: *Secret sin cannot coexist with inner peace.* Peace returns only when our sins are fully confessed and forsaken. Few grinds are more galling than the grind of an agitated, tormented conscience. It's awful! And few joys are more relieving than having our sins forgiven.

Making It Strong in Your Soul

Confession begins with a full acknowledgment of the truth . . . to ourselves first. If you have been struggling with a secret sin, write a letter to yourself naming the sinful activity, describing its effect on your life, and anticipating potential consequences in the future if it continues. Then, in prayer, present it to God.

♆

Day 4: *Psalm 32*
Sin Distorts the Truth

A s David's celebration song about God's forgiveness continues, he recognizes that confession is costly. He also acknowledges the fact that we have a window of opportunity that may, one day, close. Consequently, he prays for God's future provision.

Provision for Future Needs

Therefore, let everyone who is godly pray to You in a time
    when You may be found;
Surely in a flood of great waters they will not reach him.
You are my hiding place; You preserve me from trouble;
You surround me with songs of deliverance. Selah.
I will instruct you and teach you in the way
    which you should go;
I will counsel you with My eye upon you. (vv. 6–8)

Remember, the theme of this psalm is forgiveness. David wants to make it clear that he doesn't have a corner on this blessed experience. He therefore issues an invitation to "everyone who is godly." This includes every New Testament believer, every person who knows the Lord, having received Jesus Christ by faith. David urges all God's people to pray, even in the midst of "a flood of great waters," when all seems hopeless. He promises that when this is done, God will provide the same deliverance to us that He brought to David.

Verse 7 places full attention on God. He is the One who protects us, preserves us, surrounds us, and even gives us a song. *Selah* (again, pause and consider)! A guilt-ridden conscience casts God as a cruel deity, walking around with a club, looking for sinners to smash. That's because sin distorts the truth. Look again at verse 7. David breaks out into songs of deliverance! "You are my hiding place; You preserve me from trouble; You surround me with songs of deliverance. *Selah*."

What a comforting picture, especially to those who have been in deep sin and seek forgiveness!

The next statement is God's answer to David's invitation to all God's people. The Lord promises His guidance and counsel. The eighth verse concludes with God saying, in effect, "I will become your counselor, and guide your restoration."

Do you have the feeling that God is gone? That He doesn't care? Trust me today; He does care. He cares personally about you (1 Peter 5:7). He has His eyes on you. He may seem to be removed from you and distant, but He is near, waiting for your confession and repentance.

Making It Strong in Your Soul

What do you most fear will happen if you confess your secret sin to God? What do you most fear will happen if someone discovers your secret sin? Confession is a matter of trust, isn't it? Do you trust the Lord to transform your sorrow into joy? Earlier, you were asked to write a letter detailing your secret sin. Find a mature, trusted advisor and read the letter in private to him or her.

Day 5: *Psalm 32*

Confess and Be Cleansed

No one can tell me that Scripture, though written more than two thousand years ago, is not relevant today. David's poem is both beautiful and practical. Having celebrated the faithfulness of God and acknowledged the difficulty of confession, he scolds the reader for his or her stubborn pride.

Application to Every Believer

Do not be as the horse or as the mule which
>have no understanding,
Whose trappings include bit and bridle to hold them in check,
Otherwise they will not come near to you.
Many are the sorrows of the wicked,
But he who trusts in the LORD, lovingkindness shall
>surround him.
Be glad in the LORD and rejoice, you righteous ones;
And shout for joy, all you who are upright in heart. (vv. 9–11)

David summarizes all the lessons he wants to leave with us into three strong statements of exhortation:

First, don't be stubborn! (v. 9). When it comes to dealing with sin, don't be like a mule or any other hardheaded beast! Surrender! Keep a short account before the Lord. Don't let wrongdoing build up. Don't try to maintain a standoff any longer.

Second, make your choice! (v. 10). In reading over these concluding words, you'll notice two—and only two—paths: the path of the wicked, which brings "many sorrows," and the path of trust, which brings "lovingkindness." Consider the destination of each path and make your choice (says the songwriter).

Third, remain upright! (v. 11). Stop the downward plunge into deep, dark, convoluted, crazy-making sin by maintaining an upright walk. The Hebrew term rendered "upright" has to do with honest dealing, with God and before others. It describes someone with nothing to hide. A former colleague used to describe this kind of conduct as "clean and clear." He sought that goal with every contract, every transaction, and every decision, whether public or private.

That's a great policy. No secrets. Complete transparency. If you're looking for green pastures, you'll find them only as you deal honestly with your Lord. Remain upright. God is so gracious! He has planned a life for His children that results in inner peace, outer strength, and optimism. But we are sinful and frequently choose to walk our own way. Though He prefers that we not sin, He is willing to forgive and to guide us through our recovery and restoration. He will forgive and restore if we will completely repent; that is, confess and seek His cleansing.

Making It Strong in Your Soul

Earlier, you were encouraged to write out a full confession of your sin, to present it to God in prayer, and then to a trusted Christian advisor. Now, write down the future you would like to have once you are freed from the tyranny of a guilt-ridden conscience. Describe your relationship with God and with your loved ones. Describe the freedom and joy you would like to experience. Then, present it to God as your sincere request.

THE GRIND OF INNER TURMOIL

For the choir director. A Maskil of the sons of Korah.

As the deer pants for the water brooks,
So my soul pants for You, O God.
My soul thirsts for God, for the living God;
When shall I come and appear before God?
My tears have been my food day and night,
While they say to me all day long, "Where is your God?"
These things I remember and I pour out my soul within me.
For I used to go along with the throng and lead them in
      procession to the house of God,
With the voice of joy and thanksgiving, a multitude
      keeping festival.
Why are you in despair, O my soul?
And why have you become disturbed within me?
Hope in God, for I shall again praise Him
For the help of His presence.
O my God, my soul is in despair within me;
Therefore I remember You from the land of the Jordan
And the peaks of Hermon, from Mount Mizar.
Deep calls to deep at the sound of Your waterfalls;
All Your breakers and Your waves have rolled over me.
The LORD *will command His lovingkindness in the daytime;*
And His song will be with me in the night,
A prayer to the God of my life.
I will say to God my rock, "Why have You forgotten me?
Why do I go mourning because of the oppression
      of the enemy?"
As a shattering of my bones, my adversaries revile me,

While they say to me all day long, "Where is your God?"
Why are you in despair, O my soul?
And why have you become disturbed within me?
Hope in God, for I shall yet praise Him,
The help of my countenance and my God.

(Psalm 42)

Vindicate me, O God, and plead my case against
*   an ungodly nation;*
O deliver me from the deceitful and unjust man!
For You are the God of my strength; why have You
*   rejected me?*
Why do I go mourning because of the oppression
*   of the enemy?*
O send out Your light and Your truth, let them lead me;
Let them bring me to Your holy hill
And to Your dwelling places.
Then I will go to the altar of God,
To God my exceeding joy;
And upon the lyre I shall praise You, O God, my God.
Why are you in despair, O my soul?
And why are you disturbed within me?
Hope in God, for I shall again praise Him,
The help of my countenance and my God.

(Psalm 43)

Day 1: *Psalms 42 and 43*
A "Churning Place"

I have a "churning place." It's in my stomach. On the upper, left side, just below the rib cage. When disturbing things happen, when troubling words are said, when certain letters that contain ugly words are written or extremely critical comments are read, my inner churning starts. Do you have something similar?

One friend of mine says his spot is in his head, specifically his forehead. Another told me his "churning place" resides at the back of his neck. Most people I know have a particular region where grinding occurs, usually triggered by:

• Bad news	• Personal conflict
• Unpaid bills	• Legal problems
• Expensive repairs	• Difficult decisions
• Impossible deadlines	• Unresolved sin

I find it rather comforting that God's inspired hymnal does not omit the grind of inner turmoil. Since it is so common, I would think it strange if such a topic were not addressed. But before we uncover a few of the more practical remarks, let's take a look at some background information about Psalms 42 and 43.

The ancient songbook of the Scriptures is organized by five divisions or "books."

Book 1: Psalms 1–41
Book 2: Psalms 42–72
Book 3: Psalms 73–89
Book 4: Psalms 90–106
Book 5: Psalms 107–150

The last song in each book concludes with "Amen," or some other form of doxology. The very last song, Psalm 150, is itself an extended great doxology climaxing in praise.

All sorts of suggestions have been given to explain why these ancient songs are divided into five books. Jewish tradition explains this arrangement as a conscious reflection of the Pentateuch, the first five books of the Old Testament. A Midrash (Jewish commentary), dating from the Talmudic period, suggests:

As Moses gave five books of laws to Israel, so David gave five books of Psalms to Israel, the Book of psalms entitled *Blessed is the man* (Ps. 1:1), the Book entitled *For the leader: Maschil* (Ps. 42:1), the Book *A Psalm of Asaph* (Ps. 73:1), the Book *A Prayer of Moses* (Ps. 90:1), and the Book *Let the redeemed of the Lord say* (Ps. 107:2).[6]

In truth, no one knows for sure why the psalms are so divided. Regardless, I don't think it's any coincidence that Psalms 42 and 43 introduce Book 2. I want to suggest that these two songs should be viewed as a unit. Two observations lead me to make that suggestion. First, Psalm 43 has no superscription. Nothing by way of introduction appears before the first verse. Furthermore, it is the only psalm in Book 2 without a superscription. I believe, therefore, it flows quite naturally from the previous song. (Remember, the chapter breaks—like the punctuation markings—have been added to the text of Scripture in later centuries. God's Word is inspired . . . but not the punctuation or various paragraph and chapter divisions.)

Second, the phrase repeated twice in Psalm 42 also appears in Psalm 43. Notice 42:5, 11, and 43:5:

Why are you in despair, O my soul?
And why have you become disturbed within me?
Hope in God, for I shall again praise Him.

These three identical phrases lead me to believe that these two songs form a natural unit, revolving around a single theme. Look next at the superscription before verse 1 in Psalm 42: "For the choir director. A Maskil of the sons of Korah." You may recall that the designation *Maskil* means the song was designed to provide insight and wisdom when dealing with certain situations. In Psalm 32, the situation involved a tormented conscience.

---

6 William G. Braude, *The Midrash on Psalms*, vol. 1 (New Haven, CT: Yale University Press, 1959).

What is the situation in these two songs? Going back to the thrice-repeated statement mentioned above, we see clearly that the situation is inner despair and disturbance. In other words, these two songs have been preserved to provide the reader with wisdom and insight in handling those "blue days," that age-old grind of inner turmoil.

Making It Strong in Your Soul

Where does your "churning place" reside? What typically starts the churning? How do you respond to the onset of inner turmoil and what do you do to find relief? If you can't recall, take note the next time inner turmoil triggers your "churning place." You might consider keeping a journal of the experience.

Day 2: *Psalms 42 and 43*
Longing for God

The composition of David—preserved for us as Psalms 42 and 43—sings the following lines three times, strongly suggesting the issue at hand is inner turmoil.

> Why are you in despair, O my soul?
> And why have you become disturbed within me?
> Hope in God, for I shall again praise Him. (Ps. 42:5, 11; 43:5)

The term "despair" comes from the Hebrew word *shakhakh*, which in the literal sense means "to crouch, bow down." In the figurative sense, the verb means "to become low, be abased." This song recounts those days when we feel like curling up in the fetal position and quitting. Fortunately, David doesn't leave us on the ground. He advises how we can conquer those feelings rather than succumb to them, how to overcome feelings of inner turmoil rather than "churn" our way through life.

As I mentioned earlier, having those disturbing feelings on occasion is normal. We do a real disservice to a new Christian by telling him or her that sadness or despair is sinful. That's both unrealistic and unbiblical. David wrote many psalms while he was churning within. While we have no business wallowing for months in a pit of depression, all of us should be transparent enough to admit we have "blue" days like that. I am comforted that even Jesus Himself, on occasion, felt inwardly troubled (John 11:33; 12:27; 13:21). Charles Haddon Spurgeon wrote of "the minister's fainting fits" in his *Lectures to My Students*. Dr. John Henry Jowett, another outstanding preacher of yesteryear, was honest enough to admit in a letter to a friend:

> I wish you wouldn't think I'm such a saint. You seem to imagine that I have no ups and downs, but just a level and lofty stretch of spiritual attainment with unbroken joy and equanimity. By no means! I am often perfectly wretched and everything appears most murky. I often feel as though my religious life had only just begun, and that I am in the kindergarten stage. But I can usually trace these miserable seasons to some personal cause, and the first thing to do is to attend to that cause, and get into the sunshine again.[7]

I appreciate Jowett's vulnerability. The good news is that these two songs help us discover how to crawl out of the darkness and back into the sunshine again.

The songwriter begins his Forty-second Song with an image from the wilderness.

> As the deer pants for the water brooks,
> So my soul pants for You, O God.
> My soul thirsts for God, for the living God;
> When shall I come and appear before God? (vv. 1–2)

---

7 Arthur Porritt, *John Henry Jowett* (London: Hodder and Stoughton, 1924), 290.

David longs for God like a thirsty deer in a barren wilderness longs for a cool stream. He says he "pants" for the Lord. In Psalm 119:131 he expresses a similar thought when he writes, "I opened my mouth wide and panted, for I longed for Your commandments." God, who was considered by believers "the fountain of living waters" (Jer. 2:13; 17:13), was the sole desire of the churning singer. Being a man after God's own heart, David passionately yearned for His presence. And his opening lines suggest that his inner turmoil was a direct result of his having a distant relationship with his God.

Making It Strong in Your Soul

Think about the last time you struggled with inner turmoil. What effect do you think your spiritual life had on your perspective? If you were asked to describe your greatest desire, what would you have named? Did you want something from God, or did you long for the Lord Himself?

♮

Day 3: *Psalms 42 and 43*
Remember God's Faithfulness

David's battle with turmoil, recounted in Psalms 42 and 43, results in longing for God's presence.

My tears have been my food day and night,
While they say to me all day long, "Where is your God?" (v. 3)

God certainly has not forsaken His child, but at low, moments all of us could testify that there are times when it feels like He has! What do we do to become reassured? How can we find the hope of God's care when we are feeling low, when we are in the grind of inner turmoil? David talked to himself.

These things I remember and I pour out my soul within me.
For I used to go along with the throng and lead them
    in procession to the house of God,
With the voice of joy and thanksgiving, a multitude
    keeping festival. (v. 4)

A more exact rendering of the beginning of this verse would be: "These things I will remember . . ." or "These things I would remember . . ." David said these things to himself. Sometimes healthy, positive self-talk is great therapy. He is saying that when he is blue, he will call to remembrance past days of victory when God was very real, very present. He says, in effect, "Those were the days, my friend! Those were days of blessing, joy, and thanksgiving!" After calling to mind such days, he asks:

Why are you in despair, O my soul?
And why have you become disturbed within me?
Hope in God, for I shall again praise Him
For the help of His presence. (v. 5)

"Why," he asks, "should I feel sad and blue with such positive memories?" He admits that such vivid memories of past victory should really encourage him.

When you are "crouched" in turmoil, it helps to think back to previous victories and call to mind specific things God did for you. Remember the Lord of your past is the Lord right now.

I remember my first year at Dallas Seminary. Cynthia and I lived in an apartment on campus that wasn't air-conditioned. It stayed hot even during the early fall of the year. Knowing that summer would surely come the following year, we began to pray for a window air conditioner. In fact, we prayed through the cold winter and cool spring months for it. We told no one; we just prayed. Nothing happened for months. Zero response. Late that spring we made a trip home to Houston during a brief Easter weekend. Summer was coming, still no air conditioner. Dallas would soon be an oven! "Another hundred days of hundred-degree weather," we used to say. We didn't announce our trip home; except for our family, no one knew we were coming. We had not been home visiting Cynthia's folks for even an hour before the phone rang. On the other end of the line was a man from our home church.

Surprised, he said, "Chuck, is that you?"

I answered, "Yes."

His next words were: "Do you and Cynthia need a window air conditioner? We just installed a new central heating and air conditioning unit, and my wife and I thought you two could use the one we've replaced."

What a great God we have!

Similar things have occurred since that happened, but to this day, when I get low and blue regarding needs, I call to mind that marvelous day back in the spring of 1960 when our Lord provided for our specific need.

Making It Strong in Your Soul

Get a composition book or purchase a nice journal and keep a record of God's provision and protection. Start with your earliest memories and write out a brief account. Then, each time the Lord does something remarkable to care for you, record it. When the churning place begins to grind, read your own personal history of the Lord's faithfulness.

Day 4: *Psalms 42 and 43*

Find Solace in Nature

David's songs of inner turmoil don't offer easy answers; he's too realistic for that. David had seen the lowest of lows several times in his life, so he knew that counting your blessings won't work every time. Sometimes, we get so low that no memory will jar us loose from our turmoil. In verses 6–8, David offers another technique.

> O my God, my soul is in despair within me;
> Therefore I remember You from the land of the Jordan
> And the peaks of Hermon, from Mount Mizar.
> Deep calls to deep at the sound of Your waterfalls;
> All Your breakers and Your waves have rolled over me.
> The LORD will command His lovingkindness in the daytime;
> And His song will be with me in the night,
> A prayer to the God of my life. (vv. 6–8)

Look at that unusual expression: "Deep calls to deep." The songwriter evidently traveled from Jerusalem to northern Galilee, where the Jordan River originates on Mount Hermon. In the song, he pictures himself on one of the smaller peaks in the Mount Hermon range. In his mind he thinks of those awesome sounds and scenes surrounding him—as "deep calls to deep," as God communicates through nature and the unchanging, immutable relationship is enacted. In this case, the snow melts high upon Mount Hermon's peaks, causing the thunderous waterfalls, the rapids in streams below. He pictures his troubles as rolling down upon him like thousands of gallons of water pouring over a waterfall.

That which is "deep" in God communicates to that which is "deep" in nature, and this brings about change. It happens all around us. The "deep" in God calls to the "deep" in trees in the fall, and inevitably their leaves turn to beautiful orange, red, and yellow. Ultimately, they fall and the tree is again barren. The "deep" in God calls to the "deep" in the salmon, and millions travel back over many miles to spawn. But the psalmist is not talking about trees and fish, but rather about himself! As the breakers and waves of inner turmoil rolled over him, he was reminded of that unchanging relationship of love and joy that exists between God and us.

And again David asks in verse 11:

> Why are you in despair, O my soul?
> And why have you become disturbed within me?
> Hope in God, for I shall yet praise Him,
> The help of my countenance and my God. (v. 11)

Making It Strong in Your Soul

David found solace in nature, the divine metaphors reflected in God's creation. Perhaps it's time to change your environment, escape the routine—if only for a few hours—and let nature become your counselor. What is the nearest natural wonder? When can you get there?

🎵

Day 5: *Psalms 42 and 43*
Seek God's Truth

The source of David's turmoil, captured in Psalms 42 and 43, didn't go away after his visit to the headwaters of the Jordan River. When he returned to Jerusalem, he found his troubles waiting for him. According to Psalm 43:1–2, David suffered another personal attack. People problems were upon him, and we all know how devastating they can be! After pleading for God to intervene, David prays:

> O send out Your light and Your truth, let them lead me;
> Let them bring me to Your holy hill
> And to Your dwelling places.
> Then I will go to the altar of God,
> To God my exceeding joy;
> And upon the lyre I shall praise You, O God, my God.
>
> (Psalm 43:3–4)

Turmoil often results from having too much misinformation and not enough reliable, essential truth. Moreover, in the absence of adequate information, we fill in the gaps with what we dread most. The result is a distorted picture of the problem—a pessimistic perspective, riddled with our worst fears. In response to his turmoil, David asks for God's light and God's truth. He wanted the Lord to provide His Word (truth) and to grant him an understanding of it (light). Perhaps he sought for a specific statement from Scripture that would be fitting and appropriate for his situation, and equally important, he sought for insight into it. He needed clarity in the midst of confusion—truth to answer fiction—so he looked for wisdom in the Scriptures.

Eventually, this would bring joy and praise. When the truth of God's Word neutralized the depressing messages of his circumstances, he asked yet again (Ps. 43:5):

> Why are you in despair, O my soul?
> And why are you disturbed within me?
> Hope in God, for I shall again praise Him,
> The help of my countenance and my God. (v. 5)

Every believer in Jesus Christ must ultimately come to the place where he is going to trust God's Word completely before he can experience consistent victory. His Book is our single source of tangible truth. We try every other crutch: we lean on self, on others, on feelings, on bank accounts, on good works, on logic and reason, on human perspective. Still, the churning continues, inner turmoil continues to grind.

God has given His written Word and the promise of His light to all His children; when will we learn to believe it, and live in it, and use it, and cling to its promises?

The grind of inner turmoil will not depart forever, but its immobilizing presence can be overcome and temporarily neutralized.

I hope the lessons we learn from these two ancient songs will help to silence your churning place.

Making It Strong in Your Soul

As light penetrates darkness, so the truth of God's Word cuts through anxiety and apprehension. In response to turmoil, choose a place in Scripture—any place your instincts suggest—and begin reading. Do this each time your churning place begins acting up. Usually works for me!

The Grind of Personal Weakness

**For the choir director. A Psalm of the sons of Korah,
set to Alamoth. A Song.**

God is our refuge and strength,
A very present help in trouble.
Therefore we will not fear, though the earth should change
And though the mountains slip into the heart of the sea;
Though its waters roar and foam,
Though the mountains quake at its swelling pride. Selah.
There is a river whose streams make glad the city of God,
The holy dwelling places of the Most High.
God is in the midst of her, she will not be moved;
God will help her when morning dawns.
The nations made an uproar, the kingdoms tottered;
He raised His voice, the earth melted.
The Lord of hosts is with us;
The God of Jacob is our stronghold. Selah.
Come, behold the works of the Lord,
Who has wrought desolations in the earth.
He makes wars to cease to the end of the earth;
He breaks the bow and cuts the spear in two;
He burns the chariots with fire.
"Cease striving and know that I am God;
I will be exalted among the nations, I will be exalted
    in the earth."
The Lord of hosts is with us;
The God of Jacob is our stronghold. Selah.

(Psalm 46)

Day 1: *Psalm 46*

Human Failure

We deny it. We fake it. We mask it. We try to ignore it. But the truth stubbornly persists: we are weak and inadequate creatures! Being sinful, we fail. Being prone to illness, we get sick. Being feeble, we get hurt. Being mortal, we ultimately die. Pressure grinds the churning place. Anxiety gives us ulcers. People intimidate us. Criticism undermines us. Disease scares us. Death haunts us. This explains why Job complained, "Man, who is born of woman, is short-lived and full of turmoil" (Job 14:1). The Living Bible renders the verse, "How frail is man, how few his days, how full of trouble!" The apostle Paul writes, "We ourselves groan within ourselves, waiting eagerly for our adoption as sons, the redemption of our body" (Rom. 8:23).

How can we continue to grow in this bag of bones, covered with weaknesses too numerous to mention? We need a big dose of Psalm 46. What hope these words bring to those struggling through the grind of personal weakness! Martin Luther found courage in this song, and later composed lyrics of his own:

> A mighty fortress is our God,
> A bulwark never failing;
> Our helper He, amid the flood
> Of mortal ills prevailing.[8]

According to the superscription, the psalm was "set to Alamoth." These words are addressed to the choir director. The word *alamoth* is derived from the Hebrew noun *almah*, a term meaning

---

8 Martin Luther (1529), "A Mighty Fortress Is Our God"; transl. Frederick H. Hedge (1852).

"maiden, young woman." It's possible this means the song was composed for soprano voices or a choir of women. As far as we know, the place of worship back in the days of the psalms had no such choir. 1 Chronicles 15:20 offers a clue; it says that harps were "tuned to alamoth." The marginal reference in the New American Standard Bible says: "harps of maiden-like tone." Quite likely, this song was to be played on soprano-like or high-pitched instruments. Perhaps this was to make the psalm unique and easily remembered, much like certain lilting strains of Handel's "Messiah" ("For unto us a child is born" or "O Thou, that tellest good tidings to Zion"). This song was to be perpetually remembered.

As you were reading the lyrics, did you notice any repeated words or phrases? Verses 7 and 11 are identical, and the familiar command "Selah" appears no less than three times. As we have pointed out in our previous weekly studies, this is most likely a musical notation indicating a pause, encouraging quiet reflection. The music may have continued to play for a short interlude, allowing the audience to think about the last few lines before the singers resumed.

The three pause markings assist us in understanding this song. They are built-in hints the reader should not overlook. As in many of the psalms, verse 1 states the theme, which we might render: "God is an immediate source of strength when we're in a tight squeeze!"

The term translated "trouble" in most versions of the Bible is from a Hebrew verb meaning "to be restricted, to tie up, to be narrow, cramped." It reminds me of an expression we sometimes use. We refer to being "in a jam," or "between a rock and a hard place." It means to be in a pinch or tight squeeze. The psalmist declares that God is immediately available, instantly present in any situation, certainly at those times when we are weak!

Making It Strong in Your Soul

In what circumstances do you feel powerless or helpless? Think about those times when you want to do something—*anything*—to solve a problem or affect an outcome, but cannot. How do you typically respond? Is your response helpful or counterproductive? What is the correlation between your typical response and your faith in God?

Day 2: *Psalm 46*

A Fear Response

The psalmist was most likely a priest. As a man of letters, he would have known the history of Israel better than most. And their path had not been a smooth one. They continually faced dangers from foreign armies as well as dangers within. Consequently, the psalmist looked for help from his almighty God. In the remaining verses of Psalm 46, he develops the theme of God's omnipotent help by describing three very grave situations and then declaring his response.

Situation 1:	Nature, in upheaval.
Reaction:	I will not fear. (vv. 2–3)
	Selah!
Situation 2:	Jerusalem, under attack.
Reaction:	I will not be moved. (vv. 4–7)
	Selah!
Situation 3:	Battlefield, after war.
Reaction:	I will not strive. (vv. 8–11)
	Selah!

"I will not fear!"

In the second and third verses, the psalmist introduces some of the most terrifying scenes in all of life. The NASB translators have chosen to insert the word "though" before each of four calamities. The imperfect tense in Hebrew is often used to describe events that haven't yet happened (future) or to denote hypothetical situations. In this case, the songwriter imagines natural disasters so extreme, they challenge the imagination:

"Though the earth should change." What is more stable and predictable than the earth's landscape? It only changes under the most extreme and frightening circumstances, such as earthquakes, landslides, mudslides, and volcanic eruptions.

"Though the mountains slip into the sea." In Hebrew literature, nothing is more immovable than a mountain. To a Hebrew, a mountain falling into the sea would herald the end of the world.

"Though its waters roar and foam . . . though the mountains quake at its swelling pride." In the ancient mind, the ocean represented impenetrable mystery, often used as a metaphor for the dark, foreboding mystery of death. For this priest, it is a fearsome world in which a mighty, immovable mountain worries that the sea might overtake it.

Californians especially have become all too familiar with these scenarios; they live with the daily prospect of mudslides, earthquakes, and the massive shifting of fault lines! Even so, these natural disasters strike fear in the hearts of these residents. Those who have experienced them can identify with the psalmist's fears. He feels weak, totally helpless. As the earth beneath him shifts, rolls, and slides, his belongings instantly become insignificant and life seems dreadfully insecure. Even so, the songwriter declares, "I will not fear."

Why? How could anyone in such a threatening situation say that? Look back to verse 1 for the answer: because God, our heavenly Father, is our immediate helper, our immutable, ever-present source of strength! The psalmist resolved to reject fear in the face of overwhelming circumstances . . . but not on sheer willpower. He chose to view every situation as incapable of harm compared to the sovereign care of the almighty, awesome Lord. *Selah!*

Earlier you identified your typical response to feeling powerless or helpless. Believe it or not, that is a fear response. If God is greater than the dangers we face, why do we continue to respond from a place of fear? In what ways can you cultivate a greater confidence in the Lord's care?

Day 3: *Psalm 46*

God in Your Midst

The psalmist's response to feelings of personal weakness continues in Psalm 46 with a change of scene, which prompts another resolution.

I Will Not Be Moved

There is a river whose streams make glad the city of God,
The holy dwelling places of the Most High.
God is in the midst of her, she will not be moved;
God will help her when morning dawns.
The nations made an uproar, the kingdoms tottered;
He raised His voice, the earth melted.
The LORD of hosts is with us;
The God of Jacob is our stronghold. Selah. (vv. 4–7)

The subject? "The city of God" (v. 4). This is a reference to the Jews' beloved Jerusalem. As you read over these inspired stanzas, you quickly discover that the city is under attack. Nations and kingdoms have risen up against Israel's capital city and laid siege to the walls, yet "she shall not be moved." The reason is clearly stated in the first part of verse 5: "God is in the midst of her." Verse 7 continues, "The LORD of hosts is with us; the God of Jacob is our stronghold."

Jerusalem was a well-defended city, set high on a mountaintop, surrounded by difficult terrain, protected by high, thick walls. Later kings added a fresh water supply to extend their ability to withstand a siege. Still, the composer didn't consider embattlements and structures to be their source of safety. When he felt most powerless, he looked beyond his physical protection to find comfort in God's presence. He credited the indwelling, omnipotent presence of God!

Do you remember that account in Mark's Gospel (4:35–41) of the trip Jesus and His disciples made across the Sea of Galilee? It has been made famous by a song believers have sung for decades, entitled "Peace, Be Still!" A storm took the disciples by surprise and put them in fear of their lives. Gripped with thoughts of their own personal weakness, they woke Jesus and questioned how He could sleep at a time like that. After calming the wind and the sea, Jesus rebuked the disciples for their lack of faith. How could they sink? Why would they ever fear? They had God in the boat with them! The boat would never sink as long as God was in it. They should not have been moved, for the Lord Himself was in their midst. That's a perfect illustration of Psalm 46:5.

Look also at the term "moved" in verse 5. It literally means "to totter or shake." We have the descriptive slang expression "all shook up." I suppose it would fit here in verse 5. Because God is in me, I really have no reason to get "shook up." Do you realize that from the moment the Lord Jesus Christ became the Lord and Savior of your life, He has been living within you? In fact, Christ is called "your life" in Colossians 3:4. The hope of glory is "Christ in you." If you have placed your trust in Jesus Christ, you have the Lord God within you. In your midst! Therefore, with Him present, there is no reason to totter. God is not going to totter and shake, nor is His dwelling place. So, the next time you are tempted to panic, focus on the fact that God is literally in your midst. *Selah!*

What measures have you taken to ensure your provision and protection in the event of emergency? They can offer some peace of mind, but nothing is fail-safe. How can you develop greater confidence in the power of God living within? When bad things happen, how does this affect your trust in God's provision and protection?

Day 4: *Psalm 46*

Cease Striving

The psalmist's inner battle with the grind of personal weakness, recorded in Psalm 46, ended with a truce. He arrived at a critical decision that required every ounce of faith he could muster. He decided to withdraw from battle.

I Will Not Strive

The last four verses of his song (vv. 8–11) are nothing short of magnificent. Read them over once again.

> Come, behold the works of the LORD,
> Who has wrought desolations in the earth.
> He makes wars to cease to the end of the earth;
> He breaks the bow and cuts the spear in two;
> He burns the chariots with fire.
> "Cease striving and know that I am God;
> I will be exalted among the nations, I will be
>   exalted in the earth."
> The LORD of hosts is with us;
> The God of Jacob is our stronghold. *Selah.*

Once again, the scene changes. No longer under siege within the city walls, the songwriter now surveys a battlefield. He invites us to view the mute reminders of war, a terrain littered with bodies and debris. Chariots lie on their sides, burned, and now rusty. Dust and debris cover broken bows and splintered spears. War itself has been decimated. The song describes a scene not unlike the aftermath of World War II. The beaches of Normandy; the cities of Berlin and Hiroshima; sections of London; the islands of Iwo Jima, Guadalcanal, and Okinawa. Rusty tanks. Sunken boats covered with barnacles. Concrete bunkers. A silence pervades. It is as though our God has said, "That is enough!" When the Lord acts, He's thorough.

At this point (v. 10), the writer speaks for God, who commands,

"Cease striving and know that I am God;
I will be exalted among the nations, I will be
    exalted in the earth!"

The command "Cease striving" comes from the Hebrew imperative verb meaning "sink down, let drop, relax." Most people quote this verse in a soothing, reassuring tone, like a serene invitation to enjoy the fellowship of God. It is, in fact, a rebuke. Some scholars say it's addressed to the nations attacking God's covenant people. Others say God is rebuking the Hebrews for their lack of trust in Him. It's most likely both. The composer depicts the Lord as an angry parent breaking up a fight between siblings. While He's angry with the nations making war against His people, He's equally upset with the violence of His people, who have turned to warfare rather than a complete trust in Him. There's a subtle suggestion that their aggressive attempts to defend themselves are making matters worse rather than better.

Does this sound familiar? Do you live in strife and panic? Is there a fretful spirit about you? Have your self-protective attempts caused more harm than good? Do you know that God wants to give you rest? Hebrews 4:9 promises: "So there remains a Sabbath rest for the people of God." In response to your realization of personal weakness, God has called you to "cease striving," to end the per-petual, frenetic grind to overcome difficulties too big for you.

Does this mean we should slip into neutral and do nothing? Hardly. It means we first enter that rest He has provided (Heb. 4:11), and then face the situation without panic or strife. If He wants us involved, He will give our minds clarity, removing any doubt as to what we should do. Our responsibility is to enter delib-erately into His invisible sanctuary of rest, to trust Him completely for safety and provision. That is our best preparation for battle; to be filled and surrounded by His Sabbath rest. It is amazing what that does to stop the grind of personal weakness.

In the final analysis, it is the Lord's job to provide the vic-tory over every one of our weaknesses. He can handle whatever is needed. Our striving will never do it.

Selah!

Making It Strong in Your Soul

Take a sheet of paper—or better yet, a journal—and make a list of your most pressing problems, issues you are powerless to resolve. Make the list as long as you want. Read the first item out loud. Then (again, out loud), read Psalm 46. Officially hand it over to God as His problem to solve. Tomorrow, do this for the next item on your list. Repeat as often as necessary.

Day 5: *Psalm 46*
Comfort in God's Strength

If Martin Luther's great hymn, "A Mighty Fortress Is Our God," is any indication, he often turned to Psalm 46 for comfort. When you read his story, you can appreciate why.

In 1520, after more than three years of conflict with the Church in Rome, the Pope warned Luther in a public letter that he would be excommunicated if he did not recant his teaching that salvation is by grace alone through faith alone in Jesus Christ alone. Luther responded by burning the letter publicly and publishing a pamphlet titled, *Why the Pope and His Recent Book are Burned and the Assertions Concerning All Articles*. In 1521, Pope Leo X issued a letter announcing his excommunication, which prompted the Holy Roman Emperor, Charles V, to issue orders of arrest. Charles declared, "We want him apprehended and punished as an infamous heretic, as he deserves," and placed a generous price on his head. Naturally, this made Luther a prime target for any sovereign wanting favors from the Pope and the powerful King Charles V. Consequently, nearly every king and petty ruler in the world made Luther's capture a priority.

On his way home from the official announcement by Charles V, Luther was stopped by a masked horseman and taken to a castle in central Germany. Fortunately, he had not fallen into the hands of enemies, but was taken into the protection of Frederick III, the only man powerful enough to oppose Charles V. Luther spent the next year in the Castle of Wartburg, a walled fortress perched on a 1,200-foot precipice. From here, Luther translated the Greek New Testament into German and laid the foundation for the Protestant Reformation.

It may be from here that Luther found solace in Psalm 46. Sitting in a mighty castle, protected by a rugged terrain and a high position with only a drawbridge for access, guarded by one of the most powerful men in the world, Luther found comfort only in His God. With virtually the whole world against him, he had the truth of the gospel on his side, and that gave him confidence. He rested in the assurance of Psalm 46 and penned the words to an anthem praising the power of God. In 1853, Frederick H. Hedge translated Luther's German lyrics into the English lines we know so well.

A mighty fortress is our God, a bulwark never failing;
Our helper He amid the flood of mortal ills prevailing.
For still our ancient foe doth seek to work us woe;
His craft and power are great, and armed with cruel hate,
On earth is not his equal.

Did we in our own strength confide, our striving would be losing,
Were not the right man on our side, the man of God's
    own choosing:
Dost ask who that may be? Christ Jesus, it is He;
Lord Sabaoth, His name, from age to age the same,
And he must win the battle.

And though this world, with devils filled, should threaten
    to undo us,
We will not fear, for God hath willed His truth to triumph through us.
The Prince of Darkness grim, we tremble not for him;
His rage we can endure, for lo, his doom is sure;
One little word shall fell him.

That word above all earthly powers, no thanks to them, abideth;
The Spirit and the gifts are ours, thru Him who with us sideth.
Let goods and kindred go, this mortal life also;
The body they may kill; God's truth abideth still;
His kingdom is forever.

Making It Strong in Your Soul

David found strength in singing. The psalmists wrote songs to encourage weary worshipers. Luther wrote this anthem, which many have called "The Battle Hymn of the Reformation," because of the courage it inspires. Personally, I have memorized this grand hymn, as well as the lyrics to dozens of hymns that I regularly call to mind when gripped by fear. I urge you to memorize the lyrics to Luther's anthem about God's protection and then sing it often!

The Grind of Difficult People

For the choir director; on stringed instruments. A Maskil of David, when the Ziphites came and said to Saul, "Is not David hiding himself among us?"

Save me, O God, by Your name,
And vindicate me by Your power.
Hear my prayer, O God;
Give ear to the words of my mouth.
For strangers have risen against me
And violent men have sought my life;
They have not set God before them. Selah.
Behold, God is my helper;
The Lord is the sustainer of my soul.
He will recompense the evil to my foes;
Destroy them in Your faithfulness.
Willingly I will sacrifice to You;
I will give thanks to Your name, O Lord, for it is good.
For He has delivered me from all trouble,
And my eye has looked with satisfaction upon my enemies.

(Psalm 54)

Day 1: *Psalm 54*
People Problems

For many years, I opened the daily newspaper looking forward to another dose of wisdom from the mind of Charles Schulz, the creator of the comic strip "Peanuts." In one particular scene, Lucy chides her little brother Linus, "*You* a doctor! HA! That's a big laugh! You could never be a doctor! You know why? Because you don't love mankind, that's why!"

Linus ponders her indictment for a moment and then shouts, "I love mankind. It's *people* I can't stand!!"

There are some days I have to laugh and say "Amen!" Let's face it; most problems are people problems. You can have a job that demands long hours and great physical effort, but neither the hours nor the energy drain gives you the problems difficult people do. You can have financial difficulties, physical pain, a tight schedule, and face miles of driving each day, but these things are not the cause of our major battles. It's people, as Linus said. Difficult people are perhaps the most challenging problems of all!

Psalm 54 is David's lament over the constant grind of people problems. Take a moment to observe the superscription; you'll find it worth your while. (By the way, I hope you are learning to do that when studying the ancient songs in the Bible. The words that appear before the first verse of each psalm are part of ancient text, giving the reader some helpful hints about the song.)

In the Fifty-fourth Psalm the superscription reads:

For the choir director; on stringed instruments. A Maskil of David, when the Ziphites came and said to Saul, "Is not David hiding himself among us?"

This unusually long superscription tells us that David wrote the song. We also learn that it is a "Maskil," which should be a familiar term by now. All Maskil songs offer instruction and insight for dealing with certain situations. In this case, Psalm 54 provides some very practical advice on how to respond to problems created by other members of the human race who are just as ornery as we are!

According to 1 Samuel 23:14–26, David was being chased by

jealous King Saul, whose murderous manhunt forced the singer to take refuge in a bleak and rugged location. He feared for his life, so he was desperate to find a place of safety. But everything backfired. The spot called "the hill of Hachilah" appears safe within Ziphite territory, supposedly neutral ground. But David found no rest there. The Ziphites turned against him and reported his location to Saul, and the chase resumed. David fled to the wilderness of Maon but soon found himself surrounded by Ziphites and Saul's soldiers.

I can just picture David. He's dirty, sweaty, hungry, thirsty, exhausted, and no doubt, discouraged. He slumps beside a leafy bush or beneath the shadow of a rock to escape the searing rays of the desert sun, and he begins to pour out his feelings in a poem. Attacked and betrayed by people, he is led by the Holy Spirit to record his feelings. Those expressions are what we have today preserved in the lyrics of this song, Psalm 54.

Making It Strong in Your Soul

Which individuals cause you the most difficulties? Make a list, and beside each name, use one word to describe your feelings. For example, "Mary . . . Exasperated" or "John . . . Infuriated." Keep the list private, but close at hand; we'll do more with it later.

Day 2: Psalm 54
Consider the Source

Imagine David wilting under a bush or slumped in a cave, pouring out his feelings in Psalm 54, begging the Lord for help. The first three verses are a prayer with emphasis on the enemy. The spotlight then turns to the composer's divine defender as the next two verses form a picture. The last two verses are words of praise as David focuses on his own history with God.

The Enemy

Save me, O God, by Your name,
And vindicate me by Your power.
Hear my prayer, O God;
Give ear to the words of my mouth.
For strangers have risen against me
And violent men have sought my life;
They have not set God before them. *Selah.* (vv. 1–3)

Verses 1 and 2 appear differently in the Hebrew Bible than in our English rendering. Literally, they read: "O God, save me. . . . O God, hear my prayer."

Normally, the verb appears first in the Hebrew sentence, but in this case, each cry for help begins with "O God . . ." By rearranging the normal word order, David emphasizes his utter dependence upon God. And the emphasis is further strengthened by the repetition of His name, "O God. . . . O God . . ."

We discover immediately an example in David for when we find ourselves under attack or emotionally distressed by people: Pray first! Don't wait! Ask for His strength and stability. Normally, we pray *last*, don't we? Instinct almost compels us first to fight back. We retaliate or develop a resentment for the one who makes life miserable.

Observe that David requests deliverance and vindication on the basis of two things: God's name and God's power.

Throughout the Old Testament, God is called by at least twelve different names, each one highlighting a particular aspect of His character. As David called to mind God's attributes, he settled on the Lord's power—His omnipotence. When attacked by people, our imagination tends to stretch the truth; we begin to think our enemies have unlimited power. David found comfort in the reminder that God is more powerful than anyone or anything in the universe.

David went on to describe his problem in detail.

For strangers have risen against me,
And violent men have sought my life;
They have not set God before them. *Selah.* (v. 3)

He gives his enemies two descriptive names: "strangers" and "violent men." The first refers to the people living in the region of Ziph. Normally, people are known by their heritage. For example, the Moabites are descendants of a patriarch named Moab. The Amalekites were descendants of Amalek. But the Ziphites were of unknown origin. The term "strangers" comes from a Hebrew word that means "to scatter, disperse," characterizing them as random people known only by their current place of residence. David struggled to understand why these strangers would bother to take sides in his dispute with Saul, why the Ziphites would become spies.

I mention this because I may be writing to someone as innocent as David was, but perhaps you too are being "spied upon," sold out by people who have no known motives to betray you. It is a frightening experience to be falsely accused, especially when the accusations come from strangers. It makes you wonder if the whole world has turned against you.

It's even worse when the enemy is someone you once trusted as a friend! "Violent men" refers to Saul, whom David once served as both musician and soldier, and Saul's troops, whose mission was to bring back David's head. Other than roughly six hundred loyal soldiers, David had no support, either in Israel or among Israel's neighbors.

David further states that his enemies did not have God set before them. The Lord didn't prompt their insidious actions; fulfilling the will of God was not their motivation. They acted in self-interest without regard to "right" or "wrong," which brings up a very practical point. When people turn against you, and you are in the right, it's like being kicked by a mule. Consider the source! You were kicked by a creature whose nature is to kick.

In another psalm, a composer observes that resisting God's will is not only futile, it is to invite one's own destruction. "Why do the nations rage and the peoples plot in vain?" (Ps. 2:1 ESV) he asks. He took comfort, not only in the futility of their attacks, but in the realization that they opposed God. It's hard to take personally the attacks of someone who opposes the almighty Creator! So, when you're wrongly treated, consider the source. They have not set the Lord before them. He doesn't energize their actions. In the words of Psalm 46, "Cease striving." Relax!

Verse 3 concludes with that now-familiar command, "Selah." Pause to consider the wisdom of David's perspective in the first three verses.

Making It Strong in Your Soul

Look back at the list of names you created. Beside each one, write down what motive each has for his or her actions. Don't let paranoia gain control of your answers. Try to think objectively. What does each person stand to gain by his or her behavior? Then, evaluate each motive in light of God's will. Do you think He supports their goals?

Day 3: *Psalm 54*
Leave Vengeance to God

David could have written a whole book of poems lamenting the host of enemies surrounding him. Enemies in Saul's court. Enemies among the priests. Enemies in the surrounding territories. Enemies everywhere! But in Psalm 54, he devotes only three lines to naming his problem people. He, instead, quickly turned his mind's eye to focus on his divine advocate.

The Defender

Behold, God is my helper;
The LORD is the sustainer of my soul.
He will recompense the evil to my foes;
Destroy them in Your faithfulness. (vv. 4–5)

The English term "helper" is terribly weak, but we don't have a better term to translate the Hebrew word *ezer*, which carries the idea of rescue. An *ezer* provides indispensable help, without which a person would be hopelessly doomed. For David, the Lord is the one who supplies what he lacks to survive his enemies' attacks.

He goes on to call the Lord his "sustainer." The Hebrew term is based on the idea of leaning on a support. Think of steel beams supporting a building; without these sustaining, foundational elements, the whole structure would collapse.

The fifth verse promises the evil planned against David will return upon those who planned it. Their wrong is fated to backfire. This realization helps David maintain his integrity. Because the Lord has promised to carry out justice on David's behalf, David can concentrate on doing what's right instead of plotting revenge. So it is with the believer who maintains his integrity while under the attack of difficult people! The evil planned against us will return upon the attacker, thanks to our Defender! Thanks to His faithfulness, our attackers will be held accountable.

As I first read verse 5 of Psalm 54, it seemed awfully severe. *Surely it doesn't mean what it says,* I thought. *Surely God won't actually destroy the enemy,* I said to myself. How wrong I was! I looked up the term "destroy" in the Hebrew text. Do you know what it actually means? Are you ready for a shock? It is taken from the Hebrew verb *tzamath*, which means "to exterminate"! In fact, the verb appears in a Hebrew construction that denotes cause; literally, "to cause to annihilate"! In other words, David declares, by faith, that God will cause those who have become his enemies to be totally, completely, thoroughly removed! But I remind you that David doesn't do the removing; God does.

It is so easy to play God when we're under pressure, isn't it? We have thought about the temptation to take our own vengeance before. Romans 12:17–19 warns us against doing that:

> Never pay back evil for evil to anyone. Respect what is right in the sight of all men. If possible, so far as it depends on you, be at peace with all men. Never take your own revenge, beloved, but leave room for the wrath of God, for it is written, "VENGEANCE IS MINE, I WILL REPAY," says the Lord.

Living beyond the daily grind of difficult people requires our leaving the vengeance to the One who can handle it best.

Making It Strong in Your Soul

Go back for another look at your list of difficult people. You have acknowledged their emotional impact and you have evaluated their possible motives in comparison with the will of God. Now, grant each individual your personal pardon from retaliation. Before God, surrender your right to seek justice or restitution. This is what it means to forgive, which the Lord has commanded us to do (Matt. 6:14–15; 18:21–22).

Day 4: Psalm 54
Rest in God's Faithfulness

As David's lament over the grind of difficult people draws to a close, he turns from bitter resentment to find rest in God's faithfulness. David has named his enemies and acknowledged their sins, and he has surrendered his right to justice, placing them in God's hands. As a result, David finds peace. The tension of "Destroy them in Your faithfulness" gives way to the tranquility of "Willingly I will sacrifice to You." He has discovered the serenity of letting God be God.

Surrender

Willingly I will sacrifice to You;

I will give thanks to Your name, O LORD, for it is good. (v. 6)

The concept of surrender is difficult to grasp in our culture. It's easily confused with "giving up" and carries the implication that we're accepting defeat. That's because we typically think of surrender in terms of warfare, in which one side concedes defeat to an enemy. In the case of God, however, we're surrendering to our ally! While His ways are inscrutable, too lofty and complex to understand (Isa. 55:8–9), He is, nonetheless, *for* us. He's on our side. Therefore, we take a giant leap forward in dealing with difficult people when we say, "Thank You, Lord, for this painful experience of being maligned, misunderstood, and mistreated." David finally reached this point. He was able to give thanks to God, even in the midst of ongoing personal strife.

Let me point out that David did not live in denial. He didn't try to manufacture good feelings about his enemies. He didn't whitewash their sins or glibly excuse their sinfulness. Nor did he retaliate. He chose to focus on God's faithfulness instead. Rather than allow his mind to be consumed by the wrongdoing of others, their terrible motives, and his own imagination of God's justice coming down upon them, David devoted himself to worship. When he did this, he was able to say, "It is good," referring to God's name. David's trouble continued. His tormenters had not yet retreated. Still, he was able to declare the name and the deeds of God "good."

Making It Strong in Your Soul

Turn again to your list of difficult people. For each name, determine how God might use his or her behavior as a means of making your life better (Rom. 8:28). How might the Lord use each person to transform your character? This doesn't excuse their behavior; it merely acknowledges the faithfulness of God in *every* circumstance.

Day 5: *Psalm 54*
God's Deliverance

The final verse of Psalm 54 describes a sudden reversal. The first verses describe a dire situation, prompting David to plead for God's help. By verse 7, his despondency has turned to triumph. His declaration, "He has delivered me from all trouble," is past tense. Hebrew literature often uses the perfect tense to declare a future event "as good as done." David doesn't know how or when God will act on his behalf; nevertheless, he writes with complete confidence,

> For He has delivered me from all trouble,
> And my eye has looked with satisfaction upon my enemies. (v. 7)

According to 1 Samuel 23:26–29, God intervened to protect David from his enemies.

> Saul went on one side of the mountain, and David and his men on the other side of the mountain; and David was hurrying to get away from Saul, for Saul and his men were surrounding David and his men to seize them. But a messenger came to Saul, saying, "Hurry and come, for the Philistines have made a raid on the land." So Saul returned from pursuing David and went to meet the Philistines; therefore they called that place the Rock of Escape. David went up from there and stayed in the strongholds of Engedi.

Suddenly, perhaps as soon as David said, "I will give thanks to Your name, O Lᴏʀᴅ, for it is good," the enemy turned tail for home, removing the threat of immediate danger. Furthermore, David said his eye could now look "upon my enemies." The NASB inserts the phrase "with satisfaction" to bring clarity to this Hebrew idiom. David's choice of words reflects a man without bitterness. He could look his enemy squarely in the eye without malice or resentment. He had released them to God and God had dealt with them in His own sovereign, perfect way.

Let's declare war on those longstanding habits we cultivate against others—negative feelings, unforgiveness, resentment, competitiveness, grudges, jealousy, revenge, hatred, retaliation, gossip, criticism, and suspicion. Let's leave this rugged, ugly, well-worn road forever! The only alternative route to take is love. The longer I live and the more time I spend with the Lord (and with others), the more I am driven back to the answer to most people's problems: sincere, Spirit-empowered, undeserved love. It's called living by grace. Once Christ is in full focus, it's amazing how powerful love can be!

How beautifully Amy Carmichael reminds us of this in her small but penetrating book, *If*.

If I belittle those whom I am called to serve, talk of their weak points in contrast perhaps with what I think of as my strong points; if I adopt a superior attitude, forgetting "Who made thee to differ? and what hast thou that thou hast not received?" then I know nothing of Calvary love.

If I take offense easily, if I am content to continue in a cool unfriendliness, though friendship be possible, then I know nothing of Calvary love.

If I feel bitterly towards those who condemn me, as it seems to me, unjustly, forgetting that if they knew me as I know myself they would condemn me much more, then I know nothing of Calvary love.[9]

---

9 Amy Carmichael, *If* (London: S.P.C.K.; Fort Washington, PA: Christian Literature Crusade, 1938), 13, 44, 471.

Making It Strong in Your Soul

Once more, turn to your list of difficult people. Earlier you pardoned each person. Now take this a step further. It's time for grace and love to flow together. Pray for each person. Not just that he or she would submit to the will of God or "see the light." Petition God to protect each of your enemies from harm and to provide for his or her needs (Luke 6:28). What do you think the Lord will do to fulfill your request?

THE GRIND OF RITUAL RELIGION

A Psalm of David, when he was in the wilderness of Judah.

O God, You are my God; I shall seek You earnestly;
My soul thirsts for You, my flesh yearns for You,
In a dry and weary land where there is no water.
Thus I have seen You in the sanctuary,
To see Your power and Your glory.
Because Your lovingkindness is better than life,
My lips will praise You.
So I will bless You as long as I live;
I will lift up my hands in Your name.
My soul is satisfied as with marrow and fatness,
And my mouth offers praises with joyful lips.
When I remember You on my bed,
I meditate on You in the night watches,
For You have been my help,
And in the shadow of Your wings I sing for joy.
My soul clings to You;
Your right hand upholds me.
But those who seek my life to destroy it,
Will go into the depths of the earth.
They will be delivered over to the power of the sword;
They will be a prey for foxes.
But the king will rejoice in God;
Everyone who swears by Him will glory,
For the mouths of those who speak lies will be stopped.

(Psalm 63)

Day 1: *Psalm 63*

A Song of Quietness

How easy it is to fall into the trap of "ritual religion"! So many Christians know little of a vital, fresh, day-by-day relationship with the Lord. I did not say an *inactive* relationship. Christians have never been more active! The tyranny of the urgent is no theoretical problem. Many a believer jumps off the Sunday treadmill of activities only to hop on the weekday treadmill of meetings, appointments, functions, rehearsals, clubs, engagements, banquets, studies, committees, and retreats. I heartily agree with the one who said, "Much of our religious activity today is nothing more than a cheap anesthetic to deaden the pain of an empty life!"[10]

That's a harsh truth to ponder. As a pastor, I hope to help you cultivate a consistent and meaningful walk with the Lord Jesus Christ, a relationship that thrives without needing to be pumped up and recharged with an endless succession of activities. I would wish that we all might know our Lord in such a significant way that this divine companionship, this healthy vertical relationship, becomes a steady, serene, daily communion. We *must* find ways to live beyond the grind of ritual religion.

In *The Pursuit of God*, A. W. Tozer writes,

> I want deliberately to encourage this mighty longing after God. The lack of it has brought us to our present low estate. The stiff and wooden quality about our religious lives is a result of our lack of holy desire. Complacency is a deadly foe of all spiritual growth. Acute desire must be present or there will be no manifestation of Christ to His people. He

---

10 Howard G. Hendricks in an unpublished speech at Dallas Theological Seminary, Dallas, Texas.

waits to be wanted. Too bad that with many of us He waits so long, so very long, in vain.

Every age has its own characteristics. Right now we are in an age of religious complexity. The simplicity that is in Christ is rarely found among us. In its stead are programs, methods, organizations and a world of nervous activities which occupy time and attention but can never satisfy the longing of the heart. The shallowness of our inner experience, the hollowness of our worship and that servile imitation of the world that marks our promotional methods all testify that we, in this day, know God only imperfectly, and the peace of God scarcely at all.[11]

Psalm 63 is David's song about what it means to have a desperate longing for God, and what it means to be fully satisfied in Him alone. It is not a song of activity but of quietness. David didn't write a march to impel busy feet, but a sonnet to woo thirsty souls.

Believe it or not, many people don't know they're thirsty. You may not feel a deep longing to cultivate an ongoing personal interaction with God. That's probably because you have dulled your spiritual senses with activity. Career activity. Social activity. Religious activity. If so, your first response may be to slow your pace, to simplify.

Making It Strong in Your Soul

On a sheet of paper, draw seven large blocks and label them with the days of the week. Then write in each block your regular work hours, appointments, routine activities, etc. Try to account for every recurring activity. You may need to sacrifice something. If that's not possible, look for hidden blocks of time in your week and reserve them for solitude and silence.

11 A. W. Tozer, *The Pursuit of God* (Camp Hill, PA: WingSpread, 2006), 17.

Day 2: *Psalm 63*
The Deepest Need

David's song of the thirsty soul, preserved for us as Psalm 63, may resonate deeply with you. Perhaps you have finally come to the end of rat-race religion. Hopefully, you have decided to leave the hurry-worry *sin*drome and find complete satisfaction in the Savior, in the worship of Him alone. If so, you are rare. In fact, you are almost extinct! But, if you have come to the end of religious activity only to feel more emptiness, then this ancient song is for you. If you have not, it will sound mystical, perhaps even dull. David's quiet song, you see, is written for the few who are still thirsty—for those who prefer depth to speed.

The superscription reads: "A Psalm of David, when he was in the wilderness of Judah." David composed this ancient hymn, not while serving in the tabernacle, but in the isolation of the rugged wilderness south of Jerusalem. Most likely on the run from Saul, David found himself alone, removed, obscure, separated from every comfort and friend, acutely feeling the effects of thirst, hunger, pain, loneliness, and exhaustion. Even so, he didn't regard these as his most pressing needs. He identifies his deepest need in the first verse:

O God, You are my God; I shall seek You earnestly;
My soul thirsts for You, my flesh yearns for You,
In a dry and weary land where there is no water.

Right away we see that he was not seeking literal food, water, comfort, or rest; he needed communion with his Lord. The "dry and weary land" is a vivid picture of his surroundings in the Judean wilderness, as well as our world today. So few believers are living above the daily grind of activity. So many today are captivated by an obsession for collecting "stuff," storing their "stuff," and then pursuing more "stuff." As a result, their homes become cluttered while their souls grow more hollow. The land is indeed "dry and weary," but that only makes the yearning stronger! Since "there is no water" in that kind of land, David longs for his thirst to be quenched from above.

The next verse begins with "Thus," which is a very significant connective. The idea here is "So then" or "Therefore." Because the land is so barren of anything satisfying to the soul, David longs for God. He says, in effect, "So then, since nothing around me culti-vates a sense of closeness and companionship, I must cultivate it myself." Actually, the "Thus" of verse 2 introduces several changes David makes to find satisfaction for his inner longing, his deep desire for a meaningful walk with his Lord. I find five decisions the songwriter makes to help him find satisfaction in his Maker. Over the next couple of days, we will examine them.

The first decision involves the songwriter's imagination: *he decided to create a mental picture of the Lord (v. 2).*

Thus I have seen You in the sanctuary,
To see Your power and Your glory.

When he writes, "I have seen You," we understand he means that he imagines the Lord's power and glory in the thought pro-cesses of his mind. David couldn't go to the tabernacle to see the Lord in that sanctuary, so he spends time in the wilderness framing a mental picture of the Lord in power and glory on His heavenly throne. He takes the Scriptures he knows regarding the Lord God and allows them to "sketch" in his mind a mental image of Him. In other words, he sets his mind upon and occupies himself with the Lord. That is a great way to remove the wearisome ritual from religion.

The imagination can be a powerful instrument, for both good and evil purposes. The mind can be an instrument of pride, lust, hatred, or jealousy; we can create in our minds vivid pictures which can lead to terrible sins. This is precisely the case of "committing adultery in the heart" that our Savior mentions in Matthew 5:28. Lustful imaginings can ultimately result in illicit acts of passion. But the mind can also become an amazing means of communion with God. David spent his lonely moments in the wilderness picturing the Lord Himself.

To cultivate a closer relationship with God, use your imagination to "see" Him.

Making It Strong in Your Soul

To help stimulate your imagination, read the following passages and recreate the scene in your mind. Imagine yourself there, in God's presence, watching His interaction with His people, including you. (See Isa. 6:1–13; Ezek. 1:22–28; Dan. 7:9–14; Rev. 4:2–11.)

🎵

Day 3: *Psalm 63*
Satisfaction in Praise

David's lonely wilderness sanctuary left him thirsty and hungry, not only for food, but for meaningful interaction with his God. As his song continues, David describes a second decision he made to cultivate a relationship with the Lord: *he decided to express praise to the Lord (vv. 3–5).*

> Because Your lovingkindness is better than life,
> My lips will praise You.
> So I will bless You as long as I live;
> I will lift up my hands in Your name.
> My soul is satisfied as with marrow and fatness,
> And my mouth offers praises with joyful lips.

There's nothing mystical or mysterious about praising God. Verses 3 and 5 tell us that praise is something we do with our lips, not merely our minds. We speak something out loud so that others can hear our words of affirmation concerning the Lord, and—just as important—so that *we* can hear these words. Verse 4 says it is to be done "as long as I live," so it isn't a once-a-week matter. Moreover, where God's "lovingkindness" prompts David to praise his Lord (v. 4), praise "satisfies his soul," according to verse 5.

Yes, praise is a deeply significant aspect of our personal worship. Unfortunately, many are afraid of praise because they associate it with some sort of wild, uncontrolled, highly emotional "praise service" in which individuals faint, scream, jump around, and dance uncontrollably in the aisle. Listen, praise is important! It is not limited to organized services. Praise is a consistent flow of appreciation for God in every circumstance throughout the day. Then, when we're alone, praise is an aspect of prayer.

A prayer could be divided into five parts:

a. Confession (read Prov. 28:13; 1 John 1:9). Dealing completely with sins in our lives, agreeing with God that such-and-such was wrong, then claiming forgiveness.

b. Intercession (read 1 Tim. 2:1–2). Remembering others and their needs in prayer.

c. Petition (read Phil. 4:6; Heb. 4:15–16). Bringing ourselves and our needs to God. Remembering them and requesting things of the Lord for ourselves.

d. Thanksgiving (read 1 Thess. 5:18). Prayer that expresses gratitude to God for His specific blessings and gifts to us.

e. Praise (read 1 Chron. 29:11–13). Expressions of adoration directed to God without the mention of ourselves or others—only God. We praise God by expressing words of honor to Him for His character, His name, His will, His Word, His glory, etc.

When a man dates his wife-to-be, praise becomes an important part of courting. When he appreciates the beauty of her hair, he should express it to her verbally. He should compliment her beauty, her choice of perfume and clothing, and her excellent taste. If he enjoys her cooking or a special gift, he should freely express his appreciation. If he admires the way she expresses herself, again, he should say something. When you love someone, praise should come naturally because it's a genuine, stimulating part of a growing relationship.

Praise isn't really something we do for God; He has no ego to soothe. We praise God for what it does for us. David found personal satisfaction in expressing praise for the Lord.

Making It Strong in Your Soul

Instead of counting your blessings (plan to do that another day), create a list of affirmations concerning God. Place the words, "I appreciate the Lord for . . ." and then start writing. Keep the list in a convenient place and add praises as they come to mind this week. Read them aloud from time to time.

♪

Day 4: *Psalm 63*
Meditation and Singing

In his wilderness experience, David made five decisions that would deepen his connection with God. First, he decided to imagine the Lord's physical presence. Then he decided to express praise for God out loud. His third decision is to devote himself to a mental discipline many in the twenty-first century do not clearly understand: meditation. *He decided to meditate on the Lord (v. 6).*

When I remember You on my bed,
I meditate on You in the night watches.

Hindu and Buddhist meditation involves clearing the mind of all distractions, including conscious thought. While there's value in setting aside the mental clutter of mundane daily matters, the purpose in Hebrew meditation is to make room for thoughts about

God. The Hebrew term rendered "meditate" means "to utter, ponder, devise, plot." It's based on a verb that originally denoted "a low sound, characteristic of the moaning of a dove or the growling of a lion over its prey."[12] Imagine someone closing his eyes and saying, "*Hmmmmmm* . . ."

This kind of meditation involves a conscious considering of information gathered during the day. David "remembers" God and then puts the data together for greater understanding of the Lord and His ways. According to Psalm 49:3, the mouth speaks wisdom but when the heart meditates upon God's Word, then comes understanding.

I find it noteworthy that in this sixth verse David refers to the night watches and being on his bed when he meditates. This suggests that one of the best times to ponder God's Word and allow the mind to dwell upon Him is when we retire at night. That's the time David said he remembered the Lord. Restless, fretful nights are calmed by moments of meditation.

He decided to sing for joy (vv. 7–8).

For You have been my help,
And in the shadow of Your wings I sing for joy.
My soul clings to You;
Your right hand upholds me.

David was in the wilderness. He had no audience, nor did he seek one. God was the single object of his worship and it was to Him his soul would cling. To strengthen the relationship between himself and his Lord, David sang for joy. Rare but blessed are those disciples of David who are relaxed enough in God's presence to sing.

When I was in the Marine Corps, stationed on Okinawa, I became good friends with a missionary with The Navigators. Bob

---

12 Herbert Wolf, "*haga 467*" in *Theological Wordbook of the Old Testament*, ed. R. Laird Harris, Gleason L. Archer, Jr. and Bruce K. Waltke, electronic ed. (Chicago: Moody Press, 1999), 205.

Newkirk invested in my spiritual development at a time when I needed a mentor. It was also a critical time in his life; he was enduring a severe trial. I knew of it because he had shared it with me. I watched him to see how he would respond. He didn't seem discouraged nor did he lose his zeal. One evening I went to his home and was told by his wife that he was down at his little office in Naha, the capital city. I took the bus that rainy night and arrived a couple of blocks from his office. Stepping off the bus, I began splashing my way toward his office. Before long I began to hear singing. I realized it was his voice. The hymn was familiar. I remember the words so clearly.

> O to grace how great a debtor,
> Daily I'm constrained to be!
> Let Thy goodness, like a fetter,
> Bind my wandering heart to Thee.[13]

It was my missionary friend, singing before his Lord all alone at his study-office. He had learned the truth of this verse in Psalm 63. Under the stress of his trial, my friend sang for joy. As I listened, I felt as if I were standing on holy ground.

Making It Strong in Your Soul

Meditation—the mental discipline of comprehending God and His ways—requires solitude and silence. Tonight, before sliding between the sheets, devote thirty minutes to pondering the answer to this question: What did God try to teach me today? In fact, try this for the next several nights.

---

13 Robert Robinson [1757], "Come Thou Fount of Every Blessing"

Day 5: *Psalm 63*

Rejoice in God

David's desert song, Psalm 63, continues with a fifth decision he hoped would enhance his relationship with the Lord: *he decided to rejoice in God (vv. 9–11).*

> But those who seek my life to destroy it,
> Will go into the depths of the earth.
> They will be delivered over to the power of the sword;
> They will be a prey for foxes.
> But the king will rejoice in God;
> Everyone who swears by Him will glory,
> For the mouths of those who speak lies will be stopped.

David closes this psalm of worship with a pen portrait of his situation. To our surprise, he wasn't absolutely alone, because verse 9 testifies of those who sought his life to destroy it. Nor was he free from criticism and slander, according to the last verse. Nevertheless, in the midst of all this danger and deprivation, David chooses joy. Rather than allow his dire circumstances to dictate his attitude, he compared the long term prospects of his enemies and celebrated his destiny.

Those who sought to kill David, to prevent him from becoming the king of Israel, had condemned themselves to the grave. They lived by the sword and were fated to die by the sword. Moreover, they would not be honored as heroes upon their deaths; they would become dinner for scavengers. David, on the other hand, had been promised the throne currently occupied by his enemy, Saul. He declares, "But the king will rejoice in God" (v. 11). As the king-elect, he would not doubt his Lord's protection.

Are you as determined as young David to live beyond the grind of religious ritual? I encourage you to cultivate such a spontaneous relationship with your God that you never again fall into the predictable mold of empty religion. Once you have tasted the real thing, you'll never be satisfied with plateaus of phony piety. You will want only to be in "God's presence," regardless of your location. It is the most refreshing place to be on earth, even though, at the time, you may find yourself in a wilderness.

Making It Strong in Your Soul

People stay on the treadmill of activity—both religious and secular—because short-term thinking keeps them slavishly obedient to the tyranny of the urgent. What has God called you to do? If you don't know, now is the time to discover your purpose. Do your daily activities contribute to your calling, your purpose?

THE GRIND OF ENEMY ATTACK

He who dwells in the shelter of the Most High
Will abide in the shadow of the Almighty.
*I will say to the L*ORD*, "My refuge and my fortress,*
My God, in whom I trust!"
For it is He who delivers you from the snare of the trapper
And from the deadly pestilence.
He will cover you with His pinions,
And under His wings you may seek refuge;
His faithfulness is a shield and bulwark.
You will not be afraid of the terror by night,
Or of the arrow that flies by day;
Of the pestilence that stalks in darkness,
Or of the destruction that lays waste at noon.
A thousand may fall at your side
And ten thousand at your right hand,
But it shall not approach you.
You will only look on with your eyes
And see the recompense of the wicked.
*For you have made the L*ORD*, my refuge,*
Even the Most High, your dwelling place.
No evil will befall you,
Nor will any plague come near your tent.
For He will give His angels charge concerning you,
To guard you in all your ways.
They will bear you up in their hands,
That you do not strike your foot against a stone.
You will tread upon the lion and cobra,
The young lion and the serpent you will trample down.
"Because he has loved Me, therefore I will deliver him;

I will set him securely on high, because he has
    known My name.
"He will call upon Me, and I will answer him;
I will be with him in trouble;
I will rescue him and honor him.
"With a long life I will satisfy him
And let him see My salvation."

(Psalm 91)

Day 1: *Psalm 91*
The War with Evil

Enemy attack? There was a time in my life when I had no enemies. Once I began ministry, however, that changed. It should come as no surprise that many who serve God in full-time ministry become targets of demonic assaults, especially those who serve in regions where the powers of darkness are commonplace. But enemy attacks are by no means limited to those dark corners of the world. The adversary is working overtime anywhere he can find a relational rift to exploit or a habitual sin to manipulate. How grateful I am for this song in Scripture. It, like few other scriptural passages, comes to grips with enemy attacks and gives us hope to get beyond them.

Every ancient song, like every great hymn, has its own special tone. The magnificent hymn "And Can It Be?" has a tone of assurance. The lovely "Guide Me, O Thou Great Jehovah" has a tone of dependence and trust. The moving strains of "O Sacred Head, Now Wounded" carry a tone of passion and pain, while "I Am His, and He Is Mine" conveys love and acceptance. Psalm 91 has a unique tone in its message as well. We discover this by reading it through and looking for words or phrases that communicate similar thoughts. Let me list some:

Verse 1: shelter

Verse 2: refuge . . . fortress

Verse 4: refuge . . . shield

Verse 5: terror by night . . . arrow . . . by day

Verse 6: pestilence . . . destruction

Verse 7: a thousand may fall

Verse 9: refuge

Verse 11: guard

Verse 15: rescue

There can be little doubt about the tone of Psalm 91; it is warfare, battle, conflict, fighting. It is a song for battle in that it conveys an atmosphere of daily, oppressive enemy attack. And who is this enemy? Israel's national foes? No. A human being who opposes the writer? I don't believe so. An actual, visible war on a bloody battlefield? No, I doubt it. Look at several more verses as we identify the enemy:

Verse 3: the trapper

Verse 8: the wicked

Verse 10: evil

Then consider the promise of angelic assistance (vv. 11–12) as well as divine deliverance (vv. 14–15). When you put all the evidence together, I think it builds a strong case for a song about surviving the attacks of our spiritual enemies, Satan and his demons. It talks about a battle in the unseen spiritual realm. This explains our need for angelic and divine intervention. Because our supernatural enemy comes at us with supernatural strength, we need supernatural help.

Unfortunately, we have neither the space nor the time to examine the full spectrum of enemy attacks, but perhaps an example or two would help. There are certain people whose presence throbs with evil. Being near them unleashes depressing powers which are both frightening and unavoidable. I have encountered these individuals throughout my ministry and have never forgotten the attacks. Frequently the people have trafficked in mind-bending occult practices and/or have been heavily involved in the drug culture. I have seen weird, even bizarre things occur in my family during such times. Fitful nightmares, passionate outbursts of rebellion and arguments, a heavy cloud of depression, strange accidents, and uncharacteristic marital disharmony can follow in the wake of these attacks. I shudder as I recall those awful times.

Not all demonic attacks are overt. In fact, most take more subtle, insidious forms such as turning people against one another or keeping someone bound in habitual sin in order to destroy the lives of everyone they know. Several years ago, I witnessed the sin of just two people shake two otherwise stable ministries all the way to their foundations.

Keep this in mind as we dig into Psalm 91. The tone is warfare and the enemy is our evil adversary who comes at us with persistent regularity. Let me suggest four distinct parts to this song about divine deliverance from supernatural evil:

 I. Protection amid Evil (vv. 1–4)

 II. Attitude toward Evil (vv. 5–10)

 III. Assistance against Evil (vv. 11–13)

 IV. Security from Evil (vv. 14–16)

Making It Strong in Your Soul

What do you consider your most significant ongoing struggle in the war with evil? How does it present itself? What have you done in response to attacks? How well has this strategy worked?

Day 2: *Psalm 91*
God's Protective Care

The first verse of Psalm 91, a song about battling the forces of evil, establishes the context for everything that follows. So, let's examine these two lines closely.

Protection amid Evil

We must never forget that believers in the Lord Jesus Christ are not removed from the presence of wickedness. In fact, our Savior prayed specifically: "I do not ask You to take them out of the world, but to keep them from the evil one" (John 17:15). While it's difficult to understand the reason, God has planned that we continue to live in a hostile, wicked, non-Christian world system (*kosmos*). He deliberately did not remove us from an atmosphere of hostility. Instead, He has promised to preserve us through the conflict. He has made possible a plan of insulation, not isolation. God isn't interested in our isolating ourselves, hidden away like hermits in a cave, but rather in our living courageously on the front lines, claiming His insulation amid an evil environment.

In order for us to enjoy the benefits of insulation, we must live in the light of Psalm 91, which uses analogy and metaphor to convey spiritual truths. The secret to survival is to "dwell in the shelter of the Most High," to "abide in the shadow of the Almighty."

The word "dwell" (v. 1) is translated from the Hebrew *yashav*, meaning "to remain, sit, abide." The term conveys the idea of permanence. The verb "dwell" is used figuratively to mean "live in conscious fellowship with, draw daily strength from." In the same way someone might "live off the land," we are encouraged to draw our needs from God. This requires an attitude of continual awareness of the Lord's presence and involvement. The idea is developed further with the term "shelter" in verse 1. This original word is *sathar*, meaning "cove, covert, secret hideaway." A group of soldiers caught behind enemy lines need to find a place to rest that's hidden from view and therefore safe from the enemy. The Lord is said to be our refuge, where we can find safety and rest.

Before going any further, let me emphasize that Psalm 91 is written to *dwellers*. It promises deliverance and protection not to everyone, but to *dwellers*—those who draw daily, habitual strength from their Lord as they sustain an intimacy of fellowship and nearness with Him. Don't forget that!

We are told in the last part of verse 1 that as this close fellowship is maintained, we shall "abide in the shadow of the Almighty." Now we come upon a different Hebrew term translated "abide." It is *lūn*, meaning "to lodge, pass the night." It conveys a periodic rest or stopover for lodging.

What is verse 1 actually saying? Simply this: if we who know the Lord Jesus Christ will dwell in conscious fellowship with Him (keeping our sins confessed and forsaken, and walking in moment-by-moment dependence upon Him), we shall enjoy the benefits of living under His protective care on those occasions when rest and lodging are needed. If we maintain our walk with Him, we can count on Him and His deliverance at periodic times when the going gets rough.

The song continues to develop the idea of safety and refuge from the attacks of Satan with images of warfare.

I will say to the LORD, "My refuge and my fortress,
My God, in whom I trust!" (v. 2)

A "refuge" is a place of rest. A "fortress" is a place of defense. Notice that this does not say the Lord will *provide* these things. Rather, it says that the Lord *is* these things. This is why our dwelling in Him is essential; it is *in Him* alone that we will find rest and defense. Take time to consider the last word in verse 2: *trust*. It is a translation of the same Hebrew term found in Proverbs 3:5.

Trust in the LORD with all your heart
And do not lean on your own understanding.

This calls for total trust. A construction laborer working forty stories above the city street depends upon a lanyard to keep him from falling should he lose his balance. He trusts that the cable and harness will support him in an emergency. He must put complete trust in his safety equipment. That is the kind of trust our Lord wants from us.

Making It Strong in Your Soul

Why do you think God chose to leave His people in the world, amid evil, rather than take us to heaven immediately? How do you define "safety" from the "evil one"? Which passages of Scripture support your definition?

Day 3: *Psalm 91*

What God Does

While the first two verses of Psalm 91 depict the faithful character of God, verses 3 and 4 describe what God does. The psalmist names three actions the Lord takes on our behalf:

a. He delivers: from the snare of the trapper and
from the deadly pestilence

b. He covers: with His pinions/under His wings

c. He shields: by His faithfulness

The Hebrew sentence structure enables us to point out particular emphases in our study from time to time. In this case, the emphatic part of verses 3–4 is "He." We might render the line: "He alone" or "He it is—not anyone else!" Practically speaking, you will find no absolute assistance or deliverance from anyone other than your Lord.

Now, one at a time, let's look at the specific actions God takes to protect and sustain us when the enemy attacks. The psalmist describes these actions using three different analogies.

1. He delivers from the snare of the trapper. The first analogy imagines a bird becoming entangled in a fowler's trap, which is baited with something the bird needs. My Webster's dictionary says that a trap is "something by which one gets entangled, something deceptively attractive." The word "deliver" is translated from *natzal*, meaning "to separate, to cause removal." It suggests that the bird has already been deceived by the trap and has been caught. Certain death awaits, as described by the phrase "the deadly pestilence." Literally, from "a death of destruction." One translation renders this "a violent death."

2. *He covers with His pinions, under His wings.* The Lord is here pictured as a bird keeping close watch over its brood. Both Psalm 36:7 and Psalm 57:1 mention the protection we have under our Lord's "wings." When danger presents itself, baby ducks and geese make a beeline for their mother, who creates a shroud with her wings. The mother will then pivot to keep her young hidden from any predators.

3. *He shields by His faithfulness.* The psalmist has pictured our Lord's protection in three distinct ways in verses 3 and 4. First, in the scene of a trapper. Second, in the scene of a bird and her brood. Now, in the scene of a battle. Here he assures us that we are guarded by His faithful presence. The Hebrew word for "shield" depicts a protective barrier large enough to protect a soldier from a hail of arrows. The term translated "bulwark" comes from a term that carries the idea of "surrounding." It could be another kind of large, curved shield. Because the term also denotes a particular kind of stone, the concept of a fortified barrier, such as a castle wall, makes better sense.

Regardless, the idea is the same: in the heat of battle, when the enemy's attacks become too much to bear, the faithfulness of God is there for your protection; hide behind Him.

Making It Strong in Your Soul

Satan's primary—and at the present time, *only*—weapon is deception. How, therefore, does someone "take refuge" in the Lord? What sources of divine truth do you have available? How can you utilize these more frequently, and how can you make them more accessible in an emergency?

Day 4: *Psalm 91*
Claiming Refuge in God

In Psalm 91, the songwriter has acknowledged the Lord as his refuge when under attack by the forces of evil. Now, he sizes up his enemy and calculates his (and our) chances of surviving the battle. (Spoiler alert: we stand a 100 percent chance of victory.)

Attitude toward Evil

The majority of the song is written in the second person singular, as if composed especially for one person. That's not far from true; it was composed for you! Beginning in verse 5, the songwriter makes a series of predictions about you, presuming that you have placed your trust in the Lord and you're coming to Him for refuge from the enemy. Here are his predictions.

You will have no fear (vv. 5-6). Look over the descriptive terms that portray our enemy's tactics: terror . . . arrow . . . pestilence . . . destruction. All these describe satanic and demonic assaults against us. Notice also that these assaults take place at any time of the day or night. Our enemy will stop at nothing to make us afraid! Intimidation is one of his sharpest darts of deception.

But the psalmist assures that you won't be afraid because the truth of God's faithfulness will wrap itself around you like a warm blanket in winter. While the enemy relentlessly fires arrows in your direction, you're safely surrounded by the "bulwark" of God's fortress. The psalmist has you standing on a parapet, high above the range of the most powerful bowstring. You watch in complete peace as thousands of missiles fall pathetically to the ground before reaching you.

Your faith will prevail, while others fall (vv. 7–10). I see faith written between each line, don't you? Our Lord expects us to stand firmly on His Word—His promises—His strength. Read Ephesians 6:10–11, 16 and you'll see that the "shield of faith" is able to deflect everything the evil one throws at you. Remember, faith demands an object. There are at least four specific biblical truths for the Christian to claim when undergoing or seeking release from satanic/demonic attacks.

1. *The Cross.* Go to verses that declare Satan's defeat at Calvary and read them out loud. (See Col. 2:13-15, Heb. 2:14-15, and 1 John 3:8.)

2. *The Blood.* As you consider and claim Satan's defeat at the cross, call to mind specific passages dealing with the blood of the Lord Jesus Christ. (See Rom. 5:8-9 and Rev. 12:10-11.)

3. *The Name.* As you seek deliverance and strength amid your battle, verbally state the full name of the Lord Jesus Christ as your refuge and sovereign God. (See Prov. 18:10 and Phil. 2:9-10.)

4. *The Word.* Stand firmly upon God's written Word, as our Lord did when the Devil tempted Him to yield to his deception. (See Matt. 4:4, 7, 10 and Eph. 6:11, 17.)

If you will use this as a practical guide and claim each one by faith, you will find that you can live beyond the grind of enemy attacks.

Making It Strong in Your Soul

How does it feel to have someone predict your success in battle against all the powers of darkness? There is, of course, one condition: you must fill your mind with truth in order to refute Satan's deception. I memorized Scripture verses and committed dozens of hymns to memory. What will you do?

Day 5: *Psalm 91*
A Tactical Advantage

Having predicted your success in battle against the attacks of the devil, Psalm 91 continues with several commitments from the Lord. He has promised to give you a tactical advantage, which the songwriter enumerates in the final verses.

Assistance against Evil

God has promised to send angelic assistance when we face attacks from supernatural realms. It makes sense. Satan and the demons are supernatural beings—so are angels. We need supernatural help when dealing with supernatural enemies. In verses 11–13, the composer describes three specific activities of the angels on our behalf.

1. Angels are given "charge" of us (v. 11). The term "charge" is from the Hebrew *tzawa*, which means "to appoint, install, give command of." Other passages of Scripture suggest that the Lord has actually appointed angels—heavenly guardians—to give us aid when attacked by supernatural forces (Matt. 18:10; Acts 12:15).

2. Angels "guard" us in all our ways (v. 11). The Hebrew word *shamar* means "to keep, watch over, observe, preserve, take care of." Angels are overseers of God's people. Like silent sentries, they stand guard over those who seek refuge in the Lord, preserving our steps.

3. Angels "bear you up" in their hands (v. 12). The verb *nasah* actually means "to lift, to carry, take up." When used figuratively in reference to a person, it means "to support, sustain." In the context of Psalm 91, the angels see to your mental, emotional, and spiritual needs so that you will not be overwhelmed by the deception of the devil and his minions.

Security from Evil

For thirteen verses the songwriter has spoken directly to you. Now God speaks, committing Himself to six promises in response to your seeking refuge in Him.

- I will deliver him (v. 14).
- I will set him securely on high (v. 14).
- I will answer him (v. 15).
- I will be with him in trouble (v. 15).
- I will rescue him and honor him (v. 15).
- I will satisfy him (v. 16).

What a list of promises! From God's mouth to the psalmist's pen to your eyes. These are yours to claim. The Lord says that those who love Him and those who know Him have this secure hope in Him. The Hebrew term used for "love" is unusual and rare. Most often it is used with reference to "attaching something to something." The Hebrew term includes the idea of attaching a saddle to a horse. It would be acceptable to render Psalm 91:14: "Because he clings affectionately to Me."

Making It Strong in Your Soul

If you were to begin a battle in which your best effort guaranteed victory, how would that assurance affect your ability to fight? How would guaranteed victory affect your perspective on adversity? Psalm 91 says that taking refuge in divine truth is the key to victory. What is your battle plan moving forward? Be specific.

THE GRIND OF INGRATITUDE

A Psalm for Thanksgiving.

Shout joyfully to the LORD, *all the earth.*
Serve the LORD *with gladness;*
Come before Him with joyful singing.
Know that the LORD *Himself is God;*
It is He who has made us, and not we ourselves;
We are His people and the sheep of His pasture.
Enter His gates with thanksgiving
And His courts with praise.
Give thanks to Him, bless His name.
For the LORD *is good;*
His lovingkindness is everlasting
And His faithfulness to all generations.

(Psalm 100)

Day 1: *Psalm 100*
Abundance without Gratitude

While we have experienced financial ups and downs in the last century—some of them significant—we nevertheless benefit from an unprecedented level of abundance. Never in human history have so many people lived in the kind of comfort and security we enjoy today. And American culture leads the world in luxury. Many families have a driveway full of cars, a house full of modern appliances—many dedicated to entertainment—a closet full of clothes, and a refrigerator full of food. Unfortunately, in these days of abundance and wealth, we tend to become ungrateful, even presumptuous. Instead of thanking God, we develop a spirit of entitlement.

Please don't misunderstand. Abundance is not sinful. Scripture describes a number of people who were both wealthy and godly: Abraham, Job, Joseph, David, Solomon, Josiah, Barnabas, Lydia, to name a few. But we also find some who became enamored of their wealth and lost sight of the Lord and His right to rule their lives. There's nothing wrong with having nice things, but trouble begins when nice things have us. A spirit of entitlement can quickly overshadow an attitude of generosity and humility. Psalm 100 is a song of celebration that will help restore a spirit of thankfulness and joyful gratitude.

As we take a closer look at this song, three questions come to mind.

1. *To whom is it addressed?* Verses 1 and 5 state that it is intended for "all the earth" to sing. Psalm 100 is for everyone—all nations, all cultures, all ages, all stages. Its message is universal, for everyone to hear and apply.

2. *Of whom does it speak?* Verses 1–3, along with verse 5, give us the answer. Psalm 100 speaks of "the Lord." His name appears no less than four times in five verses. One of those times He is declared to be God Himself. This psalm directs our attention to "YHWH," the Old Testament personal name for God. You cannot appreciate Psalm 100 or apply its message if you do not know the One of whom it speaks. But the more you become intimately acquainted with the almighty, infinite Creator, the deeper this song resonates with a grateful soul. Being thankful—really thankful—begins with a right relationship with the Giver of everything.

3. *How is it arranged?* Psalms were originally written as hymns; they are poetic in form. Hebrew lyrics don't rhyme like English poetry; the psalms follow a certain style, a "meter" or "beat." Each psalm stands alone, independent of all the others. Like our present-day hymns, each one has a distinct message and arrangement.

This particular song includes seven commands or imperatives. The hymn concludes with a final verse that sums up God's character, giving us a compelling reason to obey the commands.

Making It Strong in Your Soul

How often do you stop to consider the goodness of God and how fortunate you are? What would you say is your greatest obstacle to praising God? What would you say to a billionaire who complains about not having enough blessings from the Lord?

Day 2: Psalm 100
Choose Joy

Psalm 100 wastes no time with preliminaries. Rather than try to convince the reader to praise the Lord for His goodness and our many blessings, the composer issues six commands, beginning with the first line.

The Commands

1. *Shout joyfully to the Lord (v. 1).* This is quite a beginning! The Hebrew gets straight to the point. In fact, the term "joyfully" doesn't appear in the Hebrew. Literally rendered, it's "Shout to the Lord!" The word "shout" comes from a Hebrew word meaning "to raise a noise, to give a blast (as on a trumpet)." The composer calls for the kind of shouting that erupts from a person so full of joy he can't contain his emotions, the kind of uninhibited whooping you hear from fans at a football game. He says, in effect, "Shout in joyful approval of God!"

It's hard to imagine feeling that joyful about the Lord, isn't it? Let's face it; when's the last time you shouted like a sports fan because of something you read in Scripture? When have you ever pumped your fists and shouted after a sermon on God's attributes?

I'm not suggesting we become charismatic; but certainly we should feel *some* excitement, at least a little joy. Sometimes the Lord does things that defy natural explanation, accomplishing something completely beyond our capabilities. When He comes to our rescue, don't accept this silently. Shout to Him. Lift up your voice in praise! By doing so we counteract that grind of ingratitude that so easily can climb aboard.

2. *Serve the Lord with gladness (v. 2)*. A healthy sign of the grateful life is serving. Few decisions are more effective in easing the daily grind of ingratitude than serving others. In doing God's work, we serve Him, not the local church, not the superintendent of some department, not the pastor or some board. We serve the Lord. It is He we worship and for Him we labor—not people! And please observe that the motivation is neither grudging nor guilt-ridden; we are urged to serve "with gladness." The Hebrew term for this phrase was used to describe pleasant things that gave happiness.

Now let's get real for a moment. You don't always feel like serving. Yet waiting until you feel grateful isn't a good plan; you'll never serve! (I write from personal experience.) The psalm doesn't imply we should serve only when our hearts are filled with joy. On the contrary, we are commanded to serve regardless; gladness will soon follow. In fact, when I start feeling sorry for myself or my attitude takes a cynical turn, I know it's time to serve someone who's in worse shape. It's not long before gladness pushes negativity out of my heart.

3. *Come before Him with joyful singing (v. 2)*. We have already considered this idea of singing on several occasions, so there is no need to add much to my previous remarks. Let me simply emphasize the word "joyful." I get the picture that God prefers to have us be happy people, rejoicing in His presence, for He has mentioned it in each line of this psalm thus far.

Are you joyful? Really now, is your face pleasant—is a smile frequently there? Do your eyes reveal a joyful spirit within? When you sing in church, for example, is it with joy? The next chance you get, glance at the fellow in the next car on the freeway. He is never smiling! Look at the lady ahead of you or behind you at the grocery store. No smile . . . no joy.

It's time to lighten up! After all, joy is a choice. Dress up your testimony with a genuine spirit of joy! It does the heart good and it's truly contagious.

Making It Strong in Your Soul

Do you consider yourself a joyful person? How much do you think your temperament affects your attitude? If joy is a choice, what are you doing to cultivate a joyful spirit? According to vv. 1–2, worshiping with fellow believers and serving others is a good place to start. Perhaps it's time to begin or time to make a change.

♍

Day 3: *Psalm 100*
Cultivate Relationship with God

Psalm 100 is an extended command to worship the Lord, giving specific instructions to follow. The first three commands in vv. 1–2 are directly related to cultivating a spirit of joy. The next four call for our response to the Lord's identity and character. We'll examine two of these commands today.

4. *Know that the Lord Himself is God (v. 3)*. At first glance, this seems like an odd command. A close examination of the Hebrew terms will help clarify what the psalmist intends.

The Hebrew word rendered "know" is *yada*. When used in reference to a person, it denotes a personal, experiential knowledge, not mere recognition. It's the same term biblical writers used as a euphemism for sexual intercourse (cf. Gen. 4:1; 19:8; Num. 31:17, 35; Judg. 11:39; 21:11; 1 Kings 1:4; 1 Sam. 1:19). Our knowledge of God should be personal and experiential, not merely theological.

The word "LORD" translates God's personal name, represented in Hebrew by the four consonants YHWH, and considered too holy to pronounce audibly. You may recall it's based on the verb "to be," identifying Him as the deity who actually exists. The late Christian philosopher Francis Schaeffer called Him "the God who is there" (as opposed to all the gods who are not!)

"Himself" serves to single out YHWH as the subject of the verb, emphasizing that no other name qualifies for this distinction. The sentence might just as well be rendered, "Know that YHWH, *He* is God" or "He *alone* is God." I like the additional qualification tacked on by one contemporary songwriter: "He is God (and I am *not!*)"

The English word "God" at the end of the verse translates the Hebrew term *elohim*, which emphasizes the grandeur of God, much like calling a king "His Royal Highness." So, when you put the entire command together, it could be paraphrased, "Know by personal experience that YHWH alone is the sovereign God of all."

I see two implications of practical importance here. First, God is sovereign over each of us, individually. He's not merely the ruler of the universe, having dominion over galaxies and able to command the forces of nature. He's *my* sovereign. He's *your* king. He's the boss; we answer to Him. When we surrender to that fact, life becomes much easier to understand and joy takes the place of frustration.

Second, our knowledge of God as our sovereign Lord must be gained through personal experience. That implies a personal relationship in which He leads and we follow. And through that ongoing interchange, the decision to trust Him becomes a settled, unshakable confidence. Confident people are joyful people.

5. Enter His gates with thanksgiving, and His courts with praise (v. 4). What was in the psalmist's mind? To what do the "gates" and "courts" refer? There are two possibilities. First, it could refer to the stronghold of a ruler, where he holds court, deciding cases and granting favors. If so, the invitation is to enter the great hall with praises and thanksgiving rather than seeking something from the Ruler.

The second possibility is a reference to the temple, the place where the people of God approached the Lord. In the Old Testament, the otherworldly glow of His glory—called the *shekinah* by the Hebrews—filled the Most Holy Place in the temple (2 Chr. 5:14 and 1 Kings 8:10–11). The temple had gates and courts, both of which gave access to the presence of God.

Because Jesus Christ satisfied all the requirements of the temple rituals, we no longer go to a specific place to meet God. Today, we worship "in spirit and truth" (John 4:23). So, how do we enter His gates and His courts? What is our access to His presence today? The answer is prayer. Hebrews 4:16 invites us to "draw near" to God's throne. Through prayer we come into the very presence of God. This psalm tells us to approach the Lord with thanksgiving and praise. Sometimes it's good to save our petitions and requests for another time and seek an audience for the sole purpose of praise.

Making It Strong in Your Soul

One cultivates a personal relationship with God like he or she would with another person: by listening to Him, by spending time with His loved ones, and by doing the things He considers important. What are you doing to hear the Lord speak? How much quality time do you spend with others who love God? Do you regularly join the Lord in accomplishing His work?

Day 4: *Psalm 100*
Give Thanks and Praise

Psalm 100 continues with two final commands followed by three specific reasons to "shout joyfully" (v. 1). Both of these commands urge us to speak directly to the Lord.

6. Give thanks to Him (v. 4). The Hebrew command "give thanks" is a single verb that means "to confess, praise, acknowledge, extol, thank." This is more than a mere "Thanks, God, for the blessings." This depicts someone naming the specific reasons for gratitude, telling a story with God as the hero. We do this when telling a friend about a particularly good physician who cured a long-term malady. We gush with details and gratitude. We feel unable to say enough good about the doctor. Similarly, this "giving thanks" literally can't say enough about the Lord and what He does.

If you're looking for signs of the last days, then be on the lookout for ingratitude. 2 Timothy 3:1–5 lists "ungrateful" in a list of attitudes that will mark the dark days before the end of time. Beware an ungrateful, thankless generation! Cultivating a grateful heart is no small issue with God.

7. Bless His name (v. 4). The word bless is from *barak*, which means "to kneel, praise, salute." The idea is to show honor and homage to God, recognizing His name as higher than any other name. In the Ancient Near East, a person "blessing" a superior did so while bowing or kneeling. He or she then expressed a desire for the honoree to have power, prosperity, longevity, success, etc. Of course, the Lord already possesses all power, prosperity, longevity, and will certainly succeed in all He chooses to do; by "blessing His name," we affirm His power and goodness, and we commit ourselves to joining His cause.

The two actions, "giving thanks" and "blessing His name," have a special significance deeply rooted in Ancient Near East custom. To receive the hospitality of a nobleman and to pronounce a blessing in return effectively established an alliance, a lifelong indebtedness that linked two people in a bond of friendship. In this case, the psalmist calls us to pledge allegiance to the supreme King.

Making It Strong in Your Soul

For the next few days, devote all of your prayer time to thanksgiving and praise. This doesn't come as naturally as asking the Lord for help, wisdom, strength, healing, or resources, so you may have to prepare before praying. Create a "thank you" list. Research the Lord's attributes. Then, tell the story of God's goodness to you in prayer.

♮

Day 5: *Psalm 100*
Because of Who God Is

Having called the whole world to join him in song, the psalmist declares the reason God deserves universal thanksgiving and praise. His rationale for worldwide celebration is based on three facts concerning the Lord's character.

Reasons for the Commands

Fact 1: He is good. Verse 3 told us "He is God," the one and only Creator and Sovereign of the universe; this final verse tells us "He is good." Verse 3 states His position and role; verse 5 describes the quality of His character. The Hebrew term, *tōv*, means "pleasant, agreeable, delightful, good." How different from the present-day concept many people have of God. He is not an irritated tyrant pacing the floors of heaven looking for reasons to smash our lives or squelch our happiness—like some celestial bully with a club in His hand. No! He is *good*. And His commands are for our good. Love motivates His every word and deed.

Fact 2: His lovingkindness is everlasting. "Lovingkindness" is the best English word to translate the Hebrew term *chesed*, but it is woefully inadequate. *Chesed* is perhaps the most important word in the entire Old Testament because it effectively sums up the character of God. That colorful word is so steeped in Hebrew culture and theology that it has no equivalent in other languages. That explains why *chesed* has been rendered by different translations as "mercy," "kindness," "lovingkindness," "goodness," and others. It describes God's covenant love for His people—a passionate, merciful, pursuing, unrelenting kindness that overlooks their inability to repay Him or even return His love.

The Bible is filled with wonderful, moving stories that show *chesed* in action. I think of Ruth's extraordinary loyalty for her mother-in-law, Naomi (Ruth 1:16–17). I think of Jonathan, the son of King Saul, and how he extended extraordinary friendship to David despite the enormous personal cost: the right to succeed Saul as king (1 Sam. 18:1). And when David eventually became king, he extended extraordinary mercy to Mephibosheth, the son of Jonathan (2 Sam. 9:7). Of course, we have no greater example of kindness than God Himself, who demonstrated His love in becoming a human in the person of Jesus Christ.

God loves and accepts us as we are, knowing that we have no way of repaying the debt of extraordinary kindness. His unqualified love and acceptance are behind His every command. Moreover, nothing will cancel or compromise His *chesed* love for us; it lasts forever.

Fact 3: He is faithful to all generations. The Lord is not partial. The God who commands is fair and faithful to all generations. He didn't make a limited-time offer to one generation only to rescind it from the next. He doesn't play favorites. His commands and promises apply to all people throughout all time because God never changes. He remains consistently faithful.

Note the psalmist didn't call for this joyous response to God as merely our part of a transaction. We don't praise and worship the Lord because of what we get in return. He calls for worship as a natural response to our firsthand experience of God's character.

Of course, that's based on the presumption that we actually *have* firsthand experience of God's character!

Making It Strong in Your Soul

Earlier, you were asked to create a "thank you" list for God. Review the list now. Did any of the items thank God for some aspect of His nature? For example, "Thank You, Lord, for Your unchanging nature; I am grateful that I can always count on You." Start a new list. Make this kind of thanksgiving a regular part of your prayers.

THE GRIND OF AIMLESSNESS

A Psalm of David.

I will sing of lovingkindness and justice,
To You, O LORD, I will sing praises.
I will give heed to the blameless way.
When will You come to me?
I will walk within my house in the integrity of my heart.
I will set no worthless thing before my eyes;
I hate the work of those who fall away;
It shall not fasten its grip on me.
A perverse heart shall depart from me;
I will know no evil.
Whoever secretly slanders his neighbor, him I will destroy;
No one who has a haughty look and an arrogant heart
*   will I endure.*
My eyes shall be upon the faithful of the land, that they may
*   dwell with me;*
He who walks in a blameless way is the one who
*   will minister to me.*
He who practices deceit shall not dwell within my house;
He who speaks falsehood shall not maintain his position
*   before me.*
Every morning I will destroy all the wicked of the land,
So as to cut off from the city of the LORD all those
*   who do iniquity.*

(Psalm 101)

Day 1: *Psalm 101*

A Life of Purpose

Some people seem to drift aimlessly through life, headed in no specific direction. Without clearly defined objectives, it is not surprising that many adopt a lifestyle that lacks definition and purpose.

I know a few folks who sort of take life as it comes; no big deal. Reminds me of the time I had been invited to a college campus to speak. On my way to the meeting hall, I met a fellow who was obviously apathetic. Hoping to put a little spark into his plans beyond graduation, I asked him a few probing questions. I'll never forget his answer to my asking, "Where are you going? What are your plans?" With hardly a hesitation, he responded, "Plans? Well, uh, I'm going to lunch."

How typical of those caught in the grind of aimlessness! They live from one meal to the next, without much concern beyond that evening's television programs. They drift through life like a skiff in a swamp.

According to the superscript, this is a song of David, whose life was guided by a specific purpose. He understood God's plan for him and, aside from a temporary slump into disobedience, he pursued the course laid out for him. He made decisions in accordance with his purpose, and served the Lord faithfully for many, many years. He was indeed "a man after God's own heart."

Perhaps more than any other passage of Scripture, these eight verses explain David's philosophy of life. In fact, an appropriate title for Psalm 101 might be "David's Statement of Faith." This is his credo. It declares his spiritual aims.

David committed himself to this credo without reservation. He, of course, failed at times; he wandered from the course, but he always kept the standard before him. In this psalm there is not the slightest trace of diplomatic compromise or vacillation, only simple, straightforward, devout words. Therefore, all who hope to live beyond the grind of aimlessness would do well to observe how David decided to conduct himself.

The Passage and Its Pattern

Psalm 101 could be called "the psalm of resolutions." I count at least ten "I wills" or "I shalls." It reminds me of Joshua's declaration when the nation of Israel wanted to disobey the Lord: "Choose for yourselves today whom you will serve . . . but as for me and my house, we will serve the LORD" (Josh. 24:15). For four verses David implies "as for me" and lists his resolutions in five "I wills." Following that, in verses 5–8, he turns to his kingdom, implying "as for my house" and lists seven different types of people, making a declaration about each one. An outline could look like this:

I. As for Me: Resolutions (vv. 1–4)
   A. I will sing (v. 1)
   B. I will give heed (v. 2a)
   C. I will walk (v. 2b)
   D. I will set (v. 3)
   E. I will know (v. 4)

II. As for My House: Declarations (vv. 5–8)
   A. Slanderer (v. 5a)
   B. Proud (v. 5b)
   C. Faithful (v. 6a)
   D. Blameless (v. 6b)
   E. Deceiver (v. 7a)
   F. Liar (v. 7b)
   G. Wicked (v. 8)

Making It Strong in Your Soul

What is your specific purpose in life? If you don't know, now would be a good time to ask, "Lord, why do You have me here on planet Earth; what is my specific role in Your plan?" The answer won't come in a simple reply, but through a process, beginning with the decision to serve God, above all, with your life. If you haven't already, commit yourself—without reservation or qualification—to His service.

🎵

Day 2: *Psalm 101*
Honor and Integrity

I once heard the president of a seminary express his concern over the school by saying, "I fear we may be turning out graduates with a great number of beliefs but not enough conviction." Conviction gives beliefs a backbone. David wasn't satisfied with a set of theological truths floating around in his head; he pinned them down to concrete convictions. It's as though he is saying in verses 1–4, "I'm committed to God's purpose, whatever it happens to be." In these four verses he lists four great qualities the believer must possess in order to discover clear direction. Each one assaults an aimless mindset.

Honor

> I will sing of lovingkindness and justice,
> To You, O Lord, I will sing praises. (v. 1)

Observe what he praises through song: lovingkindness and justice. These two qualities not only define God, they represent the guiding values by which He wants the world to operate. Many years later, the prophet Micah will write,

> What does the Lord require of you
> But to do justice, to love kindness,
> And to walk humbly with your God? (Micah 6:8)

The first value, translated "lovingkindness," is *chesed*, which we discussed earlier. It combines the ideas of extraordinary and unselfish mercy, love, friendship, kindness, and loyalty. The New Testament concept of grace captures the spirit of *chesed*. The companion word, translated "justice," is *mishpat*, which denotes an orderly, equitable administration of government; it describes that quality of civil rule that allows everyone to live peacefully and productively.

David resolves to make these two divine qualities the song of his life. He commits to letting them animate every decision and every relationship.

Integrity

I will give heed to the blameless way.
When will You come to me?
I will walk within my house in the integrity of my heart. (v. 2)

The first part of this verse has to do with public integrity as David says, literally, "I will give heed unto the way of integrity." The original Hebrew term translated "blameless" or "integrity" means "to be whole, complete, finished." It carries with it the idea of being totally honest, thoroughly sound. The king of Israel knew that his life before the people had to be solid and honest for the kingdom to remain strong.

The second part of this verse has to do with private integrity—he mentions being sound in "my house" and "my heart." Integrity is about authenticity, which doesn't change based on the audience or venue.

Making It Strong in Your Soul

Select a person in history you admire because of his or her accomplishments. Check an online bookstore for the most respected biography and read, taking special note of what influenced the individual, and how he or she became focused in energy and direction. Note also the roles of honor and integrity in his or her personal development.

Day 3: *Psalm 101*
Honesty and Purity

Psalm 101 names four great qualities a believer must possess in order to discern his or her divine purpose. Without these four virtues to clarify one's vision, confusion abounds. After describing honor and integrity, the song continues with two more godly qualities: honesty and purity.

Honesty

I will set no worthless thing before my eyes;
I hate the work of those who fall away;
It shall not fasten its grip on me. (v. 3)

As king, David had the political power to set any agenda and then commit the resources of the entire nation to accomplish his goal. His predecessor, Saul, used his political influence, the nation's wealth, and the might of the Israelite army to hunt down and kill David, who God had anointed as King! David, however, resolves to avoid every unworthy aim and ambition. To do anything less would inevitably lead to his "falling away" from fellowship with his Lord. Moreover, he resolved to "hate" the accomplishments of those who "fall away."

In the Ancient Near East, to "hate" something is to reject it in favor of something else. For example, Genesis 29 tells the story of Jacob's two wives and how he "loved" Rachel and "hated" her sister, Leah. The term indicates Jacob's choice to favor one over the other. He wasn't repulsed by Leah. After all, he did conceive several children with her! David has determined to choose the Lord's way and to reject the deeds of evil people, those who have fallen away from God.

Purity

A perverse heart shall depart from me;
I will know no evil. (v. 4)

David has resolved thus far that he will be a man of honor, integrity, and honesty. Now he resolves to be a man of purity—knowing no evil. This has to be one of the reasons God called David "a man after My own heart." Rare indeed are those people in this world who could say what David says in this fourth verse.

David's son Solomon also wrote of the value of personal purity in Proverbs 11:19–21:

He who is steadfast in righteousness will attain to life,
And he who pursues evil will bring about his own death.
The perverse in heart are an abomination to the LORD,
But the blameless in their walk are His delight.
Assuredly, the evil man will not go unpunished,
But the descendants of the righteous will be delivered.

Don't miss the last part of that passage. A pure life is actually a spiritual investment, the dividends being enjoyed by your children. God has a purity layaway plan, a spiritual account you establish now and your descendants later cash in on.

I cannot overemphasize the value of a pure life. We have an inordinate curiosity about perversion and evil. We are not only aware of wickedness, but we are drawn to it with interest. The news media capitalize on this interest by highlighting the evil in our world. They have found that public interest is high when it comes to impure, wicked activities. David realized, however, that "a perverse heart" would only lead to a weakening of his spiritual life.

My wife, Cynthia, and I know a young man who was in training for the ministry. He met and married a girl who had been gloriously saved out of an impure past. She had been a call girl connected with an organized ring of prostitutes in a large city. During those years she went to the depths of shame. Through a series of events she heard the gospel and came to Christ by faith. After her conversion and subsequent marriage to our minister friend, she found herself in an entirely new environment. Instead of evil there was purity. On one occasion, she shared with Cynthia the tremendous adjustment she faced and the difficulty of fully forgetting her past. She wanted to, but evil had a way of lingering in her mind. Perhaps that is the reason David resolved to "know no evil." This world's system puts a brand upon us that is the next thing to impossible to erase. How much better it is to be pure and inexperienced than to be scarred by impure memories that are quick to play back their reruns at a moment's notice.

Making It Strong in Your Soul

If investigators were to do a thorough audit of your financial and/or business dealings, what would you hope they fail to notice? If your conscience bothers you in the least, what can you do to resolve the matter? In terms of purity, what negative or ungodly influences do you regularly encounter? What can you do to insulate yourself to create a more wholesome environment?

Day 4: *Psalm 101*
Staying On Course

Having identified four qualities to cultivate, David's spiritual manifesto in Psalm 101 continues with several declarations, each intended to keep him on course in pursuit of his divine purpose. David no longer looks within, he looks around. He considers the people of his kingdom and declares his predetermined response to seven types of individual.

The Slanderer

Whoever secretly slanders his neighbor, him I will destroy. (v. 5a)

The term *destroy* comes from a Hebrew word meaning "to put an end to." The idea is that David would silence the slanderer, stop him from carrying out his secret smear campaign against another person. He would not tolerate backstabbing! People in powerful positions must have a strong policy to deal severely with those who try to advance their position by tearing someone else down.

The Proud

No one who has a haughty look and an arrogant heart
   will I endure. (v. 5b)

David refuses to abide an arrogant person. You will notice that pride reveals itself in the face, "a haughty look," but its source is "an arrogant heart." Proverbs 21:4 also links the proud heart with a haughty appearance. A practical problem associated with arrogant people is the byproduct of pride: an argumentative spirit. Show me a proud person—really haughty—and I'll show you one who brings contention and arguments into almost every situation. Pride must have its say and its way! Listen again to Solomon, the wise: "Through insolence comes nothing but strife, but wisdom is with those who receive counsel" (Prov. 13:10).

The Faithful

My eyes shall be upon the faithful of the land. (v. 6a)

I came across an interesting thought in my study of the Scriptures. On two occasions in the book of Proverbs the same question is asked—once with regard to men and the other with regard to women. The question: "Who can find . . .?" The question suggests that something is so rare, you can hardly find an example!

Proverbs 20:6 asks, "Who can find a trustworthy man?" Proverbs 31:10 asks, "An excellent wife who can find?" The two questions imply that it is hard to find faithfulness among men, and among women, strength of character is rare. (The term translated "excellent" refers to excellence of character.)

While David couldn't endure the proud, he longed to dwell with the faithful of the land. He had discovered that the faithful person, while not always in agreement, supports the leader's vision and agenda. Without faithful people to fulfill their roles, leadership cannot succeed.

Making It Strong in Your Soul

Paul warned, "Do not be deceived: 'Bad company corrupts good morals'" (1 Cor. 15:33). Write your name in the center of a sheet of paper. Then, write the names of the people with whom you spend the most time. Beside each name, describe his or her foremost quality, either positive or negative. Do your surrounding influences encourage you to become a better person?

Day 5: *Psalm 101*

Response to Others

Psalm 101, David's spiritual manifesto in song, began with a list of admirable qualities the king desired to cultivate. He then took a good look around him to determine how he would respond to different kinds of individuals based on their positive or negative influence.

The Blameless

> He who walks in a blameless way is the one who will
>   minister to me. (v. 6b)

David admits that there is a certain category of people who minister to him, who serve him. He says that they are the "blameless" people—not perfect people, but men and women whose conduct is above reproach. In my opinion, this is the single most important trait to be found among ministers—among all those who shepherd, counsel, teach, and serve others. Maintaining a standard of conduct that is above reproach must become an indispensable qualification of God's servants. When integrity breaks down—or even the appearance of it—one forfeits the ability to lead in a high-profile capacity.

The Deceiver

He who practices deceit shall not dwell within my house. (v. 7a)

David's original term for "dwell" in this verse is different from the previous verse. In this context, the term literally means "to sit." It's used figuratively the same way we might say a person "occupies a seat in Parliament" or "has won a seat in Congress." It refers to a place of responsibility or authority. David has determined that a hypocrite or deceiver will have no authority or responsibility in his administration. Deception has to do with keeping back the full story or hiding the real motive behind an action. It is the act of deliberately causing someone to be misled. If you have ever dealt with a deceiver, you know why David felt so strongly about this.

The Liar

He who speaks falsehood shall not maintain his position
before me. (v. 7b)

The king had a policy: anyone caught in a lie cannot keep his position of authority. Trust has been broken. A person who will lie once will most likely lie again. If you're in business or you occupy a leadership position, you are unwise if you tolerate an untruthful employee. Leadership depends upon reliable information. How can you steer the organization without clear sight? Morale depends upon healthy relationships, and relationships are built upon trust. You cannot maintain teamwork with even one liar in the group.

The Wicked

> Every morning I will destroy all the wicked of the land,
> So as to cut off from the city of the LORD all those who
>   do iniquity. (v. 8)

This is quite a conclusion! He has mentioned several types of people and forcefully declared himself regarding each one, but this is the strongest of all. The term "wicked" is a judicial term referring to those who commit a crime and then are found guilty by a court. This is not merely someone with bad character; the "wicked" are criminals. The phrase "those who do iniquity" are people who commit crimes. The verb "destroy" translates a Hebrew term that means "to put an end to, cut off, vanish, wipe out."

David resolves to rid the capital city of criminals by any means necessary, including execution, though not exclusively. He says, in effect, "I'm going to wipe the capital city clean of all criminals so it will be unsafe for people to commit crimes." He promises to clean up city hall.

David's credo promises to assemble an honest government administration, from top to bottom. He commits to a high degree of moral conduct personally, and he resolves to hold everyone in his government to the same standard. In doing this, he expects to discern the will of God—having cleared away the distractions of bad character—and to pursue his divine purpose to the end of his days.

Making It Strong in Your Soul

David chose to define himself by four primary values: honor, integrity, honesty, and purity. Choose four values you will cultivate as your own defining qualities. David chose to surround himself with quality people. With whom do you plan to associate more often? David rid his home and workplace of all negative influence. What needs to be removed from your home and workplace?

THE GRIND OF SORROW AND GRIEF

I love the LORD, because He hears
My voice and my supplications.
Because He has inclined His ear to me,
Therefore I shall call upon Him as long as I live.
The cords of death encompassed me
And the terrors of Sheol came upon me;
I found distress and sorrow.
Then I called upon the name of the LORD:
"O LORD, I beseech You, save my life!"
Gracious is the LORD, and righteous;
Yes, our God is compassionate.
The LORD preserves the simple;
I was brought low, and He saved me.
Return to your rest, O my soul,
For the LORD has dealt bountifully with you.
For You have rescued my soul from death,
My eyes from tears,
My feet from stumbling.
I shall walk before the LORD
In the land of the living.
I believed when I said,
"I am greatly afflicted."
I said in my alarm,
"All men are liars."
What shall I render to the LORD
For all His benefits toward me?
I shall lift up the cup of salvation
And call upon the name of the LORD.
I shall pay my vows to the LORD,

Oh may it be in the presence of all His people.
Precious in the sight of the LORD
Is the death of His godly ones.
O LORD, surely I am Your servant,
I am Your servant, the son of Your handmaid,
You have loosed my bonds.
To You I shall offer a sacrifice of thanksgiving,
And call upon the name of the LORD.
I shall pay my vows to the LORD,
Oh may it be in the presence of all His people,
In the courts of the LORD's house,
In the midst of you, O Jerusalem.
Praise the LORD!

(Psalm 116)

Day I: *Psalm 116*
Sadness Abounds

It is easy for those who are strong and healthy to forget how many tears of sorrow and grief are shed every day. All around this aching world—perhaps in your own home or in your heart this very week—sadness abounds. Tears fall. Grief has you in its grip. And it can happen so fast.

I remember speaking with a young man on our support staff at a church I once served. He was all smiles about his future, such a contagious fellow. But before nightfall that same day he was killed in an automobile-motorcycle collision. In a matter of hours, laughter turned to tears. His family suddenly found themselves grieving his absence. Such is the groan of humanity.

The composer of Psalm 116 understood the grind of grief and sorrow all too well. We don't know the details of what brought the psalmist to his knees in mourning; we can only surmise from the clues he offers in the lyrics of this ancient lament that it involved death. He states that "the cords of death encompassed" him as well as "the terrors of Sheol" (the grave). He admits that he "found distress and sorrow" in whatever he was enduring. A few lines later he declares that he was "brought low" and the Lord rescued his "eyes from tears." Then, somehow, his God put him back on his feet so firmly and brought back his perspective so clearly, he was able to write, "Precious in the sight of the LORD is the death of His godly ones" (Ps. 116:15).

Amazing! From the pit to the pinnacle . . . from agony to ecstasy. The same one who begins the song in the dark valley of sorrow and grief (vv. 1–2) ends it in the most magnificent statement of praise a Jew could utter: "Hallelujah!" (v. 19), which is translated, "Praise the Lord."

The psalmist, after passing through the deep valley of grief, sits down and recounts his experience. The song is his personal testimony; first, of his love for the Lord who saw him through the turbulent waters of distress, sorrow, and grief (vv. 1–11); and second, of his desire to return his thanks to the Lord for seeing him through it all (vv. 12–19). In outline form, the song could appear:

I. I love the Lord! (vv. 1–11)
    A. Because He hears me (vv. 1–2)
    B. Because He rescues me (vv. 3–6, 8–11)
    C. Because He cares for me (v. 7)
II. What shall I render to the Lord? (vv. 12–19)
    A. I shall proclaim His benefits (vv. 12–13)
    B. I shall pay my vows (vv. 14, 18–19)
    C. I shall praise His name (vv. 15–17)

Making It Strong in Your Soul

What event caused you the most grief and sorrow? How did it affect your perspective on life? How did it affect your relationship with God? What brought you out of that dark season? What ended your grief?

Day 2: *Psalm 116*
A Song of Sadness

salm 116 is the lament of a man surrounded by grief and sorrow, most likely because death has touched his life. Let's take a few moments this week to probe a little deeper into a song of sadness.

The first line of the psalmist's song is surprising. He writes, "I love the LORD, because . . ." (v. 1). In the nineteenth century a young English girl, Elizabeth Barrett, suffered a spinal injury at age fifteen that left her a semi-invalid for many years. Although she regained strength prior to her marriage to Robert Browning in 1846, she was hesitant to burden him with the responsibilities of caring for a disabled wife. Her love for him was beautifully expressed in her work, *Sonnets from the Portuguese*, as she wrote the immortal words: "How do I love thee? Let me count the ways." She then held nothing back as she described the "depth and breadth and height" of her love. In the same way the psalmist expresses his deepest affection for his Lord. He then counts the ways.

Because He Hears Me

I love the LORD, because He hears
My voice and my supplications.
Because He has inclined His ear to me,
Therefore I shall call upon Him as long as I live. (vv. 1–2)

1. He hears my voice.
2. He inclines His ear to me.

These are two distinct responses, not one and the same. The first, "He hears," simply means that when the psalmist speaks, God listens; God pays attention to what he has to say. The second, "He inclines," is from the Hebrew *natah*, meaning "to bend, turn aside." It implies interest, as when someone turns to face you, stops doing something to give you undivided attention, or leans closer to hear what you have to say.

For example, Solomon uses it in Proverbs 7:21–22 to describe the response of a man who is seduced by a harlot and "follows her." It appears in 1 Kings 11:4 to describe how Solomon's wives "turned away" his heart after other gods. The psalmist says that he loves the Lord because God "bends down," as it were, and "turns aside" from His infinite work . . . as He pays close attention to him in his sorrow and grief. God never turns His back on those who cry out to Him through tears. When God seems farthest away, He actually "bends closer."

Because He Delivers/Rescues Me

Take a few moments now to read vv. 3–6, 8–11 carefully.

Some tragic circumstance had surrounded the writer. Some terrible, painful experience caused him to say that he was near death. I know from personal experience that grief and sorrow can become so intense, death feels imminent. The psalmist cries out to God like a man in freefall; he even confesses to doubting the Lord and falling into sin.

I believe Spurgeon best captures the pathos of the psalmist's situation as he writes:

> As hunters surround a stag with dogs and men, so that no way of escape is left, so was David enclosed in a ring of deadly griefs. The bands of sorrow, weakness, and terror with which death is accustomed to bind men ere he drags them away to their long captivity were all around him. . . . Horrors such as those which torment the lost seized me, grasped me, found me out, searched me through and through, and held me a prisoner. . . . these were so closely upon him that they fixed their teeth in him as hounds seize their prey.[14]

14 Charles Haddon Spurgeon, *The Treasury of David*, vol. 5 (New York: Funk & Wagnalls, 1882), 281–282.

The marvelous part of it, however, is that the Lord delivered him; He rescued him. Though reduced in strength, slandered in character, depressed in spirit, sick in body, and grief-stricken, the psalmist testifies that the Lord stuck by his side! He always will. God doesn't ditch us; He doesn't leave the sinking ship; He doesn't retreat when the enemy increases strength. Our Lord is a specialist when it comes to deliverance, and you can claim that fact this moment!

We are not surprised to see that the psalmist says he will therefore "walk before the LORD" (v. 9) because of His deliverance. It is a natural reaction or desire to spend time with someone who stayed with us during some painful experience we endured.

Making It Strong in Your Soul

People enduring intense grief and sorrow often begin to doubt the Lord. Why do you think this happens? What did the psalmist do? What did you do in response to doubt? Knowing what you know now, what will you do if grief and sorrow prompts doubt in the future?

♬

Day 3: Psalm 116
A Song of Deliverance

The psalmist's lament in Psalm 116 continues with reasons to love the Lord despite the soul-crushing burden of grief and sorrow.

Because He Cares for Me

Return to your rest, O my soul,
For the LORD has dealt bountifully with you. (v. 7)

Look at that! The words "dealt bountifully" are a translation of the Hebrew *gamal*, which means "to deal fully and completely" with something or someone. Frequently, it suggests the idea of "rewarding." Today we would say, "Because the Lord takes such good care of me, I will love Him in return." In other words, God leaves nothing out when He provides for us, when He takes care of us, when He surrounds us with His watchful care. Having been lifted up and sustained in his grief, the songwriter then asks: "What shall I render to the Lord?"

In other words: *How can I return my thanks? What will possibly suffice as proof of my gratitude? God has done so very, very much, how can I adequately render my appreciation to Him? How can I possibly repay?* In response to that question, the songwriter offers three answers: (1) proclaim His benefits, (2) pay my vows, and (3) praise His name. Let's consider each one.

I Shall Proclaim His Benefits

I shall lift up the cup of salvation
And call upon the name of the LORD. (v. 13)

What does "I shall lift up the cup of salvation" mean? In the Old Testament the word "cup" is frequently used to denote plenty and abundance. You may remember that in Psalm 23:5 David claims that his "cup overflows." The term salvation actually appears in the Hebrew Bible in the plural—salvations. We would grasp the meaning better if we'd render it "deliverances." The psalmist is expressing praise to God for His abundant and numerous deliverances. So, literally, he says, "In the name of the Lord I shall proclaim." It is the idea of openly declaring that God is his Deliverer.

This matter of making a public proclamation in honor of the Lord is important. It is good. It is healthy. It is biblical. God floods our lives with abundance, yet so few Christians share their experiences publicly. So few Christians "proclaim His benefits." Let's stop holding our praise to ourselves. Share your Savior; don't be ashamed or shy. If you want to render something of value to the Lord, proclaim His benefits! It may surprise you how much it helps you to live beyond the grind of sorrow and grief.

Making It Strong in Your Soul

Take some time to review the times God has delivered you from danger or difficulty. Put a few of them in story form, rehearsing the narratives in your mind as if you're telling them at a dinner party. Then, ask the Lord for opportunities to tell the stories of God's goodness to you. Be ready! He will give you more than one occasion.

Day 4: *Psalm 116*
A Public Response

Psalm 116, a lament of grief and sorrow, takes a positive turn with the composer deciding how he will respond to the Lord's deliverance. He promised to tell the story of God's rescue; now he determines to take his public announcement to the next level.

I Shall Pay My Vows

I shall pay my vows to the LORD,
Oh may it be in the presence of all His people. (v. 14)

I shall pay my vows to the LORD,
Oh may it be in the presence of all His people,
In the courts of the LORD's house,
In the midst of you, O Jerusalem.
Praise the LORD! (vv. 18–19)

A vow is a solemn promise to which you commit yourself before God. The vows found in the Bible are quite serious and binding.

I also notice that biblical vows were always voluntary, but once made, God made them compulsory. We may want to forget our vows today, but God never does.

The psalmist declares that he can render his gratitude to the Lord by keeping his promises, preferably before the public. I recently discovered an excellent passage of Scripture regarding vows.

> Do not be hasty in word or impulsive in thought to bring up a matter in the presence of God. For God is in heaven and you are on the earth; therefore let your words be few. When you make a vow to God, do not be late in paying it; for He takes no delight in fools. Pay what you vow! It is better that you should not vow than that you should vow and not pay. Do not let your speech cause you to sin and do not say in the presence of the messenger of God that it was a mistake. Why should God be angry on account of your voice and destroy the work of your hands? (Ecclesiastes 5:2, 4–6)

Serious, isn't it? The Bible says that it is better not to vow at all than to vow and not keep your word. When you keep your vows, you bring honor to God. When you break your vow, you give the enemies of God more ammunition. The psalmist determined to show his gratitude publicly by honoring his vows.

Making It Strong in Your Soul

What promises have you made to the Lord or to others? A vow can be a verbal agreement, a written contract, an implied commitment to follow through on something, even a duty accompanying a role or position. What can you do this week to follow through on your promises?

Day 5: *Psalm 116*

From the Depths to the Heights

In just a few verses, the songwriter of Psalm 116 has climbed from the utter depths of grief and sorrow to the heights of praising God. His journey undoubtedly took many months, however. The song merely recounts his ordeal.

While his praising God marks the pinnacle of his climb, it also appears to be his means of getting there. He didn't wait until he felt better before giving the Lord praise.

I Shall Praise His Name

Precious in the sight of the LORD
Is the death of His godly ones.
O LORD, surely I am Your servant,
I am Your servant, the son of Your handmaid,
You have loosed my bonds.
To You I shall offer a sacrifice of thanksgiving,
And call upon the name of the LORD. (vv. 15–17)

Finally, the psalmist declares his thanks and praises God's name in appreciation for all His goodness. Strangely, though, the songwriter mentions "the death of His godly ones" as a part of his praise. Why? I think the answer is connected to his tragic experience mentioned earlier in verses 3–4, 6, and 8. In fact, I believe the psalmist had been delivered from death, perhaps as a lone survivor. In verse 16, he mentions himself as "the son of Your handmaid" from whom he had been "loosed." In other words, he had been loosed from the bonds of death, if I interpret this correctly. I suggest that the calamity and grief mentioned earlier quite probably snuffed out the life of several of his loved ones, likely including his mother—which resulted in his tears and grief (v. 8), sorrow and disillusionment (vv. 10-11). Even in these circumstances, he rendered his praise to God.

He calls the death of these loved ones "precious" in God's sight. I don't think this means that God took delight in the fact that they died, but that He considered their deaths honorable. Moreover, they didn't die anonymously, without the Lord's notice. He was intensely aware of their passing, and He gave value to their ordeal.

None of God's people pass from this world to the next without God's notice. When they die, He is present and He cares. According to other passages of Scripture, the goodness of God becomes their possession when they enter His presence to be with Him forever. While the composer mourns the passing of his loved ones, and laments how much he misses being with them, he knows they will no longer have to suffer the grind of grief and sorrow. They will never shed tears of sadness again.

In this way, the psalmist praised God in the midst of his own grief because he knew the Lord would raise a wonderful tomorrow from the ashes of today. That is the way it ought to be. Our praise and thanksgiving should be expressed regardless. When we learn to give thanks in everything, we will discover God's most basic lessons for our lives—even in times of distress—even in times of sorrow and grief.

Making It Strong in Your Soul

Don't wait for circumstances to improve before you begin praising the Lord. Remember His past deliverance and claim His promise of future deliverance. Make praising God a conscious decision and make plans now to join others in worship. When is your next opportunity?

THE GRIND OF LOW ENTHUSIASM

Aleph.

How blessed are those whose way is blameless,
Who walk in the law of the LORD.
How blessed are those who observe His testimonies,
Who seek Him with all their heart.
They also do no unrighteousness;
They walk in His ways.
You have ordained Your precepts,
That we should keep them diligently.
Oh that my ways may be established
To keep Your statutes!
Then I shall not be ashamed
When I look upon all Your commandments.
I shall give thanks to You with uprightness of heart,
When I learn Your righteous judgments.
I shall keep Your statutes;
Do not forsake me utterly!

(Psalm 119:1–8)

Mem.

O how I love Your law!
It is my meditation all the day.
Your commandments make me wiser than my enemies,
For they are ever mine.
I have more insight than all my teachers,
For Your testimonies are my meditation.
I understand more than the aged,
Because I have observed Your precepts.

(Psalm 119:97–100)

Day 1: *Psalm 119*
Needing More

Interesting word, *enthusiasm*. It's derived from two Greek terms, *en* (meaning "in") and *theos* (meaning "God"), carrying the idea of being inspired. In the original sense of the word, a person was so overtaken with the presence of God, he or she could barely contain the excitement. That makes sense. The truth of God applied to our circumstances brings a burst of enthusiasm nothing else can provide.

New homes, boats, cars, and clothes give us a temporary "high"—until the payments grind on. A new job is exciting, but that dries up in a few months. A new marriage partner makes us feel "up," until the daily grind begins to erode the fun memories of a fantasy honeymoon. All those things may eventually leave us feeling responsible or disappointed or disillusioned, sometimes even a little bored. We need something more than what the world can provide, something more substantial. We need "God in."

Psalm 119—the longest song in the ancient hymnal—is a song that is full of "God in" kind of statements. Over and over it affirms the value of having God's Word in our lives. It keeps pounding away on that theme with a heavy, powerful beat to the music. There is one statement after another announcing the joys, the fresh motivation, the unique benefits of God's Book in our lives. Let's get a grasp of the whole song before we concentrate our attention on a few select stanzas.

The Passage and Its Pattern
This is the longest song. Not only that, it is the longest chapter in the whole Bible, comprised of 176 verses. No other chapter even comes close in length.

The song has an unusual feature that can only be appreciated in Hebrew. Most Bibles follow the original structure of the song by dividing it into twenty-two sections, eight verses each. Each section has a title, such as "Aleph," "Beth," "Gimel," etc. These words are really not words at all, but the letters that comprise the Hebrew alphabet. There are twenty-two letters in all, which explains the song's composition in twenty-two sections. Within each section of this ancient hymn, each verse begins with the same Hebrew letter. In other words, all eight verses in the "Aleph" section of the psalm begin with the letter "Aleph." This poetical structure called "acrostic" made the song easier to memorize.

The psalm carries the Word of God as its theme. I have found only a very few verses that fail to mention the Scriptures. The composer employs several synonyms for Scripture throughout the song. Some are:

Word	Testimonies
Law	Judgments
Ways	Statutes
Paths	Commandments
Precepts	Ordinances

The purpose of the psalm is to give praise to God for His Word, and then demonstrate how we are to behave in relation to Scripture. An old German version of the Bible places the following description at the head of Psalm 119: "This is the Christian's Golden ABCs of the praise, love, power, and use of the Word of God."

Making It Strong in Your Soul

Trying to accomplish goals with a lack of enthusiasm is like trying to run with a set of weights tied to your waist. What issues or difficulties are you dragging? To help identify what's robbing your enthusiasm, think of an activity or responsibility and then answer this question by filling in the blanks:

I would enjoy _____ if _____ didn't weigh heavily on my mind.

For example, "I would enjoy *parenting* if *fear of failure* didn't weigh heavily on my mind." Identify as many issues as you can.

♔

Day 2: Psalm 119

A Spiritual Problem

The psalmist's lengthy poem about the Word of God holds the keys to regaining enthusiasm. Psalm 119 helps to identify issues that drag us down so we can address them with wisdom from above. After all, a lack of enthusiasm isn't a problem with emotions; it's a spiritual problem that can't be corrected with a pep talk or even a happy experience.

Many well-meaning folks are seeking what I would call a "spiritual high," which is really nothing more than an emotional distraction from the pain of their aching, monotonous lives. As a result, you will find people driving miles and miles to attend nightly meetings or standing in long lines to experience some high-level delight that will send them back home on the crest of ecstasy. But all this inevitably leads to deeper emotional lows.

If we think of the spirit as needing food, the problem is often malnutrition. God's Word—His written Truth—provides the Christian with all the nutrients and true enthusiasm he or she can absorb. Coupled with the indwelling Holy Spirit's motivating power, God's Word can virtually transform a life. But the effects are not instantaneous. You can't reverse the effects of physical starvation with just one meal.

Believers need to get back to the basics! If Psalm 119 says anything, it says we must be willing to consume a steady diet of truth from His Book and digest the principles it contains. Pore over it.

Pray over it. Read it. Study it. Memorize sections of it. Meditate upon it. Let it saturate your thinking. Use it when problems arise. Filter your decisions through it. Don't let a day pass without spending time alone with God, listening to the silent voice of His eloquent Word.

All other attempts to gain spiritual growth lead to frustration. I know; I've tried many of them. With each one my enthusiasm waned; with God's Word my enthusiasm grows. Nothing enables us to live beyond the grind of low enthusiasm like a daily application of His Word to our situation—absolutely nothing!

Look at an example. Turn to Psalm 119:97–100. I want to reinforce my point by considering the songwriter's words regarding the benefits of consistent scriptural input.

> O how I love Your law!
> It is my meditation all the day.
> Your commandments make me wiser than my enemies,
> For they are ever mine.
> I have more insight than all my teachers,
> For Your testimonies are my meditation.
> I understand more than the aged,
> Because I have observed Your precepts.

I once came across a powerful quote by Daniel Webster that illustrates what the composer is saying here in verse 97. In the presence of Professor Sanborn of Dartmouth College, Mr. Webster laid his hand on a copy of the Scriptures as he said, "This is *the* Book. I have read through the entire Bible many times. I now make it a practice to go through it once a year. It is the Book of all others for lawyers as well as divines; and I pity the man who cannot find in it a rich supply of thought, and of rules for his conduct. It fits man for life—it prepares him for death."[15]

---

15 Daniel Webster, quoted in Stephen Abbott Northrop, *A Cloud of Witnesses: The Greatest Men in the World for Christ and the Book* (Fort Wayne, IN: The Mason Long Publishing Co., 1894), 491.

Making It Strong in Your Soul

Using a concordance or a topical index of the Bible, search for Scripture related to the issues you listed earlier. If you know a pastor or someone very familiar with the Bible, have him or her help you find answers to the spiritual weights dragging you down. Discover the timeless principles taught in Scripture and apply them.

Day 3: *Psalm 119*
A Lack of Knowledge

Sometimes the grind of low enthusiasm results from not having sufficient knowledge to address life's difficulties. While additional training in management or finances or parenting or vocational skills can certainly help, all knowledge must be built upon a foundation of spiritual wisdom. In verses 98–100 of Psalm 119, the composer speaks of the superiority of the Word over three sources of truth held in high esteem by the world.

1. The Word makes us wiser than our enemies.

> Your commandments make me wiser than my enemies,
> For they are ever mine. (v. 98)

The world places great importance on knowledge gained from experience. In this case, the songwriter mentions experience in dealing with our enemies. But he says that the one who has a grasp of the Word is wiser than his enemies. Sometimes difficult people can drag our enthusiasm down. Divine wisdom will help us rise above the negative effects of people who drag us down.

2. The Word gives us more insight than all our teachers.

> I have more insight than all my teachers,
> For Your testimonies are my meditation. (v. 99)

The world also emphasizes the importance of getting knowledge from education. While additional knowledge in a field of study or training in a particular skill never hurts, the Lord says that the one who knows the Word possesses more insight than his educators. What good is an Ivy League education in business or law if you don't know how to live wisely? What help is a vocational certification if moral foolishness leads you astray?

3. The Word causes us to have more understanding than the aged.

> I understand more than the aged,
> Because I have observed Your precepts. (v. 100)

I wholeheartedly encourage respect for older people. I'm becoming one of them! Yet I have noticed that age doesn't necessarily lead to understanding. On the contrary, I have observed many old fools and have learned from many young sages. Verse 100 declares that one who obeys God's Word gains more understanding than many years without the benefit of the Scriptures. In Job 32:8–9, we find a similar observation:

> But it is a spirit in man,
> And the breath of the Almighty gives them understanding.
> The abundant in years may not be wise,
> Nor may elders understand justice.

A knowledge and application of the written truths of the Word will better equip us for life than the combined advantages of hard-knock experiences, dedicated teachers, and even decades of living. The Scriptures provide more than mere knowledge. From the Bible, we receive insight. Insight translates to effectiveness. Effectiveness leads to success. Success builds confidence. And confidence inspires enthusiasm.

Making It Strong in Your Soul

On a scale of 0 to 100, what would you rate your knowledge of the vocation you have chosen? Using the same scale, rate your knowledge of the Bible and its principles. What about your level of spiritual wisdom? How important is social or emotional intelligence in your line of work? What are the practical benefits of divine truth in your vocation and other dimensions of your life, such as marriage, family, finances, etc.?

Day 4: *Psalm 119*
God's Word the Cure

As I glance over Psalm 119:98–100, I see three benefits gained by those who absorb the Word: wisdom, insight, and understanding. To illustrate the meaning and distinction of each, I will use a simple diagram.

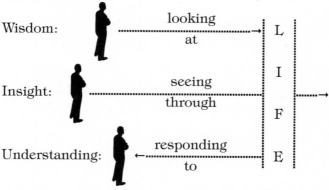

Wisdom is the ability to *look at* life and its difficulties from God's point of view. As I learn more of the Word of God and begin to get a grasp of its practical principles, I also gain the ability to look at life from a heavenly, eternal viewpoint. I see the world through the eyes of someone who is infinitely wise, entirely good, and whose agenda includes the wellbeing of all people. Consequently, I begin to see my circumstances as opportunities He has designed to develop me and train me as His vessel. This removes bitterness and irritation from my life and replaces them with gratitude and enthusiasm!

Insight is the ability to *see through* life and its difficulties from God's viewpoint. In other words, as I grow in the Word, I gain the ability to penetrate the surface level of irritations and problems. I am given insight to see the real causes for certain situations, much like God can see beneath the outer mask (1 Sam. 16:7). I can see, as it were, the inner workings of situations so that I might make strategic decisions rather than simply react. Make no mistake about it, teachers can communicate knowledge, but the Word alone can give you insight.

Understanding is the ability to respond to life's situations and difficulties from the holistic, panoramic comprehension of God's viewpoint. As I get a hold on the Word, I not only gain insight to see the inner workings of a matter, I discover how to respond to effect the best outcome. I am able to learn from my decisions, even when things don't turn out my way. I find that my attitude is as important to God as my activity—often more so!

Making It Strong in Your Soul

Low enthusiasm often results from hopelessness. Hopelessness usually results from feelings of helplessness. According to Psalm 119, regular interaction with God's Word is the cure to hopelessness and helplessness. Consider reading one chapter of Proverbs each day for thirty-one days.

♌

Day 5: Psalm 119
The Truth Perspective

As we conclude our all-too-brief examination of Psalm 119, let's put *wisdom*, *insight*, and *understanding* to the test by looking at a case study.

Let's imagine you recently got a job that has proven to be less than you expected. You prayed for employment, then, lo and behold, this job opened up. You were grateful. After a few weeks, however, you have found that the working conditions leave much to be desired. Furthermore, the fellow employees are all non-Christian and petty. Your first and natural response would be disappointment, perhaps even disillusionment. This would lead to daily irritations and possible arguments with others. Your life could soon become consumed by negative, pessimistic assaults on others—maybe even God. Exit motivation. Enter low enthusiasm.

How much better to apply some basic, biblical principles! Let's say you were deeply into God's Word, absorbing wisdom, cultivating insight, gaining understanding. You discover from Romans 8:28 that God uses all things for your good, even unpleasant experiences. You also discover from Romans 5:3–5 that God uses difficult times to help us grow mature in faith.

> And not only this, but we also exult in our tribulations, knowing that tribulation brings about perseverance; and perseverance, proven character; and proven character, hope; and hope does not disappoint, because the love of God has been poured out within our hearts through the Holy Spirit who was given to us.

This truth gives you a different perspective. You are the Lord's personal "project." His plan is to develop you into a mature, stable person. He has your good at heart. Nothing is coincidental in the Christian life; all things (even your miserable job!) are tools in God's hands, and He is lovingly shaping your character. You learn to accept that your job, with all its limitations and irritations, is a perfect place for God to mature you and make you more like His Son. Rather than resist or look for the first escape, you resolve to greet each day as another opportunity to grow in grace toward others and submission to Him. Wisdom helps you look at your situation from His viewpoint.

Then, those who work around you don't bother you as much because God's Word has taught you how to see through their surface problems. You now see that their verbal assaults are indicative of a deeper problem of inner unrest. You also learn that you need not take their abuse personally, for it really isn't directed at you personally. Soon, your insight has saved you from an ugly, irritating, retaliatory spirit. Instead of arguing with them, you find ways to help your coworkers.

You have now begun to respond to your once-irritating occupation with a positive attitude. Time spent in the Letter of James, for example, has taught you to be very careful about what you say and how you behave before those who don't know Christ personally. Furthermore, in your doing a diligent job regardless of the circumstances, you have gleaned understanding. And to your own great surprise, you have actually begun to enjoy and accept the challenge of your situation because you know it is exactly where the Lord wants you. It is an ideal place for making Christ known.

Don't misunderstand. I can't guarantee that through regular interaction with Scripture you can transform your environment. Some circumstances are beyond help. Believe me, as a pastor, I never rule out the possibility of a miraculous divine intervention, but I have become wise enough to recognize my own limitations. So, I don't want to create the impression that you can change the world by gaining spiritual understanding. I guarantee, however, that *you* will be transformed. And through your spiritual growth, the Lord may improve your environment a great deal. Regardless, you will be changed. Your attitude will change. Enthusiasm will fill the void created by helplessness and hopelessness.

God's Word is for you, my friend, not just the theologian or the pastor; it's for you! There is no situation that you cannot face if you are really serious about spending time on a regular basis in the Book of books! And a great place to start is Psalm 119, especially if the grind of low enthusiasm has begun to take its toll.

Making It Strong in Your Soul

Create your own case study based on your experience. Describe in writing a circumstance that you consider your greatest mental, emotional, or spiritual challenge. Read the following passages about trials: John 14:26–27; John 17:13–21; Rom. 8:18–25, 28–39; 2 Cor. 1:3–5; Phil. 4:12–13; James 1:2–6, 12; 1 Peter 1:6–9; 4:12–16, 19. Then, write a description of how you think each passage could be or should be applied to your specific situation.

THE GRIND OF FAMILY LIFE

A Song of Ascents, of Solomon.

Unless the LORD *builds the house,*
They labor in vain who build it;
Unless the LORD *guards the city,*
The watchman keeps awake in vain.
It is vain for you to rise up early,
To retire late,
To eat the bread of painful labors;
For He gives to His beloved even in his sleep.
Behold, children are a gift of the LORD,
The fruit of the womb is a reward.
Like arrows in the hand of a warrior,
So are the children of one's youth.
How blessed is the man whose quiver is full of them;
They will not be ashamed
When they speak with their enemies in the gate.

(Psalm 127)

A Song of Ascents.

How blessed is everyone who fears the LORD,
Who walks in His ways.
When you shall eat of the fruit of your hands,
You will be happy and it will be well with you.
Your wife shall be like a fruitful vine
Within your house,
Your children like olive plants
Around your table.

Behold, for thus shall the man be blessed
Who fears the LORD.
The LORD bless you from Zion,
And may you see the prosperity of Jerusalem
all the days of your life.
Indeed, may you see your children's children.
Peace be upon Israel!

(Psalm 128)

Day I: *Psalms 127 and 128*
Songs of Family Strength

Maybe it doesn't sound very spiritual, but some aspects of family living can be a grind! Rearing a household of busy children, maintaining good communication, living unselfishly with others day in and day out under the same roof, remaining positive and affirming, dealing with strong wills, and handling some of the other domestic challenges can be a first-class chore! Hats off to all who do their very best. To set the record straight, it is worth all the effort. Someday, parents, those children will "rise up and call you blessed." Don't count on it too soon; I said *someday*! I am pleased to discover, therefore, that the ancient songs in God's eternal hymnal do not omit words of encouragement for families.

Periodically, we come across psalms that fit together, forming a unit or a progression of thought. This is true of Psalms 22, 23, and 24. It is also true of Psalms 90 and 91 as well as Psalms 111 and 112. One psalm sets the stage, we might say, while the next resolves the drama.

This is precisely what we find in the two songs we are highlighting this week: Psalms 127 and 128. Both have to do with life in the home. They are domestic psalms. How do we know? Look at 127:1. The opening lines refer to the building of the house. Then 127:3–5 mentions children. The third verse of Psalm 128 pictures the wife, the home, and children again, and Psalm 128:6 even traces the progression of time to one's grandchildren. If you think upon this theme, you also observe the psalmist's idea of national strength being connected to the strong family unit in Psalm 128:5. A nation remains only as strong as its families. A crumbling family life is one of the signs of a crumbling culture.

Evangelist Billy Graham, in his book *World Aflame*, writes discerning yet serious words concerning America:

> The immutable law of sowing and reaping has held sway. We are now the hapless possessors of moral depravity, and we seek in vain for a cure. The tares of indulgence have overgrown the wheat of moral restraint. Our homes have suffered. Divorce has grown to epidemic proportions. When the morals of society are upset, the family is the first to suffer. The home is the basic unit of our society, and a nation is only as strong as her homes. The breaking up of a home does not often make headlines, but it eats like termites at the structure of the nation.[16]

As I mentioned earlier, these two psalms form a progression. They remind me of a historical mural that wraps its way around a room, depicting a progressive story. The progression carries us from the inception of a home all the way through to the blessings of later years. Let me suggest a simple outline:

    I. Inception of the Home (127:1–2)

    II. Children Born within the Home (127:3–5)

    III. Leading the Home (128:1–3)

    IV. Blessings of Later Years beyond the Home (128:4–6)

---

16 Billy Graham, *World Aflame* (New York: Pocket Books, 1967), 19.

Making It Strong in Your Soul

Think about your childhood. Yours may or may not have been a positive experience; regardless, think of a time when you (a) felt secure, (b) were affirmed, (c) learned a valuable lesson, and (d) your loved ones pulled together in a crisis. How can you recreate these positive experiences for your family now? Be specific.

Day 2: *Psalms 127 and 128*
Building a Strong Foundation

The pair of songs on the home, Psalms 127 and 128, begins with a look at the foundation. How does one establish a family legacy that will survive the inevitable crises, and then thrive for generations?

Inception of the Home

Unless the LORD builds the house,
They labor in vain who build it;
Unless the LORD guards the city,
The watchman keeps awake in vain.
It is vain for you to rise up early,
To retire late,
To eat the bread of painful labors;
For He gives to His beloved even in his sleep. (Psalm 127:1–2)

These two verses convey two crucial points:

1. The Lord Himself is to be the center of our home (v. 1). The emphatic repetition of the phrase "unless the Lord" tells us that God's involvement is absolutely essential. Of course, the Lord never picks up a hammer to "build the house" literally; nor does He wield a weapon that He might literally "guard the city." The meaning is that a relationship with Him, based on obedience to

His Word, must be the defining mental, emotional, and spiritual guide for every decision if the home or the nation expects to stand firm. He must be the unseen Guardian of a city, trusted completely, before a city can be considered safe. If such is not the case, all is "in vain" (also mentioned twice). In fact, in the Hebrew sentence structure, the words "in vain" appear first in each clause, emphasizing the emptiness of it all:

> . . . in vain they labor who build it.
> . . . in vain the watchman keeps awake.

Work, strive, fret, worry, plan, strain all you wish, but if a relationship with the Lord is not the very center of your home, and obedience to His Word doesn't guide every decision, no amount of your additional effort can preserve it from falling apart.

2. *The Lord Himself must be the center of our life and work (v. 2).* In keeping with the context of these two songs, verse 2 has reference to making a living—working long and hard hours. His point is that long, hard hours by themselves will never result in a godly, happy home—only "painful labors." And please note that if the Lord is first in our lives, He will reward us even in our sleep. A godly life includes times of rest and relaxation.

There is an ancient Greek motto that I learned many years ago. "You will break the bow if you keep it always bent." That is worth some thought. Do I write to a parent who has become too busy, too hurried, too stressed out? God says He will reward you even in your sleep! Though you may feel too involved to back off and rest, you'd better! And on the other hand, if the Lord is not the very nucleus of your life, all the labor of a lifetime cannot serve as a substitute for Him. Long hours and painful labors, rising early and retiring late can never replace your allegiance to the Lord and His presence in your home. Money cannot replace Christ! Neither can things, or promises that circumstances will change "someday."

So let's get this straight, right at the foundational level of in-struction on a happy home: Christ must be first. You must be a believer in the Lord Jesus Christ and you must marry one who is a believer if you wish to establish your home with full strength and stability. Then, obedience to the commands and principles of Scripture must become the defining value if you hope to build a strong family.

Making It Strong in Your Soul

Take some one-on-one time with each member of your family to dis-cuss his or her relationship with God. Has each accepted His free gift of eternal life by trusting in Jesus Christ? Does each person view the Word of God as the family's rule book for making decisions and conducting life?

🎵

Day 3: Psalms 127 and 128

The Bricks and Mortar

If a relationship with God is the foundation of a home, the chil-dren are the bricks and mortar. Wise King Solomon continues his celebration of the strong home with a focus on the value of children.

Children Born within the Home

> Behold, children are a gift of the LORD,
> The fruit of the womb is a reward.
> Like arrows in the hand of a warrior,
> So are the children of one's youth.
> How blessed is the man whose quiver is full of them;
> They will not be ashamed
> When they speak with their enemies in the gate. (Psalm 127:3–5)

The songwriter grabs our attention with "Behold!" He says, in effect, "Pay attention . . . listen up!" These three verses take us further as they address parents' proper attitude toward children.

Notice three titles the songwriter gives to children: (1) "gift," (2) "reward," and (3) "arrows." Each one calls for some analysis.

The term "gift" is a translation of the Hebrew word that means "property, possession, that which is shared or assigned." Children are the Lord's possessions. Children belong to Him; He graciously assigns to or shares with parents. Now this third verse doesn't say "some children" or even "most children," but simply "children," implying *all* children . . . your children! There is no such thing as an "accidental birth" or a "surprise pregnancy" from God's viewpoint. And wise are the parents who acknowledge the fact that their child is a personal gift from God. If you and I truly believe that each child is "assigned" by God, what a difference it can make with the child we may not have planned!

The word "reward" conveys the idea of pleasure, something given as a tangible proof of appreciation. Children are never to be viewed as punishment for God's displeasure—quite the contrary! The fruit of the womb is a token of God's love, His choice reward.

The word "arrow" is equally meaningful. You'll notice that the word picture is that of a warrior with arrows in his hand. Imagine the scene. A warrior in battle doesn't stop to make his arrows, nor does he ignore them. He uses them. He directs them toward a target. A parent is responsible for the direction of his children. A child, like an arrow, is incapable of directing himself. It is the basic responsibility of parents to direct the early lives of their children. This makes a great deal of sense when you consider that a child is born in a state of depravity and inner sinfulness. You must stop here and read Psalm 51:5 along with Psalm 58:3. Both verses verify that children are born in a state of iniquity. Solomon's saying in Proverbs 22:15 underscores this fact: "Foolishness is bound up in the heart of a child; the rod of discipline will remove it far from him." Children need parental authority.

What happens when a child isn't given direction? Proverbs 29:15 responds, "The rod and reproof give wisdom, but a child who gets his own way brings shame to his mother." On the other hand, look at Proverbs 22:6 for a moment:

Train up a child in the way he should go,
Even when he is old he will not depart from it.

God gives us children with a delegated responsibility to care for what He treasures most in the universe: people. Each child, therefore, is to be cherished as a gift, prized as a reward, and directed like an arrow.

Making It Strong in Your Soul

God has a purpose for each life He creates, and each purpose is as unique as the individual's fingerprint. If you are a parent, write the name of each child on a separate sheet of paper. In a paragraph, describe each child's talents, abilities, interests, and temperament. Then determine how you can best encourage each child to cultivate his or her strengths. This may lead to some meaningful conversations!

***

Day 4: *Psalms 127 and 128*
The Importance of Leadership

Solomon's song of the strong family, Psalms 127 and 128, continues with an emphasis on leadership. Having considered the value of children, he examines the role of leadership in the home.

Leading the Home

How blessed is everyone who fears the LORD,
Who walks in His ways.

When you shall eat of the fruit of your hands,
You will be happy and it will be well with you.
Your wife shall be like a fruitful vine
Within your house,
Your children like olive plants
Around your table. (Psalm 128:1–3)

In Psalm 127, the arrows are in our hands, needing direction. As the songwriter continues his thoughts regarding the family in Psalm 128, he says that "everyone who fears the LORD" will be blessed or happy. The context is the family, remember—specifically, the children God gives. As the progression continues in Psalm 128:1–2, we see how each arrow is to be carefully directed: 1) in the fear of the Lord, and 2) walking in His ways. Again you will notice, happiness will continue to be the surrounding atmosphere ("how blessed").

Parents who train their children according to biblical principles have the hope of ultimate happiness. As a matter of fact, verse 2 says your investment will allow you to "eat of the fruit of your hands" and "it will be well with you." The picture is, again, the hands (as it was in 127:4). Parents' hands enjoy the product of their labor as they "pick the fruit" of the domestic garden they have cultivated. As submission is caught, obedience taught, and understanding sought, the dividends come rolling in!

Verse 3 is such a pleasant picture. The father looks around the supper table. He sees his wife ("a fruitful vine") and children ("olive plants"). I notice that the children are not called "branches" but plants. This seems to emphasize that each offspring is independent, unique, one who will reproduce his own kind in later years. And the difference is also seen in that the mother is pictured as a vine, but the children as olive plants. This is a good and necessary distinction.

We as parents are unwise to assume that our children are put together exactly like we are. The father, for example, who is athletic has a strong tendency to want that same quality to emerge in his son, even to the point of forcing it. The same is true of a mother who is artistic. She persistently urges that talent in her daughter, but frequently that isn't the daughter's interest. Why? To answer with the songwriter's symbols: we are vines, but our children are olive plants. However, regardless of a child's talent (or lack of it), athletic ability (or lack of it), the training we give him or her must be that of spiritual instruction ("fear of the Lord"). A child must be directed toward faith in the Lord Jesus Christ and given an enormous amount of training in the principles of Scripture.

Making It Strong in Your Soul

What are you doing to provide spiritual training and guidance for your children? Training begins with leadership; do your children know you are a student of the Scriptures? How can you establish and maintain a Bible-centered culture in your home without it becoming trite or superficial?

♫

Day 5: *Psalms 127 and 128*
An Investment in the Future

Psalms 127 and 128 conclude with a look into the distant future, painting a portrait of a healthy, mature family. Like a farmer imagines his crop while planting seeds, Solomon helps us envision the fruit of our labor in the home.

Later Years in the Home

Behold, for thus shall the man be blessed
Who fears the LORD.
The LORD bless you from Zion,
And may you see the prosperity of Jerusalem
    all the days of your life.

Indeed, may you see your children's children.
Peace be upon Israel! (Psalm 128:4–6)

The domestic scene now reaches completion. The children are trained, reared, and launched from the nest. The psalmist paints a pleasant picture of serenity, which includes three realms of blessing:

1. Personal pleasure (v. 4). The psalmist says "for thus" happiness comes. For what? For all the hard work and consistent training invested by parents, happiness comes as God's reward. Believe me, if you determine to have Christ as the central figure of your home and His Word as the authority in rearing your children, you have your work cut out for you!

You will find that you'll be outnumbered, scoffed, considered strange by your neighbors (and a few teachers), criticized, misunderstood, and tempted to compromise. The very forces of hell will unleash their fury on you! You will be on your knees and in the Word regularly. But, if you maintain the standard (with love, gentleness, and consistency), God promises that you will look back in your twilight years and enjoy inward, personal pleasure. The converse is also true. If you relinquish your responsibilities as a parent, you can expect sad and serious consequences.

2. Civic benefits (v. 5). Even Zion will be blessed! Jerusalem will be prosperous and strong! The point is this: your offspring will be used to make a dent in society—for good! All the days of your later life, you'll enjoy the fact that your earlier direction and private contribution to the home life of your children pay off in rich, public dividends.

3. National blessings (v. 6). Now, in this final verse, grandchildren arrive on the scene. You, the grandparent, see them, and you witness a second-generation investment. Your own children pass on similar training so that the entire nation benefits and is blessed because the Lord, originally, was at the very center of your home.

Making It Strong in Your Soul

Perhaps the most encouraging thought from our study of these two songs is that we are rearing our nation's future. Take some time to talk about the future with each child in your care—what they hope to become and what they would like to accomplish. Then find tangible ways to encourage their dreams.

The Grind of Impatient Arrogance

A Song of Ascents, of David.

O Lord, my heart is not proud, nor my eyes haughty;
Nor do I involve myself in great matters,
Or in things too difficult for me.
Surely I have composed and quieted my soul;
Like a weaned child rests against his mother,
My soul is like a weaned child within me.
O Israel, hope in the Lord
From this time forth and forever.

(Psalm 131)

Day 1: *Psalm 131*
Genuine Humility

With a mere three verses, Psalm 131 is one of the shortest chapters in the Bible. If it is ever true, however, that good things come in small packages, this psalm is proof of that. Charles Haddon Spurgeon—the prince of preachers—said of this song of David:

> Comparing all the Psalms to gems, we should liken this to a pearl: how beautifully it will adorn the neck of patience. It is one of the shortest Psalms to read, but one of the longest to learn. It speaks of a young child, but it contains the experience of a man in Christ. Lowliness and humility are here

seen in connection with a sanctified heart, a will subdued to the mind of God, and a hope looking to the Lord alone.[17]

He aptly describes this little psalm. It would be missed by the hurried reader and considered of almost insignificant value to one impressed with size and choice of terms, but it nevertheless contains a timely message. David composes lyrics that address a hazardous and dangerous habit in this song: impatient arrogance. He is saying that he is not proud or haughty or interested in being seen, heard, or noticed. In fact, he is announcing his plan to move out of the limelight and away from that place of public attention.

Genuine humility isn't something we can announce very easily. To claim this virtue is, as a rule, to forfeit it. Humility is the fairest and rarest flower that blooms. Put it on display and instantly it wilts and loses its fragrance! Humility is one character trait that should be a "closet utterance," as W. Graham Scroggie puts it,[18] not something we announce from the housetop. Humility is not something to be announced. It simply belongs in one's life, in the private journal of one's walk with God, not in a book that looks like a testimony but comes across more like a "bragimony."

David, however, isn't bragging in Psalm 131; he writes this song as a part of his own devotional life. It is a conversation with the Lord that we are invited to overhear, a brief poem in which he states his convictions concerning his removal from the public eye.

We know nothing of what prompted the writing of this song. As we have already observed, the occasion leading to the writing of many of the ancient biblical songs remains a mystery. We can enter into the occasion in our imagination, however. Often we feel humbled and crushed after we have sinned and/or made a series of mistakes—after we have "blown it." At those times we are genuinely interested in finding the nearest cave and crawling in. At other times, when we get a glimpse of our own pride and become sick of

17 C. H. Spurgeon, *The Treasury of David, Volume 6: Psalms 120-150* (Bellingham, WA: Logos Research Systems, Inc., 2009), 136.
18 Graham Scroggie, *The Psalms*, rev. ed. (London: Pickering & Inglis, 1967), 273.

our deceptive attempts to cover it up, we fall before God and ask to be removed and made obscure. And then there are those occasions of heart-searching experiences: Times of sickness. Days of deep hurt. Painful waiting. Disappointing events. Loss of a loved one. Removal of a friend. Loneliness. Pressure. At those crossroads, the traffic of people seems overbearing, the flashing of lights seems so vain, and the noisy crowd, so repulsive. During such times one longs for obscurity and silent, humble communion with the Creator. Any of these occasions could have prodded the sweet singer of Israel to write this song of humility.

Making It Strong in Your Soul

Write your own definitions to the following terms:

Arrogance

Impatience

Humility

Composure

Beside each word, place the name of a prominent figure who exhibits this quality. What does he or she do to earn the label?

Day 2: Psalm 131
A Proud or Humble Heart

In a matter-of-fact fashion, David addresses the Lord in Psalm 131. Throughout the song he carries on a conversation with his God. While humility is the subject, the focus is himself. Eight times in the first two verses he uses "I," "me," and "my." The poem is a brief glimpse into David's personal journal.

Verse 1

O LORD, my heart is not proud, nor my eyes haughty;

Nor do I involve myself in great matters,
Or in things too difficult for me.

You may remember that in the Hebrew Bible whatever appears first in a clause or sentence is frequently placed in that position for the purpose of emphasis. This is especially true when the phrase is rearranged and written in an awkward, strange manner. This is precisely what we find in verse 1. There are three negatives set forth at the very beginning of three clauses: "not proud," "not haughty," and "nor do I involve myself." David is communicating the depth of his feelings. The structure of his words reveals strong passion. The terms do too.

The term "proud" comes from *gabah*, meaning "to be high, exalted." He mentions his heart first—the root source of pride down deep within. He says that as deeply as God may wish to probe, He will not find a trace of a "high, exalted" attitude within him. God may "search" and "know my heart" (Ps. 139:23) all He wishes, declares David.

The term "haughty" comes from another word having a similar meaning: "room." This Hebrew term means "to be lifted up, raised." The idea is that one who is proud within shows it in his eyes, which are "lifted up, raised." That is exactly what Proverbs 30:11–13 says:

There is a kind of man who curses his father
And does not bless his mother.
There is a kind who is pure in his own eyes,
Yet is not washed from his filthiness.
There is a kind—oh how lofty are his eyes!
And his eyelids are raised in arrogance.

The "proud look" has to do with eyes that are "lifted up." We have all seen this among the pseudo-sophisticates and on the plastic masks worn by many of the Hollywood stars and television celebrities. David declares that both his heart and his eyes will stand the test of God's scrutiny.

There are two simple and quick ways God says the true condition of the heart is revealed. (Many of us may think we can hide it, but we cannot.) The first is through the eyes (as we have seen here) and the second is through the mouth (as Jesus says in Luke 6:45). Of course, one's life is another proof of one's heart condition, but that takes longer to observe. Keen counselors and wise people are careful to listen to words (what is said as well as what isn't said) and watch the eyes of others. You soon discover that the heart is like a well and the eyes and tongue are like buckets which draw water from the same well. If true humility is not in the heart, the eyes will show it.

Making It Strong in Your Soul

Take some time to analyze how you are put together. Do you have to be the center of attention in order to feel fulfilled? Would others think of you as self-assured and confident? Or would they describe you as arrogant? If you really want a complete picture of yourself, ask people closest to you to give their honest impressions.

Day 3: *Psalm 131*
Teachability

David's song, preserved for us as Psalm 131, goes on to say that he does not involve himself in great matters or "things too difficult for him." The idea here is that he doesn't pursue places of prominence or greatness. He recognizes his own limitations based on an honest assessment of his knowledge and skills, and he feels no need to play the hero. He simply doesn't have anything to prove. He is not only willing but, in fact, pleased to be removed from the public platform of fickle applause.

This reminds me of another great man of God: Moses. According to Acts 7:22, he was educated in the finest schools Egypt had to offer. He was gifted with a powerful personality. He was a most impressive man. He was a mighty warrior—brave, brilliant, and even heroic. It was clear to many that he was destined to be the Pharaoh of the land. At age forty, however, he killed an Egyptian and attempted to deliver his people (the Jews) by his own means. Exodus 2:11–15 tells the whole story. This resulted in his fleeing Egypt for the Midian Desert—a hot, dry, forgotten place of obscurity. He lived among shepherds for another forty years, unknown and unapplauded. Think of it! Moses, a prominent member of the royal family, spending his days leading no one but flocks of woolies, utterly removed from people: shelved, sidelined, and silent. F. B. Meyer writes of this experience:

> But Moses was out of touch with God (in Egypt). So he fled, and crossed the desert that lay between him and the eastern frontier; threaded the mountain passes of the Sinaitic peninsula, through which in after years he was to lead his people; and at last sat wearily down by a well in the land of Midian. . . . and finally to the quiet life of a shepherd in the calm open spaces of that wonderful land, which, on more than one occasion, has served for a Divine school.
>
> Such experiences come to us all. We rush forward, thinking to carry all before us; we strike a few blows in vain; we are staggered with disappointment, and reel back; we are afraid at the first breath of human disapprobation; we flee from the scenes of our discomfiture to hide ourselves in chagrin. Then we are hidden in the secret of God's presence from the pride of man. And there our vision clears: the silt drops from the current of our life, as from the Rhone in its passage through the deep waters of Geneva's lake; our self-life dies down; our spirit drinks of the river of God, which is full of water; our faith begins to grasp his arm, and to be the

channel for the manifestation of his power; and thus at last we emerge to be his hand to lead an Exodus.[19]

Moses didn't choose to leave his lofty perch for the life of a lowly shepherd; his own ambition led to humiliation. Fortunately, the Lord used his humiliating experience to help the future leader gain humility. Big difference between being humiliated and becoming humble. God used Moses' failure to mold one of the greatest leaders the world has ever known.

Unlike Moses, David made a conscious choice to slip away and not involve himself in matters of greatness and public glamour. For a time at least, his was to be a life of solitude and meditation.

Making It Strong in Your Soul

We are never more teachable than when we're humble. In fact, teachability is the defining quality of a humble person. What experience has humbled you? What good resulted from this period of humility? Rather than wait to be humbled by circumstances, why not ask the Lord for a humble spirit? Does this make you nervous? If so, why?

Day 4: *Psalm 131*

Composed and Quiet

Having chosen to enter a season of quietness, stepping back from public view, David examines the effect of humility on his soul. Psalm 131 continues with several curious word pictures.

---

19 F. B. Meyer, *Moses* (Grand Rapids: Zondervan Publishing House, 1954), 32–32.

Verse 2

Was that capable and passionate man of war irritated and out of sorts because he had been reduced from captain of the team to spectator? Not in the least. He declares:

> Surely I have composed and quieted my soul;
> Like a weaned child rests against his mother,
> My soul is like a weaned child within me.

I don't find the slightest irritation in his words. The term "composed" means "to be smooth, even, level." The same Hebrew word used here also appears in Isaiah 28:25 with reference to a farmer's field that had once been rough and rugged but was now planted and "level." David is saying that his inner soul is not churning and stormy, but calm and smooth. It is a beautiful description of tranquility and patience. The result is that he is "quieted" within; he is inwardly silent and still.

After the statement declaring his inner calm condition, David gives a tender illustration of a baby quietly resting on its mother—and twice he uses the word "weaned" to describe the child. The little tot no longer strives or frets to get milk from his mother; he's no longer demanding or restless. All is calm. The roughness of self-will has been smoothed and is now calm and contented.

But wait! This isn't complete unless you see how the symbolic analogy fits into David's experience. Let's do that by answering three questions:

1. Who is the child? It is David's inward being.
2. Who is the mother? It is his public life.
3. From what is he weaned? Clearly, from the affirmation of notoriety.

David no longer craves attention. He is weaned from the desire for prominence, the place of honor—the limelight. "I no longer need that," says David. "I'm weaned!"

The term "weaned" also carries the connotation of "mature." David no longer needs the mother's milk of public attention because he is mature enough for solid food gained through humility. Note that the child is still related to the mother. David's position as king necessarily places him in the public eye. He cannot carry out his duties without standing before people. However, like a mature son, he has cut the apron strings. He doesn't depend upon mom anymore.

Making It Strong in Your Soul

David's song depicts the need for public attention as an infant's appetite. What must develop within a person in order to make him or her mature, no longer needful of public affirmation or adoration? Have you matured in this regard? What can you do to develop in areas where you need maturity?

♪

Day 5: Psalm 131
Weaned from Pride

As is true of all of us on special occasions, David had learned a truth that was so exciting he had to share it. He wanted his entire nation to enter into this joyous experience with him. As Psalm 131 concludes, David expresses his desire for the nation he leads.

Verse 3

O Israel, hope in the LORD
From this time forth and forever.

Please allow me a personal comment here. David's little song has been so comforting to me. I have loved its quiet peacefulness. I have needed its message. Perhaps you have too. It is quite possible that God is "weaning" you away from every source of pride. You may have trusted in the fleeting silver and tinsel of this world, only to have it tarnish and melt in your hands. You may have believed in someone only to have him or her fail you and even turn against you. Quite possibly, you have fallen into the trap of self-exaltation and recently failed miserably. Maybe you've been accustomed to honor and public notice, but (like Moses) all that has passed, at least for a while. Perhaps your talent is no longer in demand, or your job is not now needed, or your counsel is no longer sought.

"What's happening?" you may be asking. Arrogance refuses to accept such humbling experiences; patience must take over and consciously command our souls to be still at such times. But "Why?" you may wonder. God is answering your question in Psalm 131.

Perhaps you are being "weaned" from the mother of importance, prestige, public applause, honor, and (dare I say it?) pride. Who does the weaning? The child? No, never. The act of weaning is done *to* the child. All we can do is submit. God is responsible. He is removing every crutch upon which you would lean so you will lean hard upon Him only. (See Prov. 3:5–6.) He is changing your diet to a new kind of food—from the milk of immaturity to the meat of genuine humility. And He wants you to learn this "from this time forth and forever."

Making It Strong in Your Soul

Can you think of someone you admire for his or her genuine humility? Go to the trouble of making a creative "thank you" card that expresses your gratitude. Be specific and detailed. Leave it unsigned and then deliver the card *anonymously*.

The Grind of Lingering Consequences

By the rivers of Babylon,
There we sat down and wept,
When we remembered Zion.
Upon the willows in the midst of it
We hung our harps.
For there our captors demanded of us songs,
And our tormentors mirth, saying,
"Sing us one of the songs of Zion."
How can we sing the LORD's song
In a foreign land?
If I forget you, O Jerusalem,
May my right hand forget her skill.
May my tongue cling to the roof of my mouth
If I do not remember you,
If I do not exalt Jerusalem
Above my chief joy.
Remember, O LORD, against the sons of Edom
The day of Jerusalem,
Who said, "Raze it, raze it
To its very foundation."
O daughter of Babylon, you devastated one,
How blessed will be the one who repays you
With the recompense with which you have repaid us.
How blessed will be the one who seizes and
    dashes your little ones
Against the rock.

(Psalm 137)

Day 1: *Psalm 137*
Consequences of Bad Decisions

No one can deny the relentless pain brought on by enduring the consequences of wrong actions. It may be as quick and simple as the sting following a swat from a parent's paddle or as lingering and severe as a prison sentence. Either one, however, is hard to bear. The person who cheats on a mate and later leaves the marriage must ultimately endure the consequences. The child who runs away from home in a fit of rebellious rage must live with the painful ramifications. The politician who assures his voters of unrealistic and unachievable promises if elected must face his critics after election. The minister who compromises in the realm of ethics or morals must live with the private shame and loss of public respect. The list goes on and on.

Even though our day is characterized by an erosion of personal responsibility and attempts to soft-pedal or cover up the consequences of wrong, those very difficult days in the backwash of disobedience are nevertheless haunting realities. Sin still bears bitter fruit. Devastating consequences still await the transgressor. "Do not be deceived, God is not mocked; for whatever a man sows, this he will also reap" (Gal. 6:7) is still in the Book. Few souls live more somber lives than those who have disobeyed and must now endure the grind of lingering consequences.

Psalm 137 is the mournful song of a people enduring the grind of lingering consequences after a long history of bad decisions. The composer gives voice to the anguish of God's covenant people, removed from their Promised Land, cut off from their birthright. As a band of Jewish POWs, they have been taken by the Babylonians into a foreign land. The first lines set the scene.

By the rivers of Babylon,

There we sat down and wept,

When we remembered Zion. (v. 1)

You can skim through the next eight verses and quickly detect other terms that reveal a prisonlike experience:

Verse 3: "our captors . . . our tormentors"

Verse 4: "a foreign land"

Verse 7: "Remember, O LORD, against the sons of Edom"

Verse 8: "O daughter of Babylon, you devastated one"

Why was a Hebrew writer in Babylon? What were the events that led to his and others' becoming captives of this foreign power? Believe me, it was no accident. It came to pass exactly as God had spoken through His prophet Jeremiah:

Therefore thus says the LORD of hosts, "Because you have not obeyed My words, behold, I will send and take all the families of the north," declares the LORD, "and I will send to Nebuchadnezzar king of Babylon, My servant, and will bring them against this land and against its inhabitants and against all these nations round about. . . . This whole land will be a desolation and a horror, and these nations will serve the king of Babylon seventy years." (Jeremiah 25:8–9, 11)

For centuries, the Lord sent prophets to warn the people of Judah that continued idolatry and disobedience would lead to their exile. But they had persisted in their disobedience for more than three hundred years since the last days of Solomon's reign. The united kingdom of the Jewish nation had split after Solomon's death. A civil war followed. Ten of the twelve tribes of Israel settled in the north under King Jeroboam's leadership. Two settled in the south under King Rehoboam, Solomon's son.

The northern kingdom is called "Israel" in Scripture; the southern kingdom is called "Judah." Israel had nineteen kings during her two-hundred-plus years before she fell to the Assyrians in 722 B.C. Judah had twenty kings—only eight of whom were righteous. For many years, Judah walked a fine line between obedience and rebellion until the Lord allowed the Babylonians (also called Chaldeans) to capture the nation and hold them in bondage for seventy years, exactly as Jeremiah predicted. Psalm 137 was written during (or shortly after) Judah's captivity in Babylon.

Making It Strong in Your Soul

The Lord always warns before He chastises. Have you ever received warnings to put an end to habitual or unrepentant sin? What was (or is) your response? What eventually happened? If you are hearing warnings now, think of a trustworthy person who can help you take heed before it's too late!

Day 2: *Psalm 137*
Losing God's Blessings

The historical background of Psalm 137 is very sad. The people of God failed to heed centuries of warnings and found themselves living with the consequences of disobedience. While God had not removed His fellowship—He loved the people of Judah as much as ever—He stripped them of their covenant blessings. No longer did they live in the land promised to Abraham and his descendants. No longer could they worship in the temple in Jerusalem.

Their experience, enduring the lasting consequences of wrongdoing, has much to teach us about our walk with God. Here is my outline of the song:

   I. Memory of Captivity (vv. 1–3)
     —a personal section—
   II. Devotion to the Lord (vv. 4–6)
     —a patriotic section—

III. Plea for Retribution (vv. 7–9)

—a passionate section—

Few songs in Scripture begin with stronger emotions. The composer feels absolutely dejected! He remembers the bitter humiliation, the stinging sarcasm he and his companions had suffered. He even reminds us of a particular occasion when a representative of Babylon marched those Jews along a river and pummeled them with insults.

> By the rivers of Babylon,
> There we sat down and wept,
> When we remembered Zion.
> Upon the willows in the midst of it
> We hung our harps.
> For there our captors demanded of us songs,
> And our tormentors mirth, saying,
> "Sing us one of the songs of Zion." (vv. 1–3)

Can't you imagine that scene? With their heads hanging low, their shoulders slumped and tears streaming down their cheeks, those Jewish captives sat silent and gritted their teeth. Talk about a daily grind! This was the pit of pits. I can just hear the taunts of the Babylonian guard as he looked out over those downcast, depressed people of Judah: "Hey, how about all you Jews joining in on one of those good ol' hymns of the faith! Let's hear it for that great, big God of yours! Sing it out, now . . . and as you sing, remember Zion!"

Oh, how that hurt! It hurt so deeply the writer remembered the precise words of his tormentor.

The scoffers and critics of Christianity never stand any taller or shout any louder than when God's people publicly fall into sin and are forced to suffer the consequences of disobedience. All Satan's hosts dance with glee when believers compromise, play with fire, then get burned. We've seen a lot of that sort of thing in recent years, haven't we? The secular media have a field day as God's people are forced to take it on the chin. Those captives were getting just what they deserved, and they knew it. There was no more singing, no jokes, and no laughter in that embarrassed Jewish camp on foreign soil. One man describes the scene quite vividly:

> This is the bitterest of all—to know that suffering need not have been; that it has resulted from indiscretion and inconsistency; that it is the harvest of one's own sowing; that the vulture which feeds on the vitals is a nestling of one's own rearing. Ah me! This is pain! There is an inevitable nemesis in life. The laws of the heart and home, of the soul and human life, cannot be violated with impunity. Sin may be forgiven; the fire of penalty may be changed into the fire of trial; the love of God may seem nearer and dearer than ever and yet there is the awful pressure of pain; the trembling heart; the failing of eyes and pining of soul; the harp on the willows; the refusal to sing the Lord's song.[20]

Making It Strong in Your Soul

Do you find yourself on "foreign soil" today? Are the consequences of your sins pressing upon you? Let me urge you to lay your heart bare before your Lord. Tell Him about it. Be certain that the cause of your dreadful experience is thoroughly confessed, that you are not hiding or denying anything. Once you have claimed your Lord's forgiveness, let me urge you to claim His presence and quietly wait for relief. The consequences of sins—yes, even forgiven sins—are often difficult and sometimes lingering. But the Lord isn't cruel; His grace is sufficient (2 Cor. 12:7–10).

---

20 F.B. Meyer, *Christ in Isaiah* (Grand Rapids: Zondervan Publishing House, 1950), 9–10.

Day 3: *Psalm 137*
Remember God's Promises

After relating the anguish of lingering consequences in Psalm 137, the writer does a little self-analysis. His perspective shifts from looking outward to searching within. He asks a reasonable question in verse 4: "How can we sing the LORD's song in a foreign land?"

The question touches on two issues. First, the Jews understood their occupation of Canaan as a necessary part of God's covenant with Abraham. How could they legitimately sing about the faithfulness of God if their covenant no longer existed? But they failed to understand that their exile was temporary; seventy years, as predicted. God had said all along that their hold on the land depended upon their obedience (Deuteronomy 28). So, to answer their question, "Keep My laws, and I'll restore your land to you."

The second issue has to do with sincerity. Genuine singing is spontaneous; it cannot be forced. Nor will it joyfully burst forth from a rebellious heart or a guilty conscience. The captive Jews couldn't sing for joy naturally; they needed supernatural help. The same is true of all people. We are totally unable to experience joy as long as we're enslaved to sin. But when freed by the power of Christ . . .

Paul and Silas were chained in the Philippian jail, but the Christian melodies and songs rang out nonetheless. Physically, they were captives; spiritually, however, they were free. Consequently, they could sincerely sing with joy despite their dismal surroundings (Acts 16:25–26).

Song 137 continues with a refusal to give up hope. While their chastisement was severe, the composer would not stop trusting that God would fulfill His promises. With the zeal of a Jewish patriot, the psalmist declares his devotion to his Lord and to the capital city of his homeland, the land unconditionally promised to Abraham's Hebrew descendants.

How can we sing the Lord's song
In a foreign land?
If I forget you, O Jerusalem,
May my right hand forget her skill.
May my tongue cling to the roof of my mouth
If I do not remember you,
If I do not exalt Jerusalem
Above my chief joy. (vv. 4–6)

Notice that the pronouns change from "we" and "our" to "I" and "my." He says that he will never, ever forget the blessings and benefits of being a citizen of Judah. He says that his song would be forever silenced—he would not skillfully play ("my right hand") or spontaneously sing ("my tongue")—should he forget the marvelous benefits of home. While the composer speaks for himself, let us not forget that he wrote this hymn to be sung by the faithful of Judah. As they joined their voices, each person pledged to remember God's promise regardless of the circumstances.

If you are a believer in Jesus Christ, nothing can break your bond with God (John 10:28–29; Rom. 8:28–39; 2 Tim. 1:12). The lingering consequences of wrongdoing can, however, cause you feel like God has abandoned you. The people of Judah refused to accept this falsehood, and encouraged themselves with the promises of God. They focused on His unfailing goodness despite their faltering devotion.

Making It Strong in Your Soul

Take some time to review these promises of God.

John 14:1–3	1 Cor. 15:51–54	1 John 5:13	Rev. 7:15–17
Ps. 32:5	Prov. 28:13	John 3:17–18	1 John 1:9
Deut. 7:9	Ps. 86:15	Heb. 8:12	Rom. 8:28–39

Memorize the promises you find most compelling and recite them when discouragement begins to overwhelm you.

Day 4: *Psalm 137*
Turning to God

The composer of Psalm 137 acknowledged the sorrow of his situation, recognizing that Judah had brought this chastisement upon themselves. But he didn't stay in the doldrums. He turned from the past to focus on God's unchangeable character, His faithfulness to fulfill promises, His desire to extend mercy with every opportunity. Finally, he turned his eyes to the horizon to anticipate the future.

> Remember, O LORD, against the sons of Edom
> The day of Jerusalem,
> Who said, "Raze it, raze it
> To its very foundation."
> O daughter of Babylon, you devastated one,
> How blessed will be the one who repays you
> With the recompense with which you have repaid us.
> How blessed will be the one who seizes and dashes
>   your little ones
> Against the rock. (vv. 7–9)

It doesn't take a Bible scholar to discover that these are exceedingly emotional words. The writer feels passionate regarding the enemies of his beloved Zion. He mentions the ancient enemy of Edom in verse 7, then Babylon in verse 8. While brimming with zeal, he pronounces blessings upon those God may use to exact revenge against the enemies for their brutal and unmerciful treatment of the Jews. The critic reads this (especially verse 9) and attacks the Old Testament for its outrageous God of wrath. If you and I were of that vintage, it is doubtful that the lyrics of Psalm 137 would seem barbaric.

You probably recall the Adolf Eichmann trial of the past. One of our national periodicals covered the account in vivid detail. The journalist mentioned a Jewish man who had lost his parents and other close relatives in the horrible Nazi concentration camps. He stood abruptly to his feet in the audience of that courtroom and cursed Eichmann. He was told to sit down and restrain himself, which he refused to do. As he was escorted by force from the room, he screamed words to this effect: "Let me get my hands on that Nazi pig . . . just for sixty seconds . . . let me have him that I may torture him with my own hands!"

No one criticized that man who screamed those violent words. In fact, the magazine reporter expressed sympathy. Why? Because the man had suffered such a terrible loss, his memory was full and running over with rage. He longed for justice.

Note that the psalmist doesn't ask for divine permission to exact vengeance on his own terms, only that God might bring justice upon the heads of all who behaved cruelly toward Judah. According to Isaiah 13:14–16, the Babylonians brutally murdered the little Jewish children before their parents' eyes. With passionate pleas, the writer of this song concludes with a request for justice. By the end of the song, he rests his case with God.

Making It Strong in Your Soul

Think of a few consequences brought about by your own wrong-doing or foolishness. Pause now to thank the Lord for His mercy. He could have removed you from the earth, but He sustained you. Thank Him for His grace. The consequences didn't destroy you; they taught you.

Day 5: *Psalm 137*
God Responds

Did God respond to the plea of Psalm 137? Absolutely! After seventy years in exile, every Jew who wanted to return to rebuild the city of Jerusalem and restore the temple was allowed to do so. And the Jews learned their lesson. While they were certainly not a sinless people after their chastisement, they never again struggled with the issue of idolatry. And to this day, they prize the Old Testament Scriptures above all.

The Lord also followed through with His promise to hold Babylon accountable for its atrocities. He predicted that He would make this enormous and powerful city "an everlasting desolation" (Jer. 25:12). And, sure enough, the Persians not only invaded the Babylonians, they wiped Babylon off the face of the earth. Only the rubble of the city remains. Babylon is still a desolate, barren land of silence along the Baghdad railway, little more than a wind-whipped whistle stop for archaeologists en route to a dig in the rugged wasteland. The city is a lasting testament to the faithfulness of God to do as He has promised.

Psalm 137 is certainly relevant. It speaks to the believer who suffers the consequence of his sin, who tries in vain to "sing the Lord's song in a foreign land." It turns our hearts to Him alone, who can satisfy our deepest needs. It gives us a pattern to follow when we have been severely treated. And it reminds us that our God is fully able to bring vengeance upon those who revile and persecute and say all manner of evil against us falsely. As Romans 12:19–21 reminds us, God can and will handle our every desire for retribution, and He can do it in such a thorough way, we need only to step aside and let Him work.

If you are enduring the grind of lingering consequences following a time of disobedience in your life, you understand this song. As you read it, remember that you are not alone in your agonizing heartache. The pain may be severe and lingering, but the good news is this: it is not endless.

Making It Strong in Your Soul

Throughout the balance of this week, pray for any Christian you can think of who has fallen. A husband or wife, a politician, a minister, a leader, a friend—anyone. Ask God to bring hope and restoration to him or her. Then, think of practical ways you might be able to help ease the grind of lingering consequences.

THE GRIND OF INSIGNIFICANCE

For the choir director. A Psalm of David.

O LORD, You have searched me and known me.
You know when I sit down and when I rise up;
You understand my thought from afar.
You scrutinize my path and my lying down,
And are intimately acquainted with all my ways.
Even before there is a word on my tongue,
Behold, O LORD, You know it all.
You have enclosed me behind and before,
And laid Your hand upon me.
Such knowledge is too wonderful for me;
It is too high, I cannot attain to it.
Where can I go from Your Spirit?
Or where can I flee from Your presence?
If I ascend to heaven, You are there;
If I make my bed in Sheol, behold, You are there.
If I take the wings of the dawn,
If I dwell in the remotest part of the sea,
Even there Your hand will lead me,
And Your right hand will lay hold of me.
If I say, "Surely the darkness will overwhelm me,
And the light around me will be night,"
Even the darkness is not dark to You,
And the night is as bright as the day.
Darkness and light are alike to You.

(Psalm 139:1–12)

Day 1: *Psalm 139*
Important to God

Most folks struggle with feelings of insignificance from time to time. Larger-than-life athletes, greatly gifted film and television stars, brilliant students, accomplished singers, skillful writers, even capable ministers can leave us feeling intimidated, overlooked, and underqualified. For some, feeling insignificant is not simply a periodic battle; it is a daily grind! We know deep down inside we're valuable; but when we compare ourselves, we often come out on the short end. A well-kept secret is that many of those athletes, celebrities, authors, and preachers who seem so confident struggle with the very same feelings that plague their admirers.

Because of our rapid population explosion, we are becoming numbers and statistical units rather than meaningful individuals. Machines are slowly taking the place of workers. Computers can do much more, much faster, and with greater accuracy than even skilled specialists. Science doesn't help the problem. Our universe is viewed by scientists as being vast, so vast that this Earth is insignificant—a speck of matter surrounded by galaxies measured by light years rather than miles. The immensity of it all overwhelms an earthling at times and forces us to ask the age-old questions: Who am I? Why am I here? Where do I fit? What does it matter? This can result in an inner tailspin—one that increases rather than lessens, as we get older and the awareness of our surroundings expands. Perhaps you are among the many who are passing through what is called an "identity crisis."

If you are wrestling with this very real and puzzling perplexity, here is a song that is tailor-made for you. It is one of David's best! His lyrics describe the person who is standing alone and searching for answers regarding himself, his world, and his God. It provides the reader with a calm certainty that there is a definite link between himself and his Lord—that no one has been flung haphazardly or accidentally into time and space. This ancient song makes God seem real, personal, and involved because, in fact, He is. The crucial problems of international affairs and "global saturation" suddenly appear not half as crucial and the difficulties connected with one's identity crisis begin to fade as this wonderful song is understood.

The Passage and Its Pattern

Psalm 139 answers four questions. As we read through all twenty-four verses, we find that it falls neatly into four sections . . . six verses each. Each section deals with a different question. An outline might look something like this:

I. How well does God know me? (vv. 1–6)

II. How close is God to me? (vv. 7–12)

III. How carefully has God made me? (vv. 13–18)

IV. How much does God protect/help me? (vv. 19–24)

All twenty-four verses link us, God's creation, with our Creator. We are super-important to our Maker. We are not unimportant specks in space or insignificant nobodies on Earth, but rather the objects of His care and close, personal attention. If you take your time and think about each section, you'll find that the four questions deal with four of our most human and basic problems:

- How well does God know me? (The problem of identity)
- How close is God to me? (The problem of loneliness)
- How carefully has God made me? (The problem of self-image)
- How much will God protect/help me? (The problem of fear/ worry)

One final thought before we embark on an analysis of the first twelve verses (we'll examine the final twelve next week): all the way through these verses we read of "the LORD," "His Spirit," "God". . . as well as "me," "I," "my." To the psalmist, God is there; better than that, God is *here*. He is reachable, knowable, available, and real. All alienation is removed. All strained formalities and religious protocol are erased. Not only is He here, but He is involved and interested in each individual on this speck-of-a-planet called Earth.

Making It Strong in Your Soul

Tonight, step outside. If the air is clear and the sky cloudless, look up at the expanse of stars. Stay long enough to allow your mind to grasp the immensity of the galaxy above you. Then remind yourself that you are more significant to your Creator than all of those stars combined. They will pass away; you are eternal.

Day 2: *Psalm 139*
God's Intimate Knowledge

If you've ever been a part of a large organization, such as a multi-billion-dollar corporation or a governmental agency or a university, it's unlikely you've ever met the people at the top of the leadership chain. You may have heard their names or read their announcements, but you probably didn't know them personally. And they undoubtedly wouldn't have known you from any other person in the organization. So, it's only natural to wonder if the supreme Ruler of the universe has the slightest idea who you are.

How Well Does God Know Me?

In the first four verses of Psalm 139, we are given sufficient information to discover that God is omniscient. He knows everything.

> O LORD, You have searched me and known me.
> You know when I sit down and when I rise up;
> You understand my thought from afar.
> You scrutinize my path and my lying down,
> And are intimately acquainted with all my ways.

Even before there is a word on my tongue,
Behold, O LORD, You know it all. (vv. 1–4)

The songwriter says that God searches him. The Hebrew term that led to this translation originally meant "to explore" and sometimes conveyed the idea of digging into or digging through something. The thought is that God explores, digs into, and examines me through and through. In the next sentence David pictures himself in two phases of life—passive (sitting down) and active (rising up). Our most common and casual moments are completely familiar to our Lord. Furthermore, even our thoughts are an open book. Thoughts come into our minds through a series of distant, fleeting conceptions as microscopic nerves relate to one another in the brain through a complicated process of connections. Even those are known by our Lord. That is what David means by God's understanding "my thought from afar."

We can see thoughts enter people's heads as their faces "light up" or, in some other way telegraph the entrance of ideas. We can hear thoughts as they leave people's minds through their mouths. But we cannot see what happens between the entrance and the exit. God can. In fact, God understands what prompts us to think certain thoughts. He therefore understands the hidden, unspoken motives behind our actions.

One Christmas we bought our small children an ant city. It was a plastic ant bed filled with a narrow sheet of sand, built out of transparent material that allowed you to watch the inner workings of the insects. Normally, all you can see in an ant bed in the ground are these busy little creatures crawling in and out of their hole. But this interesting ant city allowed us to watch what happened after the ants went into their holes—we could watch these small insects as they journeyed through their tunnels. That is exactly what verse 2 is saying about our thought-life before God. He monitors the entire process.

I appreciate the New American Standard Bible's rendering of the third verse: "You scrutinize my path." The verb "scrutinize" translates the Hebrew word that means "to sift." It is the idea of submitting oneself to minute scrutiny. God carefully sifts away at our choices and decisions. As a result of this phenomenal insight, He is thoroughly acquainted with us—and I mean *thoroughly!* To put the finishing touches on the facts of God's omniscience, He knows our words even before we utter them, which causes David to write: "You know it all." God knows every word of every language in every human being on every continent at every moment of every day. Think of it!

Matthew 10:30 adds the capstone, "The very hairs of your head are all numbered." It is not that God concerns Himself with mental and verbal trivia; it is simply that He is omniscient, that He is fully and accurately aware of everything at all times, the visible as well as the invisible, the public as well as the private.

How well does God know you? These first four verses tell us that He could not possibly know you better! Just in case the grind of insignificance is still doing a number on you, ponder the fact that you are the object of the living God's attention every moment of every day of your life!

Making It Strong in Your Soul

Does the fact that God knows everything about you give you comfort, or does it make you feel uneasy? It is also true that God loves you. How does that fact influence your answer? If you could hide something from God, how would that affect your relationship with Him?

Day 3: *Psalm 139*
God Controls the Details

As David's song about the amazing attributes of God continues, he marvels at God's ability to remain in complete control of His universe.

> You have enclosed me behind and before,
> And laid Your hand upon me.
> Such knowledge is too wonderful for me;
> It is too high, I cannot attain to it. (vv. 5–6)

The Lord remains in complete control of the smallest details of His creation; He is all-knowing and all-powerful. Knowing us as He does, He puts the necessary controls upon us. The fact that He "encloses" us could be misunderstood. This is the translation of a Hebrew term used for the besieging of a city in battle—closing off all escape routes. One Hebrew scholar says it means "to be hemmed in." The idea is that God has us in inescapable situations and there steadies us, directs us, restrains us, keeps us from running and escaping from that situation. This explains why His hand is upon us. Perhaps the apostle Paul was in such a predicament when he said he and his companions were "burdened excessively, beyond our strength" (2 Cor. 1:8). The King James Version renders those words: "We were pressed out of measure, above strength." The Greek term means "to be weighed down." It's the idea of intense pressure: "We were under tremendous pressure." In pressurized situations today God shuts off all escape routes, but He stays near and steadies us with His hand so that you and I might learn valuable lessons instead of running from the difficulty. Annie Johnson Flint describes scenes familiar to all of us—times of inescapable pressure:

Pressed out of measure and pressed to all length;
Pressed so intensely it seems beyond strength.
Pressed in the body and pressed in the soul;
Pressed in the mind till the dark surges roll;
Pressure by foes, and pressure by friends;
Pressure on pressure, till life nearly ends.
Pressed into loving the staff and the rod;
Pressed into knowing no helper but God.
Pressed into liberty where nothing clings;
Pressed into faith for impossible things.
Pressed into living a life in the Lord;
Pressed into living a Christ-life outpoured.[21]

After contemplating all these truths, David exclaims, in effect, "It blows my mind!" (v. 6). So wonderful were these proofs of God's knowledge and control, he could not begin to contain his emotions. His problem of identity has begun to fade as the songwriter realizes God views His creatures as important and significant. He knows us. He scrutinizes our lives. He studies us and steadies us twenty-four hours a day. Although it blows our minds to comprehend it, it is true. How well does God know me? *Completely!*

Making It Strong in Your Soul

How do you feel about the idea that God keeps boundaries around you? What do you think is the relationship between freedom and maturity? Can you think of a good illustration of how love and restrictions work together for the good of someone or something?

---

21 Annie Johnson Flint, "Pressed," from *Poems That Preach*, compiled by John R. Rice (Murfreesboro, TN: Sword of the Lord Publishers, 1952).

Day 4: *Psalm 139*

God Is Ever Near

All right, so God knows me and controls me; He can do that at a distance, through millions and millions of light years of space. But is He near? According to Psalm 139, David's song about the amazing attributes of God, yes.

How Close Is God to Me?

God is no distant, preoccupied Deity. In fact, He is omnipresent. In verse 7, David states this in the form of two questions:

Where can I go from Your Spirit?
Or where can I flee from Your presence?

The rebellious prophet Jonah must have wondered, *Can I find any place that will remove me from God?* He found out the hard way that the answer is an emphatic "No!" David puts it in terms anyone can understand.

If I ascend to heaven, You are there;
If I make my bed in Sheol, behold, You are there.
If I take the wings of the dawn,
If I dwell in the remotest part of the sea,
Even there Your hand will lead me,
And Your right hand will lay hold of me.

In the Hebrew Bible, the pronouns referring to God are abrupt and emphatic: If I go up to heaven—YOU! If I go down to the grave—YOU!"

The next verse carries us out into the vast ocean on "the wings of the dawn." It's a beautiful expression, but what does it mean?

Most likely it describes the rays of the morning sun that flash across the sky. Perhaps we could paraphrase it more technically by saying: "If I could travel the speed of light." Just think of that! By traveling at such speed, I would get to the moon in less than two seconds—*You!* (God would meet me.) It would take about four years to reach the first star at that speed, and again—*You!* (God would be there as well.) Omnipresence simply means there is no place where He is not.

And the huge body of water we call an ocean may make me seem insignificant and remote—but still He is there. He never leaves me lonely—"even there Your hand will lead me."

The first time I grasped the magnitude of these verses I was in the Marine Corps on a troop ship crossing the Pacific Ocean, bound for the Orient. It took seventeen days. The ocean swells on stormy days were forty to fifty feet high; and when our ship was down in the bowels of the swell, the crest loomed above like a giant domed building about to fall on us. As we would rise up to the peak, we could see nothing but water all around—deep, blue-black swells, never-ending across the horizon, 360 degrees around. I remember opening my Bible early one morning to Psalm 139:7-10, and honestly, I almost shouted. I suddenly felt at ease in His presence. My loneliness seemed utterly foolish. His hand was leading me, His right hand was holding me right there in the "remotest part of the sea." Though I was literally insignificant by comparison to the vast stretches of water around me, a calm, secure feeling swept over me.

That is the point David is communicating here. God is never absent.

Making It Strong in Your Soul

God is everywhere, but in what places do you *feel* most isolated from Him? What circumstances cause you to feel distant from Him? How does reading Psalm 139 change your perspective? How can you carry the truth of this song into places and circumstances in which you feel isolated from the Lord?

Day 5: *Psalm 139*

Nothing Is Hidden from God

In verses 11 and 12 of David's song about the magnificence and nearness of God, he announces that not even darkness affects God's pervading presence.

If I say, "Surely the darkness will overwhelm me,
And the light around me will be night,"
Even the darkness is not dark to You,
And the night is as bright as the day.
Darkness and light are alike to You.

There were times in my childhood when I would become fearful at night. (You may recall having similar feelings.) At those times I would grab the covers and snatch them over my head. I can still remember tucking myself far down beneath them, thinking that I would be kept from harm. How childish, yet how much like adults! In a figurative sense, we do this when we think that doing something in secret will somehow escape the Lord's notice. This ancient song reminds us that God sees all! Even the darkness is not dark to the Lord. According to Hebrews 4:13, there is not a creature hidden from Him.

On the encouraging side of the issue, we need never feel lonely. Our Heavenly Father sees it all. He understands our complexities and quirks; He appreciates the unique difficulties we face; He "gets" us better than our closest companions. And best of all, He cares.

Because of David's great Psalm 139, we must come to terms with two of God's attributes that appear conflicted. He is transcendent, which means He exists outside of the universe, beyond the scope of space, time, and the laws of physics. He is immensely greater and more powerful than all of the mass and matter of the universe combined. Yet, God is also immanent, which means He relates intimately and personally with each and every person.

He manages the universe, yet knows every minute detail of 7 billion individual lives. I find that mind-boggling!

Making It Strong in Your Soul

I hope you find it comforting to know that God knows you, understands you, and cares about you. It might be surprising to know that the people in your life—especially if you're a leader—want to have the same feeling about you. Because you're busy, this might take some planning. So, establish a schedule that will allow you to spend time getting to know the people around you—personally and meaningfully.

THE GRIND OF INSECURITY

For You formed my inward parts;
You wove me in my mother's womb.
I will give thanks to You, for I am fearfully and
*   wonderfully made;*
Wonderful are Your works,
And my soul knows it very well.
My frame was not hidden from You,
When I was made in secret,
And skillfully wrought in the depths of the earth;
Your eyes have seen my unformed substance;
And in Your book were all written
The days that were ordained for me,
When as yet there was not one of them.
How precious also are Your thoughts to me, O God!
How vast is the sum of them!
If I should count them, they would outnumber the sand.
When I awake, I am still with You.
O that You would slay the wicked, O God;
Depart from me, therefore, men of bloodshed.
For they speak against You wickedly,
And Your enemies take Your name in vain.
Do I not hate those who hate You, O LORD?
And do I not loathe those who rise up against You?
I hate them with the utmost hatred;
They have become my enemies.
Search me, O God, and know my heart;
Try me and know my anxious thoughts;
And see if there be any hurtful way in me,
And lead me in the everlasting way.

(Psalm 139:13–24)

Day I: *Psalm 139*
God's Skill as Creator

L et's begin this week with a few words of review. Psalm 139 links us with God. This song, like few other passages of Scripture, connects us with our Creator. You'll recall it answers four of the most frequently asked questions that come to our minds about God:

    I. How well does God know me? (vv. 1–6)

    II. How close is God to me? (vv. 7–12)

    III. How carefully has God made me? (vv. 13–18)

    IV. How much will God protect/help me? (vv. 19–24)

You might not have phrased the questions quite this way, but at some level you have undoubtedly asked them. They are the most basic questions of life. Built into each of us is a curiosity that longs to be satisfied, especially regarding the One who created this world.

Last week we looked at the first twelve verses of this great song. From the first six verses we discovered that God knows us thoroughly and completely. God is *omniscient*. Furthermore, we learned that God is in full control. Nothing occurs outside the realm of His sovereign will. God is *omnipotent*. Then, in the next six verses, we found that He who knows us is always near us. God is *omnipresent*.

Now we consider the Lord's skill as a creator.

How Carefully Has God Made Me?

The song makes beautiful poetry and declares great theology, but how can we be sure it is all true? A subtle uncertainty grinds away in most of us. One of the best proofs that God exists and that He does all these things is the human body. Consider how carefully He has made you. Verses 13–16 address this. In my opinion this section of biblical truth is one of the most remarkable revelations in all of Scripture. Remember, it was written by David in a day when anatomy and embryology were relatively unknown subjects—at best, primitive. Yet here in this ancient song the prenatal stages of development are set forth with phenomenal simplicity and insight. The point David declares is this: only a God who knows us and is near us could be so intimately involved in making us.

Verse 12 tells us of darkness and the inability of humanity to hide from God. Previous verses speak of hidden or remote places as being well-known and under the perpetual surveillance of God. Verse 13 goes even further. It transports us into the womb, a place of intimacy and darkness. It is here that the songwriter builds his case.

For You formed my inward parts;
You wove me in my mother's womb.

The "You" in each declaration is very emphatic. The idea is "You, Yourself, and no other." It is neither "nature" nor "Mother Nature" who performs the miracle in the womb; it is God alone, and no other. Linger over the term "form." When this verb appears in the original Hebrew, it often carries the idea of "originate." God originates our inward parts. It may surprise you to know that those two words—inward parts—literally mean "kidneys." In ancient times the kidneys were symbolic of all our vital organs—kidney, heart, lung, liver, etc. In fact, the verse goes on to say that God did "weave me together" in the womb. The verb *sanak* suggests the idea of knitting together like an interwoven mass or thicket. God is involved in placing all the organs and various parts of our body together in such a well-ordered fashion, it forms a veritable "thicket" of muscle, tendons, bone, blood, veins, and arteries.

Let me paraphrase verse 13 in order to bring out some of the color in the original text: "For God alone—none other—originated my vital organs; You knitted my inner being together in the womb of my mother."

David chose words commonly used in the world of artists and craftsmen. What does this suggest about God's design of humanity? What does this imply about His formation of each individual? What does David's depiction of human life imply about the value of each person? Does the presence of birth defects change the value of a human life?

🎵

Day 2: *Psalm 139*

A Species of Wonder

David's song about the Lord's attributes continues with a celebration of human life, proof of God's creative genius.

> I will give thanks to You, for I am fearfully and
>   wonderfully made;
> Wonderful are Your works,
> And my soul knows it very well. (v. 14)

Isn't this true? We are a species of wonder. No one would argue that the human body is a phenomenal combination of strength, beauty, coordination, grace, and balance on the outside. But if you think the outside is remarkable, just glance inside. Talk about something wonderful! Verse 15 describes our origin.

> My frame was not hidden from You,
> When I was made in secret,
> And skillfully wrought in the depths of the earth.

We sometimes refer to our bodily shape as our "frame." The original Hebrew term here means "bony substance" or "skeleton." Our skeletons were not hidden from God when they were made in secret . . . in the depths of the earth." This is an idiomatic expression for a protected place, a concealed and safe place—as one may hide his treasure by burying it. No doubt this "secret place" is a reference to the womb. The Hebrew word translated "skillfully wrought" literally means "variegated," like a multicolored piece of cloth. Moses used the same Hebrew term in Exodus when he referred to the making of the curtains in the ancient tabernacle. The idea is similar to an embroidered piece of tapestry or a work of fine needlepoint. The picture must include the concept of our veins and arteries, "embroidered" like variegated threads within the body. God is that involved in the making of our bodies. He is like a careful, skillful artist who takes great pain with each color and stroke. Again, a paraphrase: "My skeleton and bones were not hidden from You when I was made in that concealed place of protection, when my veins and arteries were skillfully embroidered together in variegated colors like fine needlepoint."

The truth of all this was brought home to me several years ago in a conversation I had with a young man doing his medical internship. He was studying to be a surgeon. He commented on the beautiful "color scheme" God has placed within our inner bodies. He stated that there are definite colors in our various organs, that the veins and arteries almost make the inner network appear "variegated" in color. He smiled when I informed him that David used those exact words in his song centuries ago.

David then caps off this series of thoughts with a statement about God's sovereignty.

Your eyes have seen my unformed substance;
And in Your book were all written
The days that were ordained for me,
When as yet there was not one of them. (v. 16)

God's eyes were fixed upon my "unformed substance," says David. The Hebrew verb from which this descriptive statement is taken means "to fold together, to wrap up." In its noun form it appears only here in the Old Testament, and it means "embryo." In other words, David is saying: "In my very first hours and days of life after conception—when I was still wrapped up in embryonic form—God was watching over me. He was never absent nor unconcerned."

Looking at life from God's vantage point, David says that our heavenly Father marks out our days and "ordains" them even before we are born. The original term translated "ordain" is often used in the Old Testament in connection with a potter who forms clay on his wheel, shaping and pressing and pulling at it until the lump takes the shape he has in mind. God forms our days so that they are exactly the kind of days we should have to become the kind of person He wants us to be. There is little room left for insecurity once we understand His constant interest in our lives.

Making It Strong in Your Soul

Think about the implications of this section (vv. 13–16). Why is it so damaging to the proposition that abortion is morally permissible? Examine the verses closely and try to think of an argument against the biblical position that human life begins at conception.

Day 3: *Psalm 139*

Nothing Escapes God's Care

David's song about God paid close attention to His design of the human body and the individual care He gives to each conception. No individual life escapes His care, and He endows each person with a purpose. Psalm 139 carries David to the crest of ecstasy as he exclaims,

How precious also are Your thoughts to me, O God!
How vast is the sum of them!
If I should count them, they would outnumber the sand.
When I awake, I am still with You. (vv. 17–18)

Let me put these inspired lyrics together so that the paraphrase includes much of what we have discovered up to this point.

For You, God, and none other, originated my vital organs. You knitted me together in the womb of my mother. . . . My skeleton and bones were not hidden from You when I was made in that concealed place of protection, when my veins and arteries were skillfully embroidered together in variegated colors like fine needlepoint. Your eyes watched over me when I was just an embryo; and in Your book the days I should experience were all described and recorded—the kind of days that would shape me into the person You want me to be—even before I had been born. How priceless and mighty and vast and numerous are Your thoughts of me, O God! Should I attempt to count them, they would outnumber the sand on the seashore. And Your plan isn't limited just to this life. Should I die, I would awaken securely in Your arms—I would be with You more than ever before.

This leads David to consider his future. If God gave such detailed forethought into his birth, having designed his body and endowed him with a purpose, then certainly the Lord has given no less attention to his future.

How Much Will God Protect and Help Me?

The grind of insecurity begins to ease up when we grasp how perfectly God designed each one of us, and especially when we cap it off with how much He helps us. The songwriter doesn't mince his words in these verses.

O that You would slay the wicked, O God;
Depart from me, therefore, men of bloodshed.
For they speak against You wickedly,
And Your enemies take Your name in vain.
Do I not hate those who hate You, O LORD?
And do I not loathe those who rise up against You?
I hate them with the utmost hatred;
They have become my enemies. (vv. 19–22)

On six separate occasions David refers to the enemies of God in the strongest of terms. These were not moderate, passive foes of the Lord; they were unashamed, hateful, open, and blatant despisers of God and God's people. To associate with them would pollute the testimony of any saint—and David declares his independence of them, especially when he states, "They have become my enemies" (v. 22b).

Exactly what does David ask of God? "Slay the wicked!" (v. 19a). To him, the God of heaven is marvelous, pure, holy, just, and good. His desire was to be the same—just as we are told to be in Ephesians 5:1, which says: "Therefore be imitators of God, as beloved children."

Making It Strong in Your Soul

With whom do you spend most of your time? How close are you to those who defy and deny the name of your Savior? How deep a friendship have you nurtured with people who are out-and-out enemies of righteousness? How might continued association with the enemies of God affect one's feelings of insecurity?

Day 4: *Psalm 139*
Anger against God's Enemies

As David thought about God's intricate design of humanity in Psalm 139, and he pondered the Lord's loyal love for each individual He took such care to fashion and endow with purpose, the king grew angry at the enemies of God. How ungrateful. How disloyal! How outrageous that they should rebel!

He seethed with righteous anger against the ungodly. David wanted to imitate God. He longed to be a godly man—perhaps more than any other king in the history of Israel—which may explain why he was called "a man after God's own heart." The term "hate" denotes a decision to reject something in favor of something else. Unlike the English word, it does not wish harm or ill will upon another; the Hebrew concept of "hate" involves a turning away. To hate someone in the Old Testament is to turn your back upon them.

The term translated "loathe," however, is deeply emotional. It means "to be grieved, to feel revulsion." David's love for God is so great, he can barely stomach the thought of those who hate God. And, because he is aligned with the Lord, God's enemies are necessarily his enemies. But rather than take matters into his own hands and destroy the enemies of God, he asks to be removed from them.

This shouldn't be taken as a bloodthirsty, brutal plea or a self-righteous, super-spiritual gesture. He was supremely interested in being God's man, regardless. In his zeal for righteousness, he asked God's help in protecting him from those who stood against the things he held dear. To David, a man of war, the only solution for God was to "slay the wicked!" He did not hesitate to request that of Him.

Charles Spurgeon wrote, "Godless men are not the stuff out of which true friends can ever be made."[22] True words! While I am not encouraging our isolating ourselves from all lost people, I am

---

22 C. H. Spurgeon, *The Treasury of David, Volume 6: Psalms 120-150* (Bellingham, WA: Logos Research Systems, Inc., 2009), 265.

saying that a close companionship with haters of God will take a damaging toll on our spiritual life. The virus of the degenerate heart is dangerously contagious, and you cannot spend much time near those who have it without eventually suffering from the same disease. This is as true for the teenager who wants popularity at any cost as it is for the businessman who prostitutes his convictions for an extra buck. Spiritual compromise is a deadly problem! We have already looked at 1 Corinthians 15:33 on more than one occasion, but it's worth repeating here: "Do not be deceived: 'Bad company corrupts good morals.'"

In Psalm 139:20, David lists two characteristics that identify God's enemies:

1. They speak against God (they are irreverent).
2. They take His name in vain (they use profanity).

Isn't it interesting that wicked people reveal their wickedness through their tongue? Irreverence and profanity are the trademarks of deep heart problems. Mark it down: a foul, irreverent tongue is the byproduct of a foul, irreverent heart.

Because David trusted God to protect him by slaying his enemies, he did not try to take matters into his own hands. And he never attempted to clean up the lives of God's enemies. Both would be futile efforts. He left the final decision with his Lord—a very wise and biblical action to take, by the way.

Making It Strong in Your Soul

David felt such a close association with the Lord that God's enemies became his enemies, and what God loathed, he loathed. How closely would you say your values align with the Lord's? How much do your emotions track with God's with respect to good and evil?

Day 5: *Psalm 139*

Opening to God

Before David closes hymn 139, he makes a final request of God in verses 23–24. The words are familiar to many Christians.

> Search me, O God, and know my heart;
> Try me and know my anxious thoughts;
> And see if there be any hurtful way in me,
> And lead me in the everlasting way.

David no longer looks up (as in verses 1–18) nor around (as in verses 19–22); he now looks within. He wants to be God's man at any cost, so he invites the Lord to make a thorough examination of him down deep inside. The word "search" was used earlier in verse 1. The basic idea of the original Hebrew verb, you may remember, means "to explore, dig, probe." David wants God to penetrate his outer shell and dig down deeply within him. He unveils his inner being, down where unspoken thoughts dwell and unstated motives hide out in secret, and he invites God's searchlight.

Now David goes even further. He asks the Lord to put him to the test so as to discover any distracting thoughts. In other words, he is saying, "Find out which thoughts carry me away from fellowship with You, O God. Show them to me so that I can understand them and their effect on my walk with You." That was his desire. Insecurity has passed off the scene as he stands open before his Lord.

The desired result of this probing is set forth in the last verse, where David asks God to see if there is any way of pain or grief in him. It is not so that God might know the results, but that he himself—David—might know what God discovered. When you submit yourself to the scalpel of the surgeon for an exploratory operation, you do it not just for the sake of the physician. You want to know the findings yourself, don't you? You are interested in what is discovered. David finally states that it is his desire to be led in the everlasting way," meaning the path of righteousness. He wanted to be a man of God, regardless of the cost.

Do you want to be a person whose walk with God is intimate and deep? Honestly now, is Christianity simply a ticket to heaven for you, or is it the very root and foundation of your life? Is this business of Bible reading/study, prayer, church attendance, baptism, witnessing, the Lord's Table, and the singing of hymns just something to calm your guilt and/or occupy your Sundays? On the other hand, if Christ has gotten a solid grasp of your will and you've become genuinely serious about spiritual things, then you will take the truth of these verses and allow it to take root in your life. Becoming a godly person takes time, but along the way it includes occasions when you expose your entire inner being to God's searching and you welcome any insight He might give you, regardless of the difficulty involved in facing it. By and by, the daily grind of insecurity will fade and you will be saying to the Lord: "I gladly open all the closets of my life—every room and every corner. Scrutinize my thoughts and examine my motives, Lord. Show me what needs attention. Reveal to me what brings pain to You in my life."

Making It Strong in Your Soul

The final benediction of the song (vv. 23–24) is a prayer requiring a great deal of courage. Would you consider making that same request of the Lord this week? Don't take this lightly, but don't let it frighten you. Trust the Lord to do exactly what is right for you and to take care of you. Utter the words aloud. As God "searches" and "tries" you, pay attention.

The Grind of Depression

Maskil of David, when he was in the cave. A Prayer.

I cry aloud with my voice to the Lord;
I make supplication with my voice to the Lord.
I pour out my complaint before Him;
I declare my trouble before Him.
When my spirit was overwhelmed within me,
You knew my path.
In the way where I walk
They have hidden a trap for me.
Look to the right and see;
For there is no one who regards me;
There is no escape for me;
No one cares for my soul.
I cried out to You, O Lord;
I said, "You are my refuge,
My portion in the land of the living.
"Give heed to my cry,
For I am brought very low;
Deliver me from my persecutors,
For they are too strong for me.
"Bring my soul out of prison,
So that I may give thanks to Your name;
The righteous will surround me,
For You will deal bountifully with me."

(Psalm 142)

Day 1: *Psalm 142*
An Abysmal Cave

W ho hasn't struggled with those demoralizing seasons of dark sadness? Everyone suffers from grief and sorrow from time to time. But depression is a different matter. Like a disease, it's very common, but it's not "normal." Depression is an extended state of mind characterized by acute sadness that most likely will not go away by itself. It needs attention.

Depression affects individuals differently. Some get so low and stay there so long they decide that taking their lives is better than enduring it any longer. Others seem to go in and out, down, then back up again. Depression has been described as a black hole, an abysmal cave. It certainly includes discouraging feelings that refuse to go away. I know some who have fought the battle of depression for years! Earlier, we discussed the grind of despondency. Depression is much deeper, more complicated, and usually lasts longer. Despondency leaves us feeling listless, blue, and discouraged, but depression is a feeling of severe oppressiveness that is far more serious. If it doesn't lift, professional help is often necessary.

While I hope this study will help your situation, I don't pretend that what I have to share in this short space will solve your problem. If your depression has continued for an extended period of time, be smart. Contact a qualified Christian counselor, psychologist, or psychiatrist and do the spiritual and emotional work necessary to combat this serious difficulty. In the meantime, my hope is that this song from David's pen will help bring some long-awaited light into your cave of depression.

Before we begin to dig into the first verse of his great hymn, we come across some helpful information in the superscription: "Maskil of David, when he was in the cave. A Prayer."

There are four important parts to this opening statement:

1. "Maskil." Thirteen of the songs in the Hebrews' hymnal are so designated. As we learned earlier, this is from the Hebrew root verb *sakal*, meaning "to be prudent, wise, to give insight and instruction." It is an instructive psalm designed to give us help and insight in a certain area of life. It will assist us so that we may know how to handle a particular situation wisely.

Since Psalm 142 deals with a time of depression in the writer's life, it is a *maskil* designed to give us insight into handling times of great, overwhelming distress.

2. *"of David."* David composed the hymn. Although David did not write all the psalms, he wrote more in Israel's ancient hymnal than any other person.

3. *"when he was in the cave."* The phrase regarding "the cave" appears in only one other superscription: Psalm 57. Unfortunately, David does not designate which cave. Two possibilities come to mind. David spent a lot of time in the cave of Engedi (1 Sam. 24) and the cave of Adullam (1 Sam. 22). Most likely, the psalm has the latter in view.

4. *"A Prayer."* Spurgeon wrote, "Caves make good closets for prayer; their gloom and solitude are helpful to the exercise of devotion."[23] This psalm is actually a prayer, so we should handle it with respect. Prayers were not recorded in Scripture for the purpose of analysis, but to bring insight and encouragement. This psalm is a good one to consider when you find yourself in the same state of mind as David. To put it bluntly, he was back in the pits.

Making It Strong in Your Soul

If you're in a cave today, describe the situation. Spend a few minutes thinking through the reason you're submerged beneath such dark feelings and dismal outlook. Take into account a significant loss, a lingering anger, an unresolved conflict, an ongoing resentment, a dramatic change.

---

23 C. H. Spurgeon, *The Treasury of David, Volume 6: Psalms 120-150* (Bellingham, WA: Logos Research Systems, Inc., 2009), 323.

Day 2: *Psalm 142*
Crying Aloud from the Darkness

David's depression most likely resulted from an unusually long period of stress. The superscript for Psalm 142, identifying David's circumstances as "in the cave," probably refers to the cave of Adullam. To appreciate the context, observe the first two verses of 1 Samuel 22:

> So David departed from there and escaped to the cave of Adullam; and when his brothers and all his father's household heard of it, they went down there to him. Everyone who was in distress, and everyone who was in debt, and everyone who was discontented gathered to him; and he became captain over them. Now there were about four hundred men with him.

Talk about adding insult to injury! Here's our friend David, running for his life from madman Saul, finally finding relief and solitude in a dark cave. His relief is short-lived, however, as his solitude is invaded by a solid stream of "everyone who was in distress, and everyone who was in debt, and everyone who was discontented . . . about four hundred men." Just imagine! Four hundred failures. Four hundred malcontents. Four hundred plus one: David.

The four hundred were an unorganized, inefficient, depressed mob without a leader, so they attached themselves to David. Picture the scene in your mind. With a little imagination you could see how depressed he must have been. Surely he sighed as he thought, *What now?* or *Why me?* In the depth of distress, having reached the end of his rope, David talked with his Lord about his desperate situation.

In the first two verses we find David at the mouth of that gloomy cave. The depth of his anguish is clearly expressed. He comes face to face with his God in prayer. Twice he calls "to the Lord" and twice he brings his complaint "before Him."

I cry aloud with my voice to the LORD;

I make supplication with my voice to the LORD.

I pour out my complaint before Him;

I declare my trouble before Him.

What is translated in the first verse as "cry aloud" literally means "I shriek." The original Hebrew term means "to sound as thunder, to bellow." From the interior of that cave, David thunders out his pitiful needs with heartrending groans. "I make supplication" could better be rendered "implore favor." His self-image had been assaulted. He felt stripped, worthless, useless, and completely depressed. So he asks for evidence of God's favor. He needs to feel needed and necessary. He no longer had honor and respect; self-esteem was, it seemed, forever removed.

When we hit the bottom, we feel this way. Our self-image is shot! In order to be effective, we must view ourselves as God views us: favorable, loved, useful, and needed. I have found that my first step toward a solution is turning "to the Lord" and going "before Him" as David did. To stay at the bottom, lick my wounds, and roll in misery leads only to deeper despair. Call upon Him—shriek if you must—but don't sit for days in the isolation and silence of depression! God longs to hear your words. Your honest and forthright declaration is precisely what prayer is all about. It is a discipline that ignites incredible results.

Making It Strong in Your Soul

Depressed people often feel ashamed of their difficulty. Shame and isolation only make depression more acute. The best response is to be open and honest about your situation, first with the Lord. Express your thoughts and emotions to God; be as raw and as "inappropriate" as necessary. Don't worry; He's heard worse.

Day 3: *Psalm 142*
Opening to God

The raw emotion of David's prayer in Psalm 142 comes through clearly in his choice of words. In his Cave of Adullam, the beleaguered future king struggled with depression and shrieked heavenward.

I used to wonder why we ever needed to utter words in prayer since God already knows all our thoughts (Ps. 139:4). Then one day I stumbled across Hosea 14:1–2.

> Return, O Israel, to the LORD your God,
> For you have stumbled because of your iniquity.
> Take words with you and return to the LORD.
> Say to Him, "Take away all iniquity
> And receive us graciously,
> That we may present the fruit of our lips."

Did you notice the prophet's command? His charge is to "take words with you." Saying our most troubling thoughts—expressing our deep-down feelings in words—is an effective form of therapy. It's helpful to get those depressive feelings out into the open, a way to resurrect them from the prisonlike limbo of our inner being. David did exactly that. He "took words with him" as he came to terms with his depression.

In the second verse of Psalm 142 the man openly declares his problem to God.

> I pour out my complaint before Him;
> I declare my trouble before Him.

Look at that term "trouble." It comes from the Hebrew verb meaning "to be bound up, tied tightly, restricted, narrow, cramped"—or as we would say today, "I'm in a tight fix." When he says, "I declare my trouble," the Hebrew word for "declare" literally means "to cause to be conspicuous." He wanted nothing hidden.

Putting all the preceding thoughts together, the first two verses could read, "I shriek with my voice to the Lord; I implore favor with my voice to the Lord. I pour out, before Him, my complaint; my cramped, narrow way, before Him, I cause to be conspicuous."

Do you really level with God about how you feel and what you are experiencing? Do you get vividly specific? He wants to be your closest Friend, your dearest Counselor. He wants you to keep nothing from Him. Unfortunately, many who suffer lengthy battles with depression do not express what is plaguing them. Some find it almost impossible to articulate thoughts that are brimming with pain or hostility or grief. Most stay to themselves and say very little. David spoke openly of his anguish.

Making It Strong in Your Soul

Depression often prompts the victim to seek isolation, even from God. If you have trouble praying, enlist the help of friends. Take the initiative to have people regularly surround you—literally—and to pray on your behalf. Hearing the earnest prayers on your behalf will do wonders for your perspective.

Day 4: Psalm 142
Confessing Despair

In David's dark song of depression, recorded as Psalm 142, the king confesses his deepest feelings of isolation and despair.

> When my spirit was overwhelmed within me,
> You knew my path.
> In the way where I walk
> They have hidden a trap for me. (v. 3)

David feels enveloped or wrapped up in his depression, so much so his spirit feels faint and feeble. In the middle of confessing his darkest feelings of hopelessness, he acknowledges that God knows everything, even the thoughts and emotions he has not shared with any other person. David then adds that things on the outside of the cave are as depressing as on the inside. Traps were laid by Saul and his men. Spies were everywhere. He was a marked man.

Verse 4 rounds out the bleak picture.

Look to the right and see;
For there is no one who regards me;
There is no escape for me;
No one cares for my soul.

He invited the Lord to look to his right—the place for a protector and defender to stand—but no one was there. He was alone, humanly speaking. He could not escape. He felt that there was no one who understood him or cared for his soul.

Perhaps you feel down today, thinking that all hope is gone, that God has abandoned you, that the end has come. Yes, you may feel those things, but that doesn't mean your feelings are true. The Lord of heaven knows the pressure of your feelings. He understands the depths of your distress. Best of all, He is there. He cares. He understands.

David's prayer reflects a man who refuses to allow his feelings to cut off his access to the Lord and the help He promises.

I cried out to You, O LORD;
I said, "You are my refuge,
My portion in the land of the living.
"Give heed to my cry,
For I am brought very low;
Deliver me from my persecutors,
For they are too strong for me." (vv. 5–6)

His prayer includes the phrase "my portion in the land of the living." It's a double-entendre. The "land of the living" refers to existence on this side of the grave. This poetic expression says, in effect, "You, Lord, are my life and reason for living." The phrase also refers to David's share of the Hebrew birthright, given to the people of Israel through His covenant with Abraham. In this way, David respectfully reminded the Lord that the Land of Promise belongs to the faithful. David had been faithful; Saul, who continued to enjoy the privileges of kingship, was disobedient. He called for the Lord to do what is just: unseat his persecutors and give the throne to him.

Making It Strong in Your Soul

It's never wrong to ask the Lord to accomplish what He has promised or to do what conforms to His will. If you have identified at least some of the issues causing your depression, ask the Lord for what you want. Give your rationale. Not to convince Him, but for your own benefit. Once you have expressed your desires, submit them to His will, His way, and His timing.

Day 5: *Psalm 142*
Asking God for Help

David's dark song, Psalm 142, concludes with a final request and a bold prediction.

> Bring my soul out of prison,
> So that I may give thanks to Your name;
> The righteous will surround me,
> For You will deal bountifully with me. (v. 7)

In verses 5–6, David asked the Lord to change his circumstances: to deal justly with his persecutors and to honor His promise to make David king. But he also recognized the greater need for God to change his state of mind. He asked to be released from the mental, emotional prison of depression. Then his song takes a dramatic turn. It's unlikely his attitude had changed before completing the hymn. Nevertheless, he decided to change his tune—literally. The last two lines of the psalm use a Hebrew literary device in which the past tense anticipates a future event. It's like saying, "What the Lord will do in the future is as good as done." Looking into the future, David declares, "The righteous will surround me, for you will deal bountifully with me" (v. 7).

What faith! David is looking ahead and claiming, by faith, a time of genuine victory. He is declaring that God will again use him and cause others to surround him and look to him for leadership. Why? Because he trusts that God will use these distressing, difficult days to give him maturity and inner strength and stability. He rests in the assurance that healing will come, someday.

Rest assured, God doesn't use us in the lives of other people because we *do* some things, but rather because we *are* something. People do not long to be around one who *does* a lot of things as much as they want to be around one who *is* what they admire. It is greatness of character and a life with depth that earns the respect of others. Those who have been honed and buffeted, bruised and melted in the furnace of affliction, and then emerge with emotional stability and inner strength—they are the ones who have a ministry in the lives of others.

So then, in summary, if you are in the cave of depression, call upon the Lord Jesus Christ. Hold nothing back. You can trust Him to handle whatever you toss in His direction. Tell Him exactly how your situation is affecting you. If you are able, spell out precisely what you need at this time. Rely on Him. Do not doubt and do not waver. Stand firm.

Remember, you are in His schoolroom. He is the Teacher. He is giving you a lengthy examination in the crucible of suffering, and no one can give a more complete exam than our Lord! I commend this song to all who are undergoing the daily grind of depression today. It is food for your soul in the cave as the storm continues to roar.

Seek help. And don't give up, my friend. He is preparing you for a unique message and an enviable ministry. Believe it or not, that dark cave of depression which seems endless is part of His divine plan. It was for David. It is for you as well.

Making It Strong in Your Soul

God says He will use all things for the good of those who are His (Rom. 8:28). How do you think He might use this difficulty to make a better future for you? How might you use this experience to help others? How can you learn from others who have experienced depression and emerged healthy and whole? When will you ask for help?

THE GRIND OF PRAISELESS TIMES

Praise the LORD!
Sing to the LORD a new song,
And His praise in the congregation of the godly ones.
Let Israel be glad in his Maker;
Let the sons of Zion rejoice in their King.
Let them praise His name with dancing;
Let them sing praises to Him with timbrel and lyre.
For the LORD takes pleasure in His people;
He will beautify the afflicted ones with salvation.
Let the godly ones exult in glory;
Let them sing for joy on their beds.
Let the high praises of God be in their mouth,
And a two-edged sword in their hand,
To execute vengeance on the nations
And punishment on the peoples,
To bind their kings with chains
And their nobles with fetters of iron,
To execute on them the judgment written;
This is an honor for all His godly ones.
Praise the LORD!

(Psalm 149)

Day 1: *Psalm 149*
The Meaning of Praise

There are times when the hardest words in the world to utter are "Praise the Lord!" (also translated "Hallelujah!"). These words just don't flow from our lips. In fact, there are times we are turned off even when others use the words! Interestingly, each of the last five psalms in the Hebrews' ancient songbook begins with that exclamation of praise. Perhaps by focusing on one of the five, we will uncover some things that will help us live beyond the grind of praiseless times.

If you are a Christian and have spent much time in churches and Christian groups, you have heard "Hallelujah!" dozens, even hundreds, of times. But what does it actually mean? We hear it and we say it without realizing its significance. In the next few pages, I want to explore its meaning with you. These five concluding "Hallelujah Psalms" form the most beautiful scenery on the last leg of our journey through the ancient hymnal—a journey that has often included times of sadness, sin, gloom, loneliness, distress, and depression.

I recall returning to the United States after a lengthy tour of duty on Okinawa and other Oriental islands and countries. As our troop ship sailed under the beautiful Golden Gate Bridge, tears came to my eyes! All the loneliness, sadness, and distress of my previous months away from my homeland and wife and family faded from significance because of that final turn into the harbor of San Francisco. That is the way it is in our study of the songs in Scripture. The beauty and loveliness of the final scene tend to make us forget the many days the composers spent in heartache and sorrow.

"Hallelujah" is literally a Hebrew term, not English. It is a composite word made up of two smaller terms—*halal*, meaning "to boast," and *yah*, a shortened version of YHWH, the personal name of God. Putting them together, the exact meaning of *halelujah* is the command "boast in the Lord (YHWH)!" To boast is "to speak of or assert with excessive pride." Normally, it has to do with a display of pride in oneself. However, in the case of Hallelujah! it denotes a display of pride or an assertion of glory and honor in the Lord. So then, whenever we say 'Hallelujah!" we are asserting, "Let's give glory and praise to the Lord—and none other!"

This explains why some versions of the Bible prefer to translate "Hallelujah!" as "Praise the Lord!" That is what it means. Self is ignored. Magnifying the Lord is the single concern of these last five psalms. Whenever we say "Hallelujah!" let's realize what we are saying. During praiseless times, we are usually preoccupied with ourselves. We find it almost impossible to focus fully on God.

Looking at Psalm 149 as a whole, I find three significant points of interest:

1. It is written to believers—people genuinely pursuing a personal relationship with God, not merely nominal adherents to a religion. Verses 1, 5, and 9 specifically mention "godly ones."

2. It is written to Jewish believers. This becomes evident as you examine such terms as "Israel" (v. 2), "sons of Zion" (v. 2), "His people" (v. 4), and "the nations" (referring to Gentiles, v. 7).

3. It falls into three sections. Each section has to do with certain times in which we are to praise our Lord: (a) verses 1–3, times of blessing; (b) verses 4–6, times of suffering; (c) verses 7–9, times of warfare.

Making It Strong in Your Soul

What are the most common "praiseless" grinds in your life? In other words, when do you *least* feel like praising the Lord? Be specific. See if you can discover a pattern. Talk it over with family, close friends, or a spiritual leader.

Day 2: *Psalm 149*
In Times of Blessing

Psalm 149 is one of five "praise the Lord" psalms that conclude the Hebrews' ancient hymnal. Like the other four, it begins with the command "Hallelujah!" leading to a time of exalting God's goodness. In this case, the people of God are summoned to praise Him in response to three different situations: times of blessing, times of suffering, and times of warfare.

Praise the Lord in Times of Blessing

Praise the LORD!
Sing to the LORD a new song,
And His praise in the congregation of the godly ones.
Let Israel be glad in his Maker;
Let the sons of Zion rejoice in their King.
Let them praise His name with dancing;
Let them sing praises to Him with timbrel and lyre. (vv. 1–3)

Times of blessing should prompt spontaneous praise. When food fills our storehouses, when everyone is free of illness or injury, when no enemies or tragedies threaten, that's a natural time to sing our thanksgiving and shouts of praise. Consequently, the songwriter gives us three commands as he discusses times of blessing. He tells us to sing (v. 1), to be glad (v. 2), and to praise His name (v. 3). Let's look at each command and meditate upon what God is saying.

First, the psalmist urges us to sing a new song. When God brings goodness into the lives of His people, He loves to hear us respond with fresh and spontaneous expressions of delight. Even better when we gather with other "godly ones" to celebrate the Lord's blessing. After all, we openly share our times of stress and heartache—just as we should. For some reason, however, we seldom gather our friends for the sake of celebrating God's abundant blessings.

Second, the songwriter calls for God's people to be glad. Times of prosperity and/or promotion should never cause guilt. If it comes from the hand of God, we should rejoice! Unfortunately, some in the Christian ranks have begun to believe that it is more spiritual to suffer, or that only materialistic people can prosper. What a lousy testimony to a loving God! While the Lord uses suffering to cultivate godly character, He also delights to give good things to His people. Praise God when the blessings flow! They come from Him. Psalm 75:6–7 makes that clear:

> For not from the east, nor from the west,
> Nor from the desert comes exaltation;
> But God is the Judge;
> He puts down one and exalts another.

Third, the composer calls us to praise. The third verse commands us, in effect, to really "let loose." Don't stifle your praise; let it out! In the days of the psalmist, it was quite common for God's people literally to dance for joy and play on musical instruments when they were filled with praise. David danced in the street when the ark was brought back into the city of David (2 Sam. 6:12–15). Likewise Miriam, Moses' sister, danced in praise of God after the Israelites crossed the Red Sea (Exod. 15:20–21). The dancing in Scripture was done out of praise in one's heart to God for His blessings and deliverance.

The whole point of these first three verses of Psalm 149 is that we are to enjoy our times of blessing in full measure. We are to give our Lord fresh, unrestrained exclamations of praise when He chooses to pour out His abundance upon us.

Making It Strong in Your Soul

How do you typically celebrate good fortune, such as a big promotion, a financial windfall, an encouraging doctor's report, or a joyous family event? When something wonderful occurs, consider adding a time of thanksgiving and praise to your celebration. It doesn't have to become a church service. Simply offer a prayer of thanks or lead your friends in a song of praise.

Day 3: *Psalm 149*
In Times of Suffering

This song of celebration, Psalm 149, is like a rallying cry, urging all of God's people to praise the Lord regardless of their circumstances. That includes times when people aren't naturally inclined to boast on God.

Praise the Lord in Times of Suffering

For the LORD takes pleasure in His people;
He will beautify the afflicted ones with salvation.
Let the godly ones exult in glory;
Let them sing for joy on their beds.
Let the high praises of God be in their mouth,
And a two-edged sword in their hand. (vv. 4–6)

It might be helpful to begin verse 4 with "Because" instead of "For." It's a good translation of the Hebrew text and it helps to separate verse 4 from the preceding section. This also helps clarify the psalmist's meaning as the song turns to discuss times of suffering. While difficult circumstances are inevitable in life, the Lord always takes pleasure in His people. In other words, suffering is *not* the result of God's displeasure. Ever.

I notice two statements in verse 4 regarding the way God views those who are afflicted with suffering:

1. He takes pleasure in His people. The Hebrew term is *rat-zah*, meaning "to accept favorably, be pleased with, satisfied with." So often the one who is set aside feels completely unloved and useless—even rejected. He isn't contributing a thing because he can't. Not able to produce, he begins to feel as though he is nothing but a drag, a weary responsibility. That is why suffering is usually a praiseless grind! But this verse says quite the opposite! It says that God "accepts us favorably"—He is "pleased with us" even when we are laid aside and totally unproductive. That fact alone should encourage each one who is afflicted with pain and sidelined because of illness. You may be in a hospital room or alone at home. Take heart! God continues to love you and He looks upon you with favor, even though you cannot produce anything at this present time.

2. *He beautifies His people.* To be technical about it, the verse says that God "will beautify the afflicted ones with salvation" (deliverance). This is so true. The Hebrew term rendered "beautified" means "to make beautiful, to glorify, adorn." I believe it has two meanings in this context. The first is literal. When deliverance comes, when healing occurs, when the sunshine of hope splashes across the once-dismal room of the sufferer, beauty returns. The long facial lines of stress begin to fade, the light returns to the eyes, the whole countenance is lifted. God beautifies them!

In a broader, nonliteral sense, however, I want to suggest that God brings glory to many who live long years with affliction. Some of the most beautiful people I have known are people whose lives have been scarred by disease, pain, and paralysis. Stationed upon their bed or limited to a chair, these "beautiful sufferers" have a radiance that shines like the quiet, faithful beam from a lighthouse across troubled waters. Often I go to minister to them, but I soon discover that the beauty of their lives ministers to me! Their attitude toward suffering prompts me to give praise to God.

The Lord will also beautify and glorify His suffering saints with the ultimate deliverance: eternity with Him in a place where there is no suffering, no pain, no illness, no death, and no tears.

Making It Strong in Your Soul

Praising God is not a natural response in times of suffering. It requires supernatural help, as well as the help of loved ones. I don't recommend trying to cheer up the afflicted by helping them see the "silver lining" or by quoting Romans 8:28. Instead, help them join others in praise and worship. Immerse them in an atmosphere of praise. If you can't get them to a service, bring a service to them!

Day 4: Psalm 149
In Times of Warfare

Psalm 149 is not only a call to praise the Lord in times of blessing, and encouragement to praise Him in times of suffering, it's also a call to arms.

Praise the Lord in Times of Warfare

Let the high praises of God be in their mouth,
And a two-edged sword in their hand,
To execute vengeance on the nations
And punishment on the peoples,
To bind their kings with chains
And their nobles with fetters of iron,
To execute on them the judgment written;
This is an honor for all His godly ones.
Praise the LORD! (vv. 6–9)

In verse 6, the people of God were told, in effect, "While you're singing praises, keep your sword ready!" This may be a word picture drawn from the days of Nehemiah, where the Jews rebuilding the walls of Jerusalem sang praise as they worked and maintained battle-readiness against marauders. The visual picture is a worker with a mason's trowel in one hand and a sword in the other. In other words, "Don't drop your defenses, don't become disheartened, and don't give up! Victory is inevitable for those who remain faithful."

In practical terms, the message is, "Stay faithful to the Word of God—the sword of the Spirit (Eph. 6:17), the two-edged sword (Heb. 4:12)." Sickness and suffering have a tendency to weaken our faith if we fail to feed our thoughts with God's Word. Praise, like a fragrant blossom, wilts quickly. The sufferer is encouraged to hold fast to the sword of truth—good counsel. This is one of the reasons a visit with those who are ill should include sharing a portion of the living Book, the Bible. It helps the sufferer keep a firm grip on the two-edged sword.

Verses 7–9 are the most difficult in the song to understand. As I stated earlier, it is important for us to interpret this psalm historically, with the believing Jew in mind. You see, the enemies of Israel were enemies of God, so Israel was trained to be a militant, aggressive force against wrong (and they still are!). Once they were given the land of Canaan, they were never permitted by God to conquer other lands, only to defend their own.

The land given to Abraham and his Hebrew descendants was considered holy ground, the territory owned by the kingdom of God. Therefore, invaders were subject to God's judgment. Consequently, He used Israel to "execute vengeance on the nations and punishment on the peoples" who desecrated the kingdom of God. This work of judgment was actually "written" (v. 9) in such passages as Deuteronomy 32:41-43, Joel 3, and Zechariah 14.

Practically, however, verses 7–9 exhort the Christian today to stand and fight against Satan and all his hosts of demons. Our warfare is not in the realm of the seen, but the unseen; not in the tangible realm of guns and bombs, but the spiritual realm of Satan's deception and sin's temptation. This is precisely what 2 Corinthians 10:3–5 is saying:

For though we walk in the flesh, we do not war according to the flesh, for the weapons of our warfare are not of the flesh, but divinely powerful for the destruction of fortresses. We are destroying speculations and every lofty thing raised up against the knowledge of God, and we are taking every thought captive to the obedience of Christ.

So then, let us be just as aggressive and militant against our spiritual foe as Israel was against its national foes. After all, "this is an honor for all His godly ones" (v. 9). To think that God would even allow us to be a part of His combat unit is an honor, indeed! May He be praised for equipping us for battle, empowering us for the fight, and encouraging us with the absolute promise of victory. Praiseless times are often times of demonic warfare, but the victory is ours!

Making It Strong in Your Soul

Make no mistake, we are at war. In what ways have you experienced the enemy's attack? How did you respond? When deception or temptation strike, change your physical location for a period of time and immediately begin praising God, either in song or through prayer. Before returning, read something from God's Word.

Day 5: *Psalm 149*
Praise at All Times

Psalm 149 encourages the people of God to praise Him at all times, regardless of circumstances. In times of blessing, praise Him! In times of suffering, praise Him! In times of warfare, praise Him! When we come to that enviable place in our Christian experience that we can honestly say, "Praise the Lord!" in every situation—and genuinely mean it—we will have assimilated the full thrust of this magnificent hymn of praise—and *all* the songs in Scripture. May that day come soon, and may it never end.

During the eighteenth century, Charles Wesley wrote numerous hymns. It has been estimated that during his lifetime he composed more than eight thousand! "O for a Heart to Praise My God," one of his finest and oldest, has been put to the familiar tune of "O for a Thousand Tongues to Sing," another Wesley hymn. It is a fitting conclusion to our study of the songs in Scripture.

> O for a heart to praise my God,
> A heart from sin set free,
> A heart that always feels Thy blood
> So freely shed for me!
>
> A heart resigned, submissive, meek
> My great Redeemer's throne,
> Where only Christ is heard to speak,
> Where Jesus reigns alone.
>
> A heart in every thought renewed,
> And full of love divine;
> Perfect, and right, and pure, and good,
> A copy, Lord of Thine!

Making It Strong in Your Soul

Read the following New Testament promises and rejoice.

> Therefore, my beloved brethren, be steadfast, immovable, always abounding in the work of the Lord, knowing that your toil is not in vain in the Lord. (1 Corinthians 15:58)
>
> But thanks be to God, who always leads us in triumph in Christ, and manifests through us the sweet aroma of the knowledge of Him in every place. (2 Corinthians 2:14)

When you were dead in your transgressions and the uncircumcision of your flesh, He made you alive together with Him, having forgiven us all our transgressions, having canceled out the certificate of debt consisting of decrees against us, which was hostile to us; and He has taken it out of the way, having nailed it to the cross. When He had disarmed the rulers and authorities, He made a public display of them, having triumphed over them through Him. (Colossians 2:13–15)

Submit therefore to God. Resist the devil and he will flee from you. (James 4:7)

You are from God, little children, and have overcome them; because greater is He who is in you than he who is in the world. (1 John 4:4)

About the Author

Charles R. Swindoll has devoted over four decades to two passions: an unwavering commitment to the practical communication and application of God's Word, and an untiring devotion to seeing lives transformed by God's grace. Chuck graduated *magna cum laude* from Dallas Theological Seminary and has since been honored with four doctorates. For his teaching on *Insight for Living*, he has received the Program of the Year award and the Hall of Fame award from the National Religious Broadcasters, as well as multiple book awards. He and his wife of over half a century, Cynthia, live in Texas. You can find out more about Chuck at www.insight.org.

WORTHY
PUBLISHING

IF YOU LIKED THIS BOOK . . .

- Tell your friends by going to: http://www.livingthe psalms.com and clicking "LIKE"

- Share the video book trailer by posting it on your Facebook page

- Log on to our Facebook page, click "LIKE" and post a comment regarding what you enjoyed about the book

- Tweet "I recommend reading #LivingthePsalms by @charlesswindoll @Worthypub"

- Hashtag: #LivingthePsalms

- Subscribe to our newsletter by going to www.worthypublishing.com/about/subscribe.php

WORTHY PUBLISHING
FACEBOOK PAGE

WORTHY PUBLISHING
WEBSITE